# MIDNIGHT

Also by

Victoria Shorr

*Backlands: A Novel*

# MIDNIGHT

Three Women

at the Hour

of Reckoning

## VICTORIA SHORR

W. W. Norton & Company

*Independent Publishers Since 1923*

NEW YORK | LONDON

For information about permission to reproduce selections from this book,
write to Permissions, W. W. Norton & Company, Inc.,
500 Fifth Avenue, New York, NY 10110

For information about special discounts for bulk purchases, please contact
W. W. Norton Special Sales at specialsales@wwnorton.com or 800-233-4830

Manufacturing by Lake Book Manufacturing
Book design by Marysarah Quinn
Production manager: Beth Steidle

ISBN 978-0-393-65278-9

W. W. Norton & Company, Inc., 500 Fifth Avenue, New York, N.Y. 10110
www.wwnorton.com

W. W. Norton & Company Ltd., 15 Carlisle Street, London W1D 3BS

1 2 3 4 5 6 7 8 9 0

TO MY Mother

*Who always vindicated the Rights of Woman,*
*and like Joan of Arc's mother, kept the faith*

# CONTENTS

# AUTHOR'S NOTE

I wrote the Jane Austen piece first and called it "Jane Austen at Midnight." Midnight is literal in that case. Jane Austen alone in her room with her candle dripping. Soon to sputter out and leave her in the dark.

But then, as I sat to write the others, that very word, *Midnight*, the toll of it, came to mean more than an hour on the clock.

It was, rather, the time of reckoning, the moment when one's life stands stark before one's eyes. Sometimes there is a choice, as with Austen and Joan of Arc; sometimes there is simply one's fate, as with Mary Shelley, and the test becomes how one meets it. That time is always midnight, even if the sun is high in the sky.

# MIDNIGHT
# AND
# JANE AUSTEN

# I.

B leak midwinter, 1802; doubly bleak, as Jane Austen was now essentially homeless. She and her sister, Cassandra, had arrived at Manydown in the snow by borrowed carriage, from a grueling season, with their parents, as houseguests, tossed from relation to relation. Sometimes welcomed, sometimes tolerated, but even when welcomed, when explicitly invited, still seated at what she called "the lower end of the table" and expected to play cards into the night. To show interest in all, and expect none for herself—in other words, to play the part of unmarried woman without a penny to her name.

Although if she'd had a penny, which in this case would have meant an income of at least £200 per year, a figure often mentioned in her novels as minimal for keeping up the lifestyle to which she'd been born, she probably wouldn't have been unmarried to begin with. A state of affairs, by the way, that had come upon her both gradually and by surprise, because it wasn't as if Jane Austen had thought herself marked out for spinsterhood. Though she was not a standout beauty, she was no worse than the lot of married ladies, had lively brown eyes, was funny and smart, loved to dance, could sew a fine seam, and came from a family as good as the rest. Her favorite book was *Tom Jones*—which seemed to form a backdrop, a sort of laughing, rollicking scenery for her first flirtation, with Tom Lefroy, a boy who was visiting her friends and neighbors, when she was twenty.

He loved *Tom Jones*, too, she thought worth mentioning in a letter to Cassandra. Meaning that he was both a reader and a rollicker himself, so exactly the kind of man Jane Austen expected to marry.

That she would marry she never doubted. As a teenager, she had tried out a few names in an old parish registry that her father, the parson in the local church, left lying around—inscribing her engagement first to a "Henry Frederic Howard Fitzwilliam of London," and then to an "Edmund Arthur William Mortimer of Liverpool." Gentlemen both, they sounded, along the lines of the Austens themselves. Not quite nobility, though capable of rising to it should the chance come, as it did for some of her brothers. As for her, she was prepared, clearly, to take her place in London or Liverpool society as either Mrs. Fitzwilliam or Mrs. Mortimer, although on another line she penned, "Jack and Jane Smith, late Austen," followed by, "Of God knows where." Already Jane Austen.

She didn't try out "Jane Lefroy," because she was twenty by then. Moreover, as soon as it was noticed that the two of them were dancing together so much, and, when not dancing, sitting together in gales of laughter that evinced, even more dangerous, a meeting of the minds—engaging, in fact, in "everything most profligate in the way of dancing and sitting down together," as she would write in the kind of teasing letter with which she would transmute bitterness all her life—the young man was sent away at once, before Christmas. This was partly to spare the feelings of the young Jane Austen, since there was no way that Tom Lefroy could marry her. She was too poor.

And he, too, had no money, though what he did have were a mother and sister to support. He needed an heiress, and he got one, and went on to become Lord Chief Justice of Ireland, and lived to say that he'd liked Jane Austen very much, perhaps even half loved her, "with a boyish love." But marry her, no, he couldn't—none of them could. She wasn't pretty enough for a man to lose his head over, and she didn't bring enough of anything else to the table.

No title for a rich man, no money for a poor one. Her sister had gotten engaged—it has been said that she was prettier. Maybe she was. We have a straight-on sketch of Jane Austen, but only a profile of her sister Cassandra. The only description we have is from some nieces, who laughed at them, the two "girls," as the family called them, in their matching caps. Quite dismissive, with no understanding of what it meant to be wearing matching caps. That two caps had to be cut from the one piece of cloth that could be afforded.

Or even what it meant to wear a cap at all—that one had no ladies' maid to fix one's hair. That one had to resort instead to the expedient of pulling on a cap. That one was an old maid.

Though before Cassandra Austen was an old maid, she was a fiancée, engaged to a lovely young man, who also had no money but had secured a "living," as they say in the books of the day, as a country parson. This meant he was attached for life to a village church, chosen and supported by the local nobleman, and given what looks to us today like a very nice house. The problem being that the smaller churches offered salaries too small for a man with a family, so that a parson with a wife had to scrabble together two or three of these "livings," which was precisely what Cassandra Austen's parson was in the process of doing.

And though no one could have called the match a "triumph," still everyone was pleased, and at that point Cassandra had the prospect of a home of her own, much like the one her clergyman father had provided for them growing up, and, if God willed, a happy family. Cheerful if slightly improvident, with lots of rosy-cheeked children and a maid or two to milk the cow and make the beer. A carriage, eventually, if things progressed as they often did.

Which looked to be the case, since the nobleman who supported the fiancé's living then invited him to come along as ship's chaplain while he went out to the West Indies to suppress a slave rebellion. This boded well for the young man's future, and the Austens took it as a very good sign.

The problem being that there was yellow fever in Saint-Domingue, as Haiti was then called, and he caught it and died. Cassandra Austen got the news months later, by tattered letter. The nobleman who took him out there was sorry. He hadn't known the young man was engaged to be married; if he had, he never would have asked him to come on such a risky mission, he wrote.

Which was probably true, but on the other hand, that was it for Cassandra Austen. She put on mourning clothes, and her cap, and set about waiting to die. Nursing this friend through childbirth, that one through illness, caring for the children, and the old ones—refusing to consider the several other suitors who tentatively raised their heads. Maybe she nurtured hopes of reuniting with her young man in heaven.

But at least in this life she had had her invitation. Someone had at least asked her. Though she hadn't in the end married, she had not walked the long and lonely road entirely alone.

But Jane—"Not at all pretty," an older cousin dismissed her. A neighbor remembered a girl "slight and elegant, but with cheeks a little too full" for her face. Her best feature seems to have been her "fine eyes," not unlike her own Elizabeth Bennet, the heroine of *Pride and Prejudice*, who is also a young woman of more wit than beauty, also without a fortune. But Lizzy Bennet had Jane Austen to write her a Mr. Darcy, a fabulously rich nobleman who could see beyond the social strictures of his day and was smart enough to prefer the bold, lively intelligence of a girl with no money to a dull little life with a garden-variety heiress. A man who was willing to look twice, willing to look hard enough to see beyond the obstacles that blocked Lizzy Bennet's way—her family, his aunts, and all the ladies in the county with their eligible daughters and nieces—to the real and lasting light in her eyes.

Jane Austen, however, had no one pulling those strings for her, and even though she was the smartest girl in the room, always, and the funniest, and daring, willing to dance all night, and surely the one who would have, given the chance, climbed the fence on an outing, like the bold, ambiguous Mary Crawford in her *Mansfield Park*, in utter disdain for the creeping Victorian morality, she never had the chance. No one ever invited her to walk across the downs with him. No one looked across the room and really saw her. No one even turned his head, intrigued, at anything she said.

Not that there really ever was anyone smart enough for that in her circle. She grew up in Hampshire, which was great fun when she was a girl, what with all the hunting and riding and country dances, but where the men were either prigs or talked, as she would write, "nothing but horses." Which would provide us with some very good laughs in her books.

But what did it do for her? As the years went on, it was as if she had wandered into one of those circular mazes in a truly bad dream. If there'd been someone who'd wanted her when she was young—if one of those handsome horse-talkers in a brightly colored jacket, the kind she liked, and the deep yellow breeches she fell in love with in *Tom Jones*, if someone like that had tried to kiss her one night after one of the dances, and then come by the next morning, when the blood from their hearts was still clouding their minds, then she might have—would have—married him, and become one of the minor characters in her own novels, the smart, kind women with too many children who are there mostly to help her heroines.

But there were no kisses, not even with young Lefroy that time, or at least none that was written up with that killing humor. That humor that could kill or bite or sting anyone who might harm her or her sister, and as there was no one to stop her, no hand seeking hers, pulling her back, ever further into that crystalline maze of the seer she was left to wander.

Where everything, everyone, is magnified, with no mercy, and where, though somehow invisible herself, she could see them all, ever more clearly, in that "bright white glare," as she would call it. And where she found herself increasingly alone.

# II.

By the time she and her sister pulled up to Manydown that winter day, she was nearly twenty-seven, the age at which Anne Elliot finally married for love in *Persuasion*, and poor Charlotte Lucas resigned herself to Mr. Collins in *Pride and Prejudice*. But outside of the great Jane Austen novels, twenty-seven in 1802 was beyond the pale. Women didn't marry at twenty-seven, they died at twenty-seven, of serial childbirth, for the most part. Since they married at seventeen.

It had been a bad season for Jane Austen, a long, bad season. Her parents had decided to leave the house where she'd been born and grown up, her home, and go, essentially, on the road. Her father, the rector of the church at Steventon, still held his position and was entitled to the house—and the income that went with it—but his son James, Jane Austen's older brother, was also a clergyman with a wife and growing family to support. The Austen parents resolved to relinquish the house and income to the son, and retire to the resort town of Bath, the Palm Beach or Palm Springs of their day—pick the place you'd rather live less. That's how it was for Jane Austen.

There had been no discussion, no consultation. One account claims that she came home from a visit with her friend Martha and was greeted by her mother, "Well, girls, it is decided." All accounts agree that she fainted dead away when she heard.

And it wasn't just that she hated the thought of shallow, boring Bath; there was also the fact that she loved her home, loved the surrounding nature, the countryside there. Loved the trees, the elms and beeches, and her flower garden—she mentions wanting to plant syringa, "iv'ry pure," as in one of the Cowper poems that her father used to read them of an evening, from the books she was informed they would also be leaving behind for her brother and his wife. Not to mention the walks, the hills she knew so well she could "explain" them, as she once put it.

Since, one may imagine, she'd had lately to turn to them for rather more than in her younger days. When she had walked those hills with all the hopes of any perfectly nice-looking girl, mulling over the mystery of her own likely marriage, her still-undisclosed Mr. Mortimer or Jack Smith, or even dreaming of some wildly improbable meeting, as must have happened now and again, as it did in *Sense and Sensibility*, when a Willoughby appeared out of the blue to take a Marianne in his strong young arms.

But by the time the Austens decamped from the region, Jane Austen would no longer have been walking in quite that same expectation. And as the years rolled by—she was twenty-three, twenty-four, twenty-five—what she sought in and took from those hills must have been, increasingly, consolation.

And inspiration, too, which she would carry back to the room in the house where she'd always lived, the room she shared in perfect sympathy with her sister, who anyway traveled quite a lot, and even when there, left Jane Austen in the requisite security from intrusion once she had sat at her desk with pen and paper. This, along with the quiet rhythm of country life, allowed her to cultivate what Picasso would call "seclusion," so crucial to any artist, so precious to any woman.

And what had come to her of the last few years of her seclusion in that room with its desk, the quiet brown carpet, her own dear piano, and the little oval mirror between the windows that looked out on the elms she so loved, seemed some compensation, even justification, for what had not. For what she had now were three manuscripts—"Elinor and Marianne," "First Impressions," and "Susan," the future *Sense and Sensibility*, *Pride and Prejudice*, and *Northanger Abbey*, respectively.

They told stories that she thought had not been told in quite that way till then, about real people, the ones she knew well— "3 or 4 Families in a Country Village," as she would put it to a niece some years later. Seen with the hyper-clarity that only the lonely can muster, the one who has been left to take measure of both the charm of those country families and the narrowing of their eyes. Who goes to their dinners though she will be seated well away from any honor, far from the host. Whose name still remains unadorned by Mr. Fitzwilliam's or even Mr. Smith's, and who expects, with increasing certainty, that she will leave their dances as she came to them, alone.

Her own fate, then, she was having to conclude, and not what she'd imagined for herself, or would have chosen. But on the other hand, there seemed to come with it an awareness— was it a gift? She had written a few little books and stories when she was younger, half as spoofs, romps, taking off from the family theatricals that had enlivened the Austen household—but what she'd been doing lately felt qualitatively different. These were serious books—the same people as before, though written not by a joking girl but a clear-sighted woman. Who was still laughing but in a more knowing way, at her dumb old rich, her sharp new rich, her would-be rich, whom she eventually drags off the scene, to our satisfaction, still clawing the parquet.

And we laugh with her at them, though laugh less at her less rich, her disinherited girls, the ones trying in discreet desperation to maintain the gentle forms—renting a pianoforte when the piano is sold, sitting fine and tall on borrowed horseback when the carriage can no longer be maintained. The girls slipping down from the gentle perch to which they'd been born, through no fault of their own—a father's death, a thwarted marriage; girls whose best prospect is suddenly entering the governess market, "the slave trade," as one of them, Jane Fairfax, shudders in *Emma*; nice girls, smart girls, even pretty girls, slipping down past the luckier ones, the less smart, and less nice, even less pretty, but firm in their fortunes, who have nothing to offer beyond the occasional spiteful meddling.

Unless Jane Austen stopped them, which was precisely what she could and did do in the solitude in her room at home. Here the wrongs of outside were righted, and the last laugh went to her girls. Her "own children," she would call them privately to her sister, her "suckling" babes, but they were more, they were her ladies fair, and she was their knight in armor. They were coming to life right there at her nice old desk, at the end of her sharpened plume pen, where she sat with them, day in, day out, without, again, much fear of interruption, and no need to think about dinner or tea, for the household managed that, and left her with her Marianne, and the dreadful Fanny Dashwood, and bright Lizzy Bennet, and stiff, unseeing Darcy who didn't consider her worth a dance at first. This was Jane Austen's world, where justice reigned, as it rarely did outside those walls. But here the stiff-necked and cruel got at least some comeuppance, and girls like her married both well and for love.

But without that room? Without any room? For apparently

in Bath they were going not even to a rented apartment, but to a relative's house, to pitch up for a while, while they looked for a place that was both affordable and not, her mother hoped, dreary. A place where appearances could be maintained without the requisite expense. Which might, in a resort town like Bath, take some time.

In the meantime, "the girls," Jane Austen and her nearly thirty-year-old sister Cassandra, were to pack their bags and come away with what they could carry. The rest they would leave in the house for their brother and his wife, a former friend whom Jane Austen was liking less all the time. When it was suggested she give her desk to one of her nieces, even a favorite niece, she bristled, though, as always, with that wit. "You are very kind in planning presents for me to make," she wrote to her sister, "& my Mother has shewn me exactly the same attention— but as I do not chuse to have Generosity dictated to me, I shall not resolve on giving my cabinet to Anna till the first thought of it has been my own."

But what she chose or didn't choose had ever less to do with anything or anybody. She was one of the "girls," dependent, unmarried; a nice aunt to the nieces and nephews who laughed at her bonnet behind her back. A looming problem to her brothers and their wives, who were concurring among themselves that the moment had passed for her, that brief time when young women stood, all in a row, on the stage of life with the world's eyes upon them with some interest, and one pair of eyes, if all goes correctly, with enough interest to stop roving down the row and remain fixed.

That hadn't happened with Jane. She'd been eyed, tentatively, a few times, but the eyes had always kept moving. Already, in 1799, she was writing to her sister, about a ball at nearby Basingstoke, "I do not think I was v. much in request. People were rather apt not to ask me till they could not help it; one's consequence, you know, varies so much at times w/out apparent reason."

And that was when she was twenty-three. When her parents gave up their house, she was already twenty-five, and the family had been cognizant that her chances of a marriage proposal were diminishing, geometrically you might say, for years by then. Which meant that they—her parents, her brothers, their wives—would have to support her for the rest of her life.

It crossed no one's mind that she might actually earn a living. They all knew she wrote; they loved her little pieces. She read them aloud sometimes in the evening, and the family found them charming and funny and delightful. Shortly before the move, her father had even sent "First Impressions"—the early version of *Pride and Prejudice*—to a London publisher, who sent the manuscript back, unread, by return post. If she was disappointed, we have no record. She bundled that manuscript into a carrying case with the other two, "Elinor and Marianne" (*Sense and Sensibility*) and "Susan" (*Northanger Abbey*) and took them with her to Bath. By Greyhound, so to speak—in this case, a sort of stagecoach. Since her parents, on giving over most of their income to her brother, found they could no longer afford a carriage. Thus she was left to depart her lifelong home, with nothing boding well and little more in hand than her manuscripts, her few clothes, and her scrimped little savings, stuffed into a case.

Bad enough, but at one of the stops along the way it was discovered that her case had been transferred to a coach for Southampton, along with some other bags, to be shipped out to the West Indies. A rider went off in pursuit, and arrived just as her case was being loaded onto the ship. If he hadn't, she'd have lost *Pride and Prejudice* and *Sense and Sensibility*—but she didn't, we didn't. But she almost did. That was her life then. Barely under control.

It was sunny when she and her mother first arrived at Bath, but she hated it at first sight. "I think I see more distinctly through rain," she wrote to her sister. "The sun was got behind every-thing, and the appearance of the place was all vapour, shadow, smoke, and confusion." She mentioned that at her aunt's, she was given her "room," in quotations, and then trudged around the next day with her father, looking for suitable places to rent. It seemed there were none to be found that were both somewhat presentable and not creeping with damp.

As for daily life besides the ongoing house hunt, Bath offered the drinking of sulfuric waters, some nice walks when the weather was good, and then, come evening, an unending series of small, repetitive parties, to which Jane Austen, as a less-rich, long-term guest of a quite rich, insatiable aunt and uncle, was obliged each night to trot.

Before long she would be writing to her sister, "Another stupid party last night; perhaps if larger they might be less intolerable, but here there were only just enough to make one card-table, with six people to look on and talk nonsense to each other."

For what else was there to talk about in Bath, beyond the minutiae, the "nonsense," of a resort town, where no one was doing much except going to the spa by day and each other's par-ties in the evening? There was no farming, and no politics, since daily life, real life, had been left behind, "back home," wher-ever that might have been. Here there were no serious house-holds being run, so no cheese or beer or ongoing charity, and few babies, since those who alighted in Bath were mostly too young or too old. And since the town was constructed anyway on a new model, with the rich neighborhoods isolated from the poorer ones, there was little chance for snatches of conversation with people from the other side of life, where much of the fun of the world is to be found.

But Bath—you might call it the proto-gated-community effect—was deadly in its social fragmentation, and Jane Austen was bored. The public squares were too far away to attract the public, the open assemblies were losing ground to private parties, and there wasn't even any hunting, so not even the passionate arguments about horses and dogs that she at least could laugh at in her stories. In fact, the only ones in Bath talking about horses were the careless young gamblers who'd come down looking for a nice rich bride to pay their stable bills. Which is to say, not Jane Austen.

Though there were plenty of other candidates for these young men—that was the other problem with Bath. It served as a sort of marriage marketplace of the last resort, particularly for young ladies on the high end of the age curve. Which was precisely where Jane Austen was mortified to find herself, at almost twenty-five, in 1800, and she had an uncomfortable suspicion that this was one of the reasons her parents had fixed on the place. Maybe they were thinking there was hope for her yet; that they would still find her someone. It was what her grandparents had done with their own daughter, her mother, who had also found herself getting on—she was twenty-three—when they'd brought her to Bath; and then, *voilà*. There had been Mr. Austen, himself age thirty-three and just at the precise point in his life where he was both prepared to take a wife and disabused of any dreams of an heiress, and they were married right there in Bath, at the lovely church.

So why not poor Jane? She was still nice and slim, with

cheeks still pink, and those sparkling clear eyes that all her nieces and nephews were to mention in later years. And in truth there seemed to be no one for her in the country. Her news of the dances there had been, increasingly, no news, or even bad news, which she turned, Jane Austen–style, into good reading. For example, "There was one gentleman, an officer of the Cheshire, a very good-looking young man, who, I was told, wanted very much to be introduced to me, but as he did not want it quite enough to take much trouble in effecting it, we never could bring it about."

Anyway, there seemed to be "a scarcity of men," she would write that year, the eighth year of war on the Continent, "in general & a still greater scarcity of any that were good for much." And as the move to Bath was set anyway, she indulged in a rare bit of optimism, speculating that, perhaps, "We have lived long enough in this Neighbourhood, the Basingstoke Balls are certainly on the decline, there is something interesting in the bustle of going away."

And perhaps there would be someone in Bath for her. She had a new dress made—"a round gown, with a jacket, like Catherine Bigg's, to open at the side"—and went on to her sister for some paragraphs, about fronts "sloped round to the bosom," and "a frill . . . to put on occasionally when all one's handkerchiefs are dirt—and low in the back," even including a little sketch, to convey the full effect.

All this with the faith, the renewal, the new hopes, that stir to life in all bosoms "sloped round" by a new dress. And, thus attired, she went out to the balls of Bath.

She wasn't old yet, she was still twenty-four. And it wasn't as if she went without partners there—she had her partners in Bath, men who asked her to dance, old men, married men, Bath-types. "Toughs," she would come to call them, chillingly, once she knew them a little better. And though she was an avid dancer at the country balls among people she knew, though she loved dancing with a passion, "could just as well dance for a week together as for half an hour," as she'd written when she was twenty, she found the dances at Bath "very stupid," with "nobody worth dancing with and nobody worth talking to." She would later have her heroine in *Northanger Abbey* enter and leave the balls in Bath "without having inspired one real passion, and without having excited even any admiration but what was very moderate and very transient."

Jane Austen would fix that for her.

But who would fix it for Jane Austen? Her friends had sustained her at home in Hampshire, but they didn't seem to have "freindship," as she often misspelled it, in Bath. What they had was acquaintanceship, fine for the beautiful, rich, and married, but to an unmarried, not quite young, and close to poor woman, this was a form of pure ordeal. Jane Austen had been sheltered from this kind of thing at home, where everyone knew her. There were no strange eyes on her there, no offhand or harsh summings-up.

But in Bath, there were new drawing rooms to walk into, new faces, hard and white, to take her measure. She soon knew the drill. There would be the introduction, and then the quick appraisal. She was no one—though from a good enough family, and therefore suitable for an extra at table, or to stand among them at one of their dances. Someone who could be asked, but would not, on the other hand, be missed if she regretted.

All this every time she entered a drawing room in Bath.

That first spring she was still hoping, still thinking, that disguised among this crew there might be a possible friend. There was a Mrs. Chamberlayne, with whom she went out walking, several times, in May of 1801. The first time, the woman walked so briskly that Jane Austen was impressed, and thought perhaps there might be something interesting in her athleticism.

"It would have amused you to see our progress," she wrote to her sister. "We went up by Sion Hill, and returned across the fields. In climbing a hill Mrs. Chamberlayne is very capital; I could with difficulty keep pace with her, yet would not flinch for the world. On plain ground I was quite her equal. And so we posted away under a fine hot sun, she without any parasol or any shade to her hat, stopping for nothing, and crossing the church-yard at Weston with as much expedition as if we were afraid of being buried alive. After seeing what she is equal to, I cannot help feeling a regard for her."

But that proved chimerical—for the next time they walked together, Jane Austen was bored. It "was very beautiful," she wrote, "as my companion agreed, whenever I made the observa-tion." This is Austen-ese, spoken only between the sisters, for "the woman had nothing whatever to say for herself."

Her letter continued: "And so ends our friendship, for the Chamberlaynes leave Bath in a day or two."

Which was just as well. "I cannot anyhow continue to find people agreeable; I respect Mrs. Chamberlayne for doing her hair well, but cannot feel a more tender sentiment. Miss Langley is like any other short girl, with a broad nose and wide mouth, fashionable dress and exposed bosom. Adm. Stanhope is a gentleman-like man, but then his legs are too short and his tail too long."

Austen-ese for, *I am in despair.*


Not that it did her any good to hate it there. Her parents were doing quite well in the place. If Jane wasn't finding a husband, well, that was what it was. "Poor Jane," but the waters were helping her father's gout. He bought a new cane, easy to come by in Bath. He didn't mind the "toughs," nor did he find their parties "stupid," since he never minded sitting down among them for a hand of cards.

"Intolerable," Jane Austen wrote to her sister, but a game of whist was just as pleasant to the retired Reverend George Austen at Bath as it had been at home in Hampshire.

# III.

A nd so it went, for the next two years. The Big Clock struck
twenty-five, then twenty-six, was rounding on twenty-
seven. Jane Austen was at the outer limit, as even she saw it,
of marriageability. When she pulled up in a borrowed coach
at Manydown that day, all she had in the way of money was an
allowance from her parents—worth about $1,000 per year—but
not an income.

Nor was there any way—outside of marriage—for her, or any
respectable woman of the gentry class with living male relatives, to get an income. The two options open to gentlewomen
of that day were teaching or becoming a governess, but both
offered lives bleak and downtrodden, a "sacrifice," as Jane
Austen would call it in *Emma*, "a retirement from all the pleasures of life, of rational intercourse, equal society, peace and
hope, to penance and mortification for ever."

Less careers than hard judgments, on one's family as well,
exposed as incapable of supporting an unmarried sister, and so
naturally shunned by anyone with elsewhere to turn. Both gov-
ernesses and teachers were subject to offhand scorn by those they
served—"served" being the operative word. They were servants—
smart servants, fallen servants, poor gentlewomen servants who

had had the worst luck of all, true, but servants, and if they were so smart, why weren't they rich or at least married? Was it the length of the nose, or perhaps the pallor of the cheeks, "a bit too full," their vapid, silk-clad, bejeweled employers could almost be seen wondering.

Not that they ever asked. Nary a question beyond the references, which these impoverished gentlewomen always had, stellar references, from the vicar, from the bishop, even, because their grandfather had once been rich and had endowed the parish—but that was history, and who cared for history? Outside the schoolroom, that is, from where these ever thinner, ever paler, always shabbier—didn't they care?—shades rarely strayed, except for the obligatory dinners, Christmas, the family birthdays, when they shook out the one good dress—again?—and took their seat at the far end of the table.

"Dear old Sharpe" or "Fairfax" or "Eyre," but not Austen, not yet, her father was still alive, and though by no means rich, he could still support her on his retirement stipend. He loved her, respected her even, enjoyed her stories, and would keep her from the governess trade.

But he was her father, not her husband, and he was old. And he had moved her against her will out of what she had thought of till then as her home—but it turned out that it wasn't her home. It was his home, and when he decided to leave, they left. So though it could have been worse for her, much worse, though she was neither a teacher in a school nor a governess to the stupid rich, she was still a single woman with no way to make any money beyond hoping for it, as she and Cassandra often did in their letters—"I do not know where we are to get our Legacy—but we will keep a sharp look-out"—and with no home at all at this point.

. . .

W hat she had, though, were her friends from Hampshire. There were five of them who mattered to her, five women whom she probably couldn't even remember having met, since she had known them all her life. This was what friendship was to Jane Austen—deep and lifelong, friendship with women with links not just to her but to her entire family. And three of the five lived at Manydown.

They were the Bigg sisters, Catherine, Alethea, and a widowed sister, Elizabeth, who had invited the Austen sisters to spend a few nice long leisurely weeks with them, as people did then. The Bigg house, Manydown, was a lovely old place with plenty of room for all, and plenty of people employed there to make it all easy, set in a lovely old park, in Hampshire, Jane Austen's favorite part of England, a short ride from what she still called "home." It was winter, and she arrived hoping for "a hard black frost," which would make the crisp fast walks she loved possible, with no mud, no puddles, and then, after that, true comfort. "To sit in idleness over a good fire in a well-proportioned room is a luxurious sensation," she'd written earlier, and to sit thus, in that kind of comfort, and with friends, real friends, must have seemed to her, after Bath, like she'd fought her way in from the blizzard.

And then there would be the dinners, delightful, small, with no low end of the table, stretching into long pleasant evenings, since there was, unlike at Bath, nowhere to rush off to. The moment itself could be the thing. And the Biggs knew her, they loved her, there was no judging, only deepening conversation, among the women and also their father, Lovelace Bigg, a widower, who lived there with them, and whom she liked so much. He was jolly, one of those Hampshire dog-and-horse men, that cozy old type she'd come to miss in Bath. An old-time lord of the manor, devoted to his place and his people—family, staff, and tenants—with "a character so respectable and worthy," as Jane Austen had once written to her sister, leading a life so rooted, so free of the self, so big, in stark contrast to the petty pursuits of health and pleasure that had emptied her hours since her family had left home.

A "life so useful," she called it, the kind of life she herself aspired to, considered worthiest, worth living. A life with both substance and leisure—which for her had meant, when she still lived at home at Steventon, active help for the poor with both money and food and warm handmade clothing, and time in the afternoon to sit and write. Both of which had been taken from her by the uprooting to Bath. Both of which flooded over her once again as she arrived at Manydown.

"We spend our time here quietly as usual," she wrote. "One long morning visit is what generally occurs." She herself was described by one of the sisters, Alethea, as "pleasant, cheerful, interested in everything about her." Happy, that is. Even if just on reprieve, just for the moment. Even if Manydown was just a port in the storm that was now her life.

They made seven at dinner, an agreeable number, enough but not too many. Still, with seven, someone always had something new to bring to the table—an observation from a walk, some news from town, and when that failed, Napoleon, and Pitt, and the terrible Mr. Fox. There was just the right degree of disagreement on the small things to keep it all lively, although the seventh member, the younger brother, Harris, sat mostly in silence, because of his stutter—and his father. His stutter, his father—and where one began and the other left off, no one knew, but in those days, overbearing fathers and stuttering sons were taken more in stride. Just one of the permutations of extended families living together in elaborate, multigenerational houses.

Jane Austen certainly didn't think anything of it, either way. She'd known Harris for most of his life—had even taught him to dance, years ago, when she'd come to a ball at Manydown, unforgettable, since they'd illuminated the greenhouses. This at a time when light in the night still took one's breath away—it was so rare and expensive.

That was in 1796, when Jane Austen was twenty, and caught in that brief whirl with her Irish friend—you could say boyfriend—Tom Lefroy. When life itself had seemed a merry dance to her, and one she danced well. And since she danced so well, with grace and real lightness, never tiring or walking through the long numbers, none of the heaviness you saw in some of the other girls, the richer girls, should she have denied herself all expectations from the start? Was she so wrong to have thought that there might have come something for her from it all?

Nearly seven years ago. He, Harris, had been little over fourteen then, and terribly shy, since he wasn't sent to school, but educated at home by tutors, to spare him the teasing, what with the stutter. Still, they were old friends, she and he, or at least she was his sisters' old friend, so no one for the backward boy to worry about, no one to judge or be judged by. And she'd taught him both the spirited country dances and the formal minuet, so at least he could join in with the others. Most often with his sisters as partners, or sometimes Jane herself. She would eventually write the scene, by the way, in her unfinished "The Watsons," except that the little boy there was adorable, charming.

But as for Harris, though he had little "beside his height" to recommend him, as one of her nieces would write, he was twenty-one in 1802, and since his older brother had died, heir to Manydown. He had even taken his rightful place, despite the stutter, at Oxford, though had not finished his degree.

But the only ones who needed degrees in those days were the clergy, and Harris wasn't going to be a clergyman, he was going to hire a clergyman, like Jane Austen's father or brother. Give the man a good living, as a proper lord of the manor would do. Which was to be Harris's lot, his luck, in life. To be lord of the stately splendid Manydown when his father died, and live as pleasant a life as could be had in England, and maybe the world, in those days.

And to live it in as pleasant a place as could be imagined. Manydown was a stone mansion, built around a courtyard, not just grand but also graced with history. The family had held the house for more than a hundred years before the first Queen Elizabeth, with one wing dating from Tudor times. They are mentioned in the Domesday Book, and an ancestor had bought a piece of their land from Henry Wriothesley, Shakespeare's patron.

And the house had been modernized, too, with its famous ironwork staircase and grand reception room on the first floor. Jane Austen loved the place, loved the combination of old and new, real grandeur, not opulence but beauty, and she loved the park surrounding it as well, the two hundred acres of ancient oaks and the famous cedar—with another 1,500 acres of farmland beyond, all of which made for wonderful walks and views. She had spent many a day and night there, first as a girl after the dances at nearby Basingstoke, and now as the unmarried—was it too soon to say spinster?—friend of Harris Bigg-Wither's unmarried sisters.

S he might have written an account of the night—we don't know. All the letters she wrote from around that time were burned by her sister, Cassandra. But Cassandra was there, and told their nieces, afterward, how it had all played out.

It seems that Harris's sisters knew what he was intending, and they let Cassandra in on the plot, and together the four women contrived to leave Jane Austen alone with the young man. This was on their second night there, just before supper. Somewhere in that grand vast house, Harris Bigg-Wither cornered Jane Austen and asked her to marry him.

She was taken completely by surprise. She saw her life, in that moment, flip from black to white. Everything became, all at once, its opposite. She was poor; she would be rich. She was last at the table; she would be first. She had no home; she would have the grandest home of all. Her carriage would be the best one. She would never have to think of that again.

Never have to think about any of it—she would no longer be one of "the girls." No more "poor Jane." That would be over, just like that. All in one stroke—lucky Jane, happy Jane, perhaps even eventually Lady Jane. She would return to Hampshire— they would all return to Hampshire. Thanks to dear happy married Jane, her sister, her mother and father, even, would have a home, and what a home. A home with their good friends, for they would all continue to live together. Harris's sisters, his charming father, Jane and Cassandra, her parents when they were not in Bath—all of them. They would be her guests, for she would be the mistress of the house.

And the estate—mistress, too, that meant, to all the workers, the laborers. And a charitable one, as she'd already proved herself, when it was a hardship. She always reserved between 5 and 10 percent of her own meager yearly allowance for the poor. Imagine what she could do with real money, how beloved she would be, what an object of gratitude. And not just from the poor—from her brothers as well, for their careers in the navy were always needing a connection to move them up the ladder. Now, rather than needing a hand, she would be able to extend one.

And she would have children of her own too, not just nieces and nephews. She would not just marry, but make a brilliant match. Unheard-of, at her age, and in her situation—a woman of no money and no consequence, well on her way to being an old maid, already treated like an old maid, raising no eyes when she entered a room, causing not a ripple in the social current, unnoticed, unconsulted, unmarried. "Poor Jane."

And now, here was a chance that even a beautiful young girl in her social position could scarcely dream of. Besides, she knew Harris, he didn't frighten her, he was younger, the younger brother of her good friends. There would be no dreadful family to confront, none of the petty jealousies and wranglings she would chronicle so minutely in her books.

Did his sisters know he was going to ask her? she asked him. Did her sister?

Yes, he told her. Knew and supported. All of them.

Then yes, she said.


That evening passed as in a dream. There were the whoops, the shouts, the congratulations to the happy couple! Tears of joy, genuine joy, from the sisters, hers and his. His father brought out a French claret, a rare luxury in those days of homemade orange wine and mead, and they toasted the two, Jane and Harris. Long may they live. Happy forever.

She floated through it all. She was amazed, stunned, could hardly believe any of it. She would be married—she! Herself, Jane Austen, married! Just as she'd thought when she was young—not to Jack Smith of "God knows where" but to Harris

Bigg-Wither of Manydown. It was hard almost to fathom, so sudden, so unexpected. So radical a change of circumstances, well beyond even the happy endings that were starting to come from her pen. For all the good that pen sought to do, it had never yet attempted such an out-of-the-blue, high-and-wild a leap as this one.

She floated up to bed. Her sister kissed her good night. They had shared a room all their lives, but here they had separate bedrooms. Maybe if Cassandra had slept with her that night, rubbed her temples, seen her to sleep—but she didn't. All she did was kiss her and tell her how happy she was, how happy they all were, and then continue down the hall to her own room.

And Jane Austen closed the door.

O h, God, if she'd only had someone in the room, to brush away the demons that must have come at her from every side. She knew that what Cassandra had said was true, that she was happy, that they were all happy. And how happy would be those who didn't yet know, her own family, the ones who worried about her and, worse, faced the prospect of keeping her for the rest of her life. Here was her way out of that dreadful position, and more than that—her chance to turn the trick back on them, to become, like magic, at the stroke of twelve, their benefactor.

Eventually, she would put the very words that must have crossed her own family's minds in the mouth of Sir Thomas in *Mansfield Park*, to the unhappy Fanny Price, as she turns down a rich suitor: "The advantage or disadvantage of your family, your parents, your brothers and sisters never seems to have held a moment's share in your thoughts . . . throwing away such an opportunity to be settled in life, eligibly, honourably, nobly settled as will, probably, never occur to you again."

She knew that. It would never occur to her again. As her niece Caroline would write many years later, "All worldly advantages would have been to her, and she was of an age to know this quite well. My aunts had very small fortunes, and on their father's death, they and their mother would be, they were aware, but poorly off. I believe most young women so circumstanced would have gone on trusting to love after marriage."

As did her own sweet Marianne, in *Sense and Sensibility.* Jane Austen married her off to Colonel Brandon, and we are happy about it—what other options were there for her? After the fiasco with Willoughby?

None, nor were there for Jane Austen, but who was there right then to marry her off to Harris Bigg-Wither? No one.

And in the still of that dark night, she found she couldn't do it. Despite everything—just could not. In the dark of night, it was suddenly not them all but her, and not just her, but her and Harris, a big young man whom she did not love. Barely liked. Might have grown to love "after marriage," but until then? What would she do in his bed? That became the toughest angel of all, in her wrestle that night: What would Jane Austen, the one who had sat alone in a room once, happy with her pen in hand, do in that young man's bed?

She was dressed and packed and downstairs waiting by the door in the morning when the first of the household arose. She excused herself and begged forgiveness. She was in tears. She had to renege, take back her word, she could not marry Harris. She begged the sisters to bring round the carriage and take her off, right away, to her brother who lived closest, in her old house, in Steventon.

The household was shocked, offended. Her sister hastily

gathered her things, and the two Austen women left in disgrace. The Bigg sisters accompanied them in the carriage. Her brother and his wife were likewise shocked to see them pull up, so soon after leaving, shocked to see the four women embracing each other in tears, and then turning away from each other. Shocked further when they heard the reason. Her brother's wife, Mary, felt Jane had made an incomprehensible mistake, the mistake of her life. She could not refrain from voicing this.

And what answer was there for Jane Austen to give her, to give them all? None, no answer, since there wasn't one, not yet. For the one and only time in her life, she insisted that her brother take her in his carriage, immediately, back to Bath. It was bad timing for him—a Saturday, he had his sermon to write, and then preach on Sunday. He would have to somehow wrangle a substitute at very short notice. If she could wait till Monday—

But she wouldn't wait till Monday. For the only time on record, Jane Austen would not wait. She begged her brother to take her away from there, that day, right then. To his credit, he did.

# IV.

After that it went from bad to worse. Jane Austen scholars call this part of her life "the silent years." She was basically homeless, a guest here, lodgings there, for the next nine years. Nine years. Her father died in 1805, three years after she refused Harris Bigg-Wither, the pension stopped, and then she and her mother and sister became family charity cases. Her brothers—their wives—subscribed annual amounts for their upkeep. That, cobbled together with Mrs. Austen's minimal stipends, amounted to about £460 a year for the three of them.

They were truly poor now, as well as beholden. When invited to their brothers' establishments, they had no choice but to go. Jane Austen felt her situation most acutely when she was called to the richest of her brothers, at his grand estate. In "The Watsons," she speaks of "the dreadful mortifications of unequal society." She doesn't even have the money to properly tip the servants there. "I cannot afford more than ten shillings for Sackree"—her sister-in-law's maid—she frets to Cassandra. To her shame—there must be a name for this. Virginia Woolf, a century later, is mortified by the same phenomenon, the maids unpacking her shabby nightgown and old stockings, on a visit to a grand country house. That shame—irrational, unfair, laughable even, when faced with it, pen in hand, in one's own room.

But, confronted in a sister-in law's house, face-to-face with a sister-in-law's maid—a rich sister-in-law, rich because her, Jane Austen's, relatives had made her rich, had given Jane Austen's brother their property and fortune without a thought of his sisters—hard to muster the humor there. Jane Austen and this sister-in-law in fact didn't much like each other. Her heroine in "The Watsons" rails against "hardhearted prosperity, low-minded Conceit & wrong-headed folly."

But Jane Austen didn't rail. "Dinner is pleasant at the lower end of the Table," she wrote gamely from her brother's grand house to Cassandra, but she would come right out with it in *Mansfield Park*, creating the evil aunt to say it, straight, to Fanny Price: "Wherever you are, you must be lowest and last."

Lowest and last. Not that she sought to be first among them, or among them at all. "They mostly discuss food. You know how interesting the purchase of a sponge-cake is to me," she joked to Cassandra. Tried to joke. But finally she broke off. "I feel rather languid and solitary . . . I am sick of myself and my bad pen."

Sick. She wanted to go home, but she didn't have a home, she didn't even have a ride. She couldn't afford one. So there she sat, at the low end of the table, served by maids who would know her by her undersized tip, sipping the bitter broth of the poor relative, even when it was "French wine and ices," until, like a child or the dependent she was, she was informed one fine morning that her visit was over, they were shipping her back. She had not been consulted. She was thirty. "Till I have a traveling purse of my own, I must submit to such things," she wrote to Cassandra.

. . .

Jane Austen abandoned "The Watsons" around then. She'd had enough of "hardhearted prosperity" out in the world. She couldn't face it in battle alone in the night, at a wobbly table in some insufficient rented room. One of her stuffy, Victorian nephews wrote after her death that the Watson characters were "too low" for their illustrious aunt. But were they? Why? Just because the older sister says out loud, "We must marry . . . it is very bad to grow old & be poor and laughed at."

Jane Austen had solutions at hand for the Watson girls— had already marshaled the requisite suitors, and set them moving toward their transformative proposals. But one gets the sense that she somehow couldn't pull it off this time. Had ceased, in those days, those long years, to believe, even in her own solutions.

Life was bleak, life was an unending struggle to make ends meet and maintain appearances. To lead a gentrified life with no money. She has her protagonist in "The Watsons" say to one of the stupid rich who inquires why she does not ride, "Female Economy will do a great deal my Lord but it cannot turn a small income into a large one."

"Female Economy"—that was Jane Austen's lot. Trying to turn "a small income into a large one." It was exhausting, and there was that feeling, those years, of real futility. If one is sick of oneself and one's "bad pen."

After five long dreary years in Bath, though, she, along with her mother and sister, finally left, with "happy feelings of escape." But what kind of escape was it, when all they were doing was moving to another coastal town, into a shared house with a recently married brother and his young wife? He had offered them rooms in the house he'd rented in Southampton.

He was a naval officer and expecting to ship out before long, and thus it was thought that they'd make good company for his wife.

And they probably did—what choice did they have? But still, to have to charm, on a daily basis, a young married woman with no particular charm or culture of her own, but she their hostess, and they her guests? It was better, though, than Bath, and better, too, than the far end of the rich brother's table. But no place to summon the high spirits requisite for serious writing. No place to confront a cast of newly impoverished young gentlewomen, needing to marry their way out of poverty.

Hard to go on, hard to believe. Hard to go on when one doesn't believe. There had been one ray of light, real light, in all this—in 1803, a publisher in London, Benjamin Crosby, had bought her manuscript *Northanger Abbey*, then called *Susan*, for £10, which nearly doubled her income for that year. He promised "early publication," and even advertised that the book was "in the press."

And then, nothing.

Five years later, she wrote to him discreetly, under the name of Mrs. Ashton Dennis. She mentioned his promise of "an early publication" and protested, nicely, that this had not come to pass. She wondered if the manuscript was "by some carelessness to have been lost; & if that was the case, am willing to supply You with another Copy if you are disposed to avail Yourselves of it, & will engage for no farther delay when it comes into Your hands. . . . Should no notice be taken of this Address, I shall feel myself at liberty to secure the publication of my work, by applying elsewhere."

That was fine with Crosby, he responded by return mail. She could have her manuscript back for the same £10 he'd given her.

Ten pounds or a million—Jane Austen didn't have it. We do have her account of how she spent her £50 allowance that year:

"14: Clothes." That would be about $910 in today's dollars. Fabric, dressmakers, hats, shoes. It is worth noting that in her time, there was no such thing as cheap clothes. A pair of silk stockings, for example, cost the equivalent of about $60, and there was no alternative. Nylon hadn't been invented.

"8: laundry." About $520. An interesting expense. Dyes were not color-fast then, and fabrics shrank at different rates. If you read the descriptions of how to wash a "good" dress in those days, the laundress started by removing the trimming and the buttons. Then she separated the lining from the garment itself (picking the seams). If the skirt was full enough that the weight of the wet fabric would cause it to stretch unevenly, she took the skirt off the bodice and took the gores apart at the seams. Then she washed it, dried it, checked to see if the lining and the garment still matched up in size, made any necessary adjustments, and sewed it all back together.

"4: postage." About $260. One paid in those days upon receiving letters, in her case mostly from Cassandra. This was a significant expense, but as her protagonist says in Emma, "Oh! the blessing of a female correspondent when one is really interested in the absent!"

"6: presents." $400. Mostly for her nieces and nephews.

"3.10—charity." $200.

"2.13—rent a piano." $145.

"1 on plays and waterparties." $65. For her two nephews whose mother had just died. She took them boating on the river in Southampton.

True, if she hadn't taken the boys boating, and had cut out the rest of the presents and all that charity, she could have mustered the £10.

But, despite being "sunk in poverty," that never crossed her mind. The Austens gave charity, she had always given charity, and if she stopped giving, then who was she? Someone she wouldn't know.

And what would she do with the manuscript anyway, if she did get it back? That was the worst part—Crosby was the only one who'd ever accepted any of her work. Suppose she did buy it back—where would she turn with it? What else could she do?

Nothing—that was the thing, nothing. That was her life—nothing, or almost. All she could control were the few presents for others, a little piano music to cheer her in the morning, a gift of alms to the poor. The only writing she could manage in these dark wandering years were the letters to her sister, some of them—more of them—on the cross side.

After sneering at a rich aunt's health complaints—"What can vex her materially?"—and insisting her sister-in-law's widowed brother, seeking another wife, had "no right to look higher than his daughter's Governess," she turned her writer's eye, and relentless humor, on herself, admitting that "I am forced to be abusive for want of subject, having really nothing to say. I expect a severe March, a wet April, & a sharp May."

"You could not shock her more than she shocks me," wrote W. H. Auden. "I would rather not find myself alone in the room with her," wrote Virginia Woolf. D. H. Lawrence calls her "mean," and "old maidish." Harold Nicolson sees a mind "like a very small, sharp pair of scissors." E. M. Forster hears the "whinnying of harpies."

But what were they smoking? Jane Austen was, true, in her way, "abusive" in these letters to a wholly sympathetic and confidential confidante; but these were years of exile, when she couldn't sit to write her books, maybe would never sit to write again, and what was life then?

What was life? Without that half smile that played around her face as she sat, writing at her own little desk in her corner?

Without those "3 or 4 Families in a Country Village" as her starting point, families she knew, Hampshire families rooted in her own Hampshire ground, with those subtle distinctions that make all the difference, as with those gnarled vines that produce magical wine in their own terroirs in Burgundy or Bordeaux, and don't do anything special anywhere else.

Hampshire, home—Jane Austen's terroir, from which had sprung that precise variety of human comedy that connected her, a woman alone, to the world, and not just any world, but the world she loved, and connected her, too, to Johnson and Richardson, Fielding and Wollstonecraft, all of them somehow there, in her bedroom as she wrote.

But away from Hampshire, nothing took root. Nothing seemed quite right, or made sense.

She was lost, unhappy, dependent, an exile, and, worst of all, confused. Overcome with "languor," as she put it, writing unhappily from her rich brother's house. "When are calculations ever right?" she cried, in ink, to her sister. "Nobody ever feels or acts, suffers or enjoys, as one expects."

Does Forster hear his "whinnying of harpies" here? He is mistaken, then, they are all mistaken, though she would have preferred their dislike to their pity. Would have been glad that no one saw a terrified, brilliant woman for whom everything, somehow, had gone wrong. A woman who believed in love— "Nothing can compare to the misery of being bound without love," she wrote to a niece. Her best characters disdained pursuing "a Man merely for the sake of situation." They considered it "wretched . . . unpardonable, hopeless and wicked" to "marry without affection." Which seemed fine on the page, but when carried into real life?

Well, there was Jane Austen nearly thirty-three. Unmarried. Childless. Alone. Homeless. Worse, open to those fraught, precarious charges—"harpies"; "old maidish"; "mean." They'd burned women at Exeter a mere hundred and thirty years before.

Though her brothers would protect her.

Unless it was between her and one of the brothers' wives? Then what? But she knew what. Because wives came first, and children, of course, naturally. And she only after. She knew that even in her dreams—bad dreams. The kind where the dog at the party bites only you.

But that's how it was with unmarried women. "Always in the way, unequal to anything and unwelcome to everybody," she'd joked to her sister a few years before, about an old woman in Bath. But that was when she was in her twenties, and now, in her thirties—with nothing to her name, and nothing to hope for, nothing to show for her bold rejection of wealth and protection and a splendid home of her own where she would be first not last, and in the way of no one, neither harpy nor old maid but rather mistress of all she surveyed and any dog at the party wouldn't bite her, but would be hers—now the joke seemed very much on her.

# V.

B ut that wasn't how it ended.

True, she never married, there would be no fatherly husband, the kind she came to like best, a Mr. Knightley or Colonel Brandon, for her.

But it turned out she didn't need one, because one fine day in 1808, Jane Austen and her mother and sister were offered a house. Not just a house, but a wonderful house, called Chawton Cottage, with six bedrooms, a garden, and in Hampshire, no less, so not just a house, but a home. In the land she loved, the hills she could "explain," only about fifteen miles from Steventon, where she'd grown up. It had come to her rich brother from his benefactor, and now it occurred to him that it might serve for his mother and sisters, and then, just like that, their exile was over.

Jane Austen was almost giddy with joy. She wrote, of the house, to another of her brothers:

> . . . *how much we find*
> *already in it to our mind;*
> *And how convinced, that when all complete*
> *It will all other Houses beat,*

*That ever have been made or mended,*
*With rooms concise, or rooms distended.*

And, "Yes, yes," she wrote to her sister, "we will have a pianoforte, as good a one as can be got for 30 guineas, and I will practice country dances, that we may have some amusement for our nephews and nieces."

Nephews and nieces whom she loved and was loved by. "Aunt Jane and I walk every day in the garden." "Aunt Jane and I drove about shopping." "Aunt Jane and I very snug."

"The whinnying of harpies"? "Mean" Jane Austen? Or a single woman sheltered at last? In out of the "white glare" with its pitiless appraisals, sheltered enough to think once more of the pleasures of her own life, of playing her beloved country dances on her new pianoforte, and then, finally, and at last, that half-secret, most intense of all pleasures of which she was essentially deprived all these long silenced years—her work.

The Austen women moved into Chawton Cottage in the winter of 1809. They invited a close friend, Martha Lloyd, to join them, partly because that was how women lived in those days, and partly so Jane wouldn't have to be alone with her mother when Cassandra was traveling. The logistics of having Martha while leaving guest rooms for those nieces and nephews meant that Jane and her sister would have to share a room, but they likely would have anyway. "They are wed," their mother would, annoyingly, say. But they were wed, in a way—bound by sheer inclination even beyond the blood tie of being sisters. They truly liked each other, trusted and missed each other, shared tastes, opinions, and a private laugh at the world. Put into words by Jane.

There was no dressing room off the bedroom at Chawton for a desk, but it was a house of women, and quiet enough that

Jane Austen found she could write downstairs and be mostly unbothered. Unbothered enough so that the first year at Chawton, she sat and revised "Elinor and Marianne" into *Sense and Sensibility*. Her brother Henry, living in London and mixing with a fashionable set, got it sold and published for her, and the small edition sold out. That was in 1811.

Meanwhile, she was "lopping and chopping," as she put it, "First Impressions" into *Pride and Prejudice*. This was published in 1813.

Suddenly life was less bleak; life was, one might even say, beautiful. All the doubts, all the slights, subtle or less so, had been transmuted into art, and turned out to be just what she needed, what she drew on, to preserve her light touch from superficiality. The depths under her thin black ice.

Even her unmarried state, her childlessness—true, there were no little replicas of her own clear hazel eyes, her pink cheeks, "too full." But had she married—let's say Harris Bigg-Wither, to whom she'd said yes that strange night eleven years before—would she have been our Jane Austen? Harris himself did marry a few years later; went on, in fact, to father ten children, five girls and five boys. Would Jane Austen Bigg-Wither, in the throes of perpetual pregnancy, have found a moment to turn "First Impressions" into *Pride and Prejudice?* Would she have even survived all that childbirth? Many—very many—didn't.

But she—she suddenly found that from being "least and last," she somehow now had it all. Money of her own, and the exaltation that brings to one who has been so long dependent. It wasn't even that it was much—she received for the four books published in her lifetime £684—but it was hers. She rushed out to buy beautiful material for gowns for herself and Cassandra. "Remember, I am very rich," she joked to her sister. No more

dowdy caps for them. Her new money had made her "less indif-
ferent to Elegancies. I am still a Cat if I see a Mouse."

"Old maidish"? Then bring on the old maids, and their
children. "I have had my own darling child from London,"
she exulted to Cassandra, *Pride and Prejudice* proofs in hand.
She had even seen one of the characters, she teased, at an
exhibit of paintings in London, a Romney portrait that
seemed to her a perfect Jane Bennet, and "there never was a
greater likeness. She is dressed in a white gown, with green
ornaments, which convinces me of what I had always supposed, that green was a favourite colour with her." Lizzie, on
the other hand, would be "in yellow."

There was no Lizzie to be found, though, not even among
the late portraits by Sir J. Reynolds. "I can only imagine that
[Darcy] prizes any picture of her too much to like it should be
exposed to the public eye. I can imagine he would have that sort
of feeling—that mixture of love, pride, and delicacy."

Ha, ha. So what if D. H. Lawrence didn't get it? She
wasn't the only one, by the way, thinking about Lizzie and
Darcy, Marianne and Elinor. The Regent's daughter, Princess
Charlotte, thought that she and Marianne were "very like in
disposition, the same imprudence . . . I must say it interested
me much." Her father, the future George IV, insisted on sets of
both books at each of his residences.

The books had, by the way, been published anonymously,
as "by a Lady," but her brothers were hard-pressed to keep the
secret. Charles Austen, the naval commander, wrote that when
he "praised [Sir Walter Scott's best-seller] Waverley highly, a
young man present observed that nothing had come out for
years to be compared with Pride and Prejudice, Sense and
Sensibility. As I am sure you must be anxious to know the
name of a person of so much taste, I shall tell you it is Fox, a

nephew of the late Charles James Fox," the great opposition leader in Parliament.

And who on board ship wouldn't own all, as did Charles? But so did brother Henry, a banker in London, with less excuse but more temptation—when he heard his sister's novels praised, he, too, spilled the beans and basked in her growing glory.

And though unwilling at first to be viewed as a "lady novelist," "a wild Beast," as she put it, she found herself beginning to take a breath on the whole thing, beginning to uncurl a bit in that sun. She even wrote to a niece of "the pleasures of vanity . . . at receiving the praise which every now and then comes to me, through some channel or other."

She went to a dance and found herself in "the same room in which we danced fifteen years ago," she wrote to her sister. "I thought it all over, and in spite of the shame of being so much older, felt with thankfulness that I was quite as happy now as then."

Quite as happy—happier, even proud. She had chosen her work over what you might call "life"—marriage, children, security, riches—and how many do that? Especially women then—who had the guts? No one. Statistically no one.

What women do is to go on "trusting to love after marriage," and it works, they learn to love their nice rich husbands whose features smile up from the crib by their sides. But she didn't, she couldn't, she trusted to something else, something bigger, and mostly that doesn't work out. Mostly, in life, she would have lived and died quiet as a mouse, unnoticed, unknown, at the far end of the table, "last and least."

But this time, the work, that spark she'd trusted, had caught fire, and lit her life. And she was happy, she found, "a Cat," on her own terms, and even the weather was wonderful. November in England, but "I enjoy it all over me," she wrote to her sister, "from top to toe, right to left, long, perpendicularly, diagonally."

And there they all are, her own brave fighting girls, Lizzie and Marianne, Emma and Anne Elliot, and even Eliot's future Maggie Tolliver and Brontë's Cathy Earnshaw and on and on, all of them enjoying November, from top to toe with Jane Austen.

# VI.

One might wish to see a map of Jane Austen's stars from 1809 through 1816. Posthumous offense has been taken for her plight at having to write in the living room, on paper small enough to be covered by a blotter upon intrusion. But how many among us, with paneled private studies and nice windows and doors that lock, write like she did in that common room in Chawton?

For here is the list:

JULY 7, 1809: moves to Chawton Cottage. Begins rewrite of *Sense and Sensibility*.

OCTOBER 1811: *Sense and Sensibility*, by "a Lady," is published. She starts her rewrite of *Pride and Prejudice*.

JANUARY 1813: *Pride and Prejudice* is published. She starts writing *Mansfield Park*.

MAY 1814: *Mansfield Park* is published. She begins work on *Emma*.

DECEMBER 1815: *Emma* is published.

In 1816, she starts work on "The Elliots." Puts it down, picks it up again, rewrites the last two chapters, and finishes *Persuasion*, as we know it, on August 6, 1816.

Room of her own or not, Jane Austen knew what she'd been born for, that shining time at Chawton. She had been born to write, she'd laughed at the world to write, she'd turned down a brilliant marriage to write, she'd sat alone and low at the sorry end of every dinner table at every dinner she was obliged to attend to write, she'd scrimped and saved and raged and hurt, badly, under insult to write, and write she did. Write she had, as no one had before her. Of a world that was hers to know and to reveal, as exotic and interesting in its way, if you knew it as she did, as Marco Polo's China.

And write successfully, too—because it turns out there is that in her story. The first edition of *Sense and Sensibility* sold out. *Pride and Prejudice* was an immediate success and went into a second edition. *Mansfield Park* sold out in six months, and *Emma* was dedicated, by royal request, to the Prince Regent. With that book, she moved to John Murray, the best publisher in London.

Who published *Persuasion*, and would also take, she hoped, the next one, already in the works, that she was calling "The Brothers." It had swum into sight, and was starting to take watery form at her table—when she could sit at her table, without her eyes hurting, or, for some strange reason, her face. She had always hated illness, disdained complaint, but there had come upon her, she had to admit, a weakness where there had been none. And she, who had always enjoyed a walk in the evening, found suddenly, in the summer of 1816, that she couldn't bear the night air on her face.

And when that ameliorated somewhat, she found herself too weak for her afternoon walks. Nor had she much appetite for her dinner, or even the will to sit at her desk. Her nieces would find the avid writer stretched awkwardly across three chairs in the living room—never on the sofa. That she left for her mother, the sick one, the complainer, who would outlive her by a full ten years.

But Jane Austen wasn't sick, not really, she argued. She had simply appeared "ill at the time of your going," she wrote to her sister in September of 1816, due to the "very circumstance of your going." It was all nothing but "agitation, fatigue," and she was quite well again and "nursing myself up now into as beautiful a state as I can, because I hear that Dr. White means to call on me before he leaves the country." Well again meaning well enough for a small joke, though there is the stark fact that the doctor was himself worried enough to come back.

As well he might have been, for this turned out to be the last letter between the sisters.

"I have certainly gained strength through the winter," Jane Austen wrote to her niece Fanny in March of 1817. "Sickness is a dangerous indulgence at my time of life." She was able to work on "The Brothers," and had finished the first twelve chapters by the middle of March.

But then she found herself sick again. "Bile," she wrote to a friend, "rheumatism," but by this time she could hardly walk. Addison's disease, say most doctors now, or Hodgkin's disease. Bovine tuberculosis. Brill-Zinsser.

All curable now, none curable then. By mid-April, she was pretty much in bed, pale, an invalid. On April 27, she made her will (leaving almost everything to her sister), but a doctor from nearby Winchester held out hope for a cure. Her sister and brother Henry took her there in the pouring rain toward the end of May. They rented an apartment, and thought the treatment was working. On May 27, she joked to a nephew that "Mr Lydford says he will cure me & if he fails I shall draw up a Memorial & lay it before the Dean and Chapter &

have no doubt of redress from that Pious, Learned & Disinterested Body."

Still Jane Austen.

But not for much longer. The ailment proved fatal, and on July 18, 1817, after a night of faintness and a feeling she somehow could not describe, she died in her sister's arms. She was forty-one.

The real success came after her death, the adulation later still. She was buried in Winchester Cathedral, with a nice plaque that nods to the "extraordinary endowments of her mind," without quite bringing itself to mention her books.

It was written by her brother James, the one with the meanspirited wife, Mary. Jane Austen would have understood, could have written the scene herself. Good Jane. Modest Jane. Better to stick to her "benevolence of heart" and "sweetness of temper" than risk any mention of her surpassing achievements, her life's work, her books.

Now, however, there's another plaque, bigger, brass, and a stained-glass window in her memory. People come to Winchester Cathedral to see her grave. Her books are sold in the gift shop. She would have had a laugh at that, too.

They make more in a month there than she made in a lifetime. She is by now well in the way of supporting Winchester Cathedral. Though it's no stretch to imagine that she would have preferred her posthumous endowments to shower down upon her former home, Steventon, and her remains to molder in the churchyard there. But Harris Bigg-Withers's sisters were living in Winchester then, and one of them was the widow of a canon of the cathedral. They thought it fitting and proper that she lie among the kings and bishops there, and had the clout to make it happen.

And this time there was no Jane Austen to face them, grave and quiet, dressed in gray in the morning, to tell them no, that it wouldn't do for her. For others, but not for her. This time, they had their way.

# MARY SHELLEY ON THE BEACH

# I.

What did it mean, she wondered, to dream about a bird in a room? Trapped, fluttering around, too high to catch and free? Did it bode ill, as the people here said? An impending omen, another death, or was it more a portrait? Herself, trapped and fluttering, beating away from any chance to get free?

Either way, she thought as she looked out, either way. It was the twelfth of July. Shelley should have been back days ago—three days, if he'd kept to their plan. Two days, yesterday even, if something had arisen. Caught his eye, his imagination. There was a chance of that, always.

She took a breath, tried to get up again, but couldn't quite. Maybe later, if someone brought tea. She had barely gotten herself out here, onto the terrace, early, just at daybreak, with the morning star still in the sky. It had taken some doing—but it was good to be here now alone, which meant without Jane Williams, and especially without Claire.

*Breathe in*, she told herself, *breathe out*. She was still slightly amazed to be alive that July morning. It was how long since the miscarriage? June 16—so nearly a month. Barely time for her to come back, in spirit as much as body, from the other side, to where she had herself sailed and nearly made land.

She could hardly recall how it had all started—was it first the bleeding or first the fevers? They had sent for the doctor, but the doctor was far—that was another problem with this place. No help should help be needed, and with a woman, or was she still a girl? Age twenty-four, so a woman by age, but pregnant five times, five, over the past eight years, so in some ways she felt as vulnerable, as out-of-control as the girl she'd been at sixteen when she'd run off with Shelley. But woman or girl, or both, pregnant, and no doctor near, nor any wise woman among the neighbors. She'd seen them on the beach at night, "singing or rather howling," she wrote a friend, "the women dancing about among the waves that break at their feet." No one to turn to.

Except her two nemeses—her far-too-constant companion, stepsister Claire Clairmont, and her co-inhabitant of this boat-house, Jane Williams. Wife of Shelley's sailing partner, and current object—yes, she knew—of Shelley's "platonics," as she'd come to call them. Both women worthy of her scorn, if not her active distrust, both, she might even say, open to question as to their true heart's intentions vis-à-vis her life or death.

Not that any of that mattered once it had started, taking over not just her body but all the time and space around her, the way birth does, as she knew by now. Though it wasn't quite "know-ing," at least not like she knew her father's *Enquiry Concerning Political Justice* or her mother's *Vindication of the Rights of Woman*. Or maybe it was more in the biblical sense, the physical, the violent—the men in the Old Testament "knowing" a woman, by stealth or by force. So yes, taken like that, she *knew* birth, and knew, too, that this time it wasn't going as before, with the pains strong perhaps but essentially progressing, toward the custom-ary and successful outcome. This time, she was dying.

And so she would die. She knew that, too, as she slipped

in and out of consciousness, now and then aware of bustling activity around her, worried faces, tears, sweat, and the blood, hers, and so much of it. Sheets being wrung into buckets, carried away, new sheets slid under her, and then they, too, carried away, drenched in what was clearly too much blood. As it flowed from her, she felt herself flowing with it, flowing off, only occasionally opening her eyes to other eyes, which seemed to be darkening, along the scale from alarm to real fear.

She, too, had attended childbirth, not so long ago for Jane Williams herself, who was at her bedside. She, too, had shot frightened glances out of doors and windows for a doctor who was late, who hadn't come. But she had been lucky—she'd never been witness to a fatal outcome, never had to carry out the sheets dripping with blood. There had been blood, of course, always, but dark, not the clear red she was seeing in her sheets. Lifeblood that was telling its own tale, even while those clustered around her bed—her bier—still held out hope.

Maybe it was better from where she lay that day, outside it all. "Where can the doctor be?" she heard them whispering with desperation. She opened her eyes for a moment—Claire, Jane Williams, and then Shelley.

Still her love, even then. She filled her eyes with his face, still beautiful to her. His blue eyes, too big, really. His soft brown hair, his thin form, leaning forward, gazing on her, very still, unmoving, among the activity, the sheets, the chaos, the fear. *I'm dying, Shelley*, she wanted to whisper, not to scare him, but to bring him in, as it used to be between them. To let him know that she wasn't afraid, that it was all right. She had no fear. She wasn't happy to die, but she wasn't *unwilling*. That's how she would have put it to him.

But by then she couldn't muster the strength even to whisper, and maybe she didn't have to, maybe he knew. He had been read-ing Plato lately, learning, he'd told her, "all that could be said on the immortality of the Soul." And though that would have, she thought, prepared him for her loss—for her transfiguration, as it was feeling to her then, from body to spirit—Shelley, rather than submitting to her death, took action.

He somehow managed to get a load of ice brought to their isolated beachhead from one of the nearby *nivieras*, the ice caves, and had it dumped into the tin bathtub. Then, with Claire and Jane arguing against it, arguing that the shock might kill her, he swooped her up and carried her, sheets dripping, to the tub, where he sat her, fainting and bleeding, in the ice.

And it was shocking, but it saved her. Stanched the bleed-ing, which stopped the fainting, and before long she could open her eyes, sip some brandy, and feel death receding, sip by sip. And when the doctor finally arrived, there was nothing left for him to do, as Shelley wrote to their friends the Gisbornes, "but applaud me for my boldness."

Which was why she was alive this dawn, to lie on this sofa and keep watch out over the troubled waters of the Bay of Spezia, which were coming to look, more and more, to her like a grave. Treacherous waters, which swept under the house at high tide, more changeable than they had first appeared. Storms, she was seeing, came up here in the summer out of nowhere, impossible to predict. From the Alps, people said—the cold air clashing with the heat, unsettling the sea.

And them, too—unsettled, strangely. When she'd last writ-ten to the Gisbornes, she had considered telling them about the nightmares that had recently been plaguing Shelley, mostly to see if they had any thoughts, any similar experiences. In the hopes of getting an answer from the dear wise Maria along the lines of, *Oh, yes, John had the same kind of dreams*, though she knew he hadn't.

Not dreams like Shelley's. One night, it was that their housemates, Ned and Jane Williams, were covered with blood, their bones sticking through their skin, running, crying that the sea was flooding into the house. Another night, he saw himself strangling her. He'd come screaming into her room, "yet he dared not approach the bed." His eyes were open, but he couldn't speak, just stood with such a haunted look on his face that she, terrified herself, though still unable to stand after the miscarriage, had somehow managed to crawl into the Williamses' bedroom, to get Ned to help her. He'd carried her back to bed, and brought Shelley some brandy, managed to calm him.

But the very next day, he'd come to her again, awake this time, with tears streaming down his face. He'd seen himself, he told her, walking on the terrace. He took courage and approached the vision, who had turned to him and asked, "How long do you mean to be content?" That had chilled her, too, not that she feared it as a haunting, but more as an interior call to arms. "How long do you mean to be content?"


It was Friday, the day the mail came—such was the isolation here. Mail only Monday and Friday, and who could blame the postman? She, too, hated to come here, though it had looked beautiful at first, from the water. The white house, the terrace with its five arches, the green trees behind, the chestnuts and scrub oaks she'd come to love in Italy.

But once they'd arrived, once they'd moved in, she'd seen that it was scarcely more than a boathouse, set right on the sand, where, she wrote, the "sea came up to the door" and "the howling wind swept round unremittingly." The ground floor was nothing but dirt and sand, since it flooded at high tide, which left only the upper floor for both them and the Williamses, whom Shelley had convinced to join them, along with their children and household help. This left no place for a dining room—dinner was served in a dark narrow hallway between the bedrooms.

"It would be complete madness to come," she had recently written to Shelley's friend Leigh Hunt, who had just arrived in Pisa. Adding, incautiously but she had to—had to—"I wish I cd break my chains & leave this dungeon."

Afterward she wished she hadn't written that, lest Hunt show the note to Shelley; Shelley who not only liked this place, but loved it, for precisely what she hated. For the gales, the squalls, the way the sea came in and the salt speckled the windows. "This divine bay," he called it. He was happy here "reading Spanish dramas and sailing."

Yes, sailing. She, too, had sailed with him a bit now and then, around the bay for fun, but with him it wasn't diversion, it was his passion, what he lived on. Because he'd fallen into that despair that always hit him when he was writing little. Silenced, once again, by spending too much time with Byron. "Albé," as they called him between themselves, slightly mocking, Frenchifying his initials, L.B., their answer to the way he made a point of the "Lord." "Lord Byron," even with them he couldn't leave it—it was absurd. As if Shelley would go around insisting on the "Sir," once his father finally died and he inherited the title.

But Byron—always "my lord." His crest everywhere, on the doorposts of his house, on his gates, his carriage, his guns. Was it because of his bad foot, she sometimes wondered, that he woke up every morning slightly unsure of it all? Needing to be deferred to on a daily basis, even by them, his closest friends?

If they ever really were friends. If there could be the possibility of friendship with mythological horses and ancient mot-

tos blocking that narrow way, like Milton's covering cherubs.
Friendship, tenuous enough, she had found, with all ways clear,
all doors wide, but with Byron, *Lord* Byron, strait was that gate,
too narrow, anyway, for Shelley, who'd found the "demon of
mistrust and pride lurks between two persons in our situation,
poisoning freedom."

Not to mention another demon. Even that summer as Shelley
found himself wondering if he'd ever write another line worth
the ink and paper, fearing that he'd "lived too long near LB and
the sun has extinguished the glow-worm," Byron was turning
out page after page of his latest work, his *Don Juan*, which he
read aloud to the suffering Shelley at their midnight suppers in
Pisa. And it was great work, maybe his best, relaxed, sure, teasing, challenging:

> *Thou ask'st if I can love? be this the proof*
> *How much I have loved—that I love not thee!*

But it wasn't Shelley. How could anyone compare Byron's
"Sultana's sensual phantasy," or his "tigress robbed of young,"
with Shelley's:

> *Or thou, immortal Childe, with him that saw,*
> *Islam's revolt, in rapt prophetic trance—*

One came from a picture book, a beautiful one, granted, the
other from the depths of soul. From mystery, by miracle, but
Byron didn't work that way. She had seen him six years ago, that
summer on Lake Geneva—he could write almost half chatting
in a room, almost in public, as if his sources were in the air. As
if Byron gave voice to the midnight dreams of literary London.

And Byron, unlike Shelley, was popular, famous, lionized.

"I awoke one morning," as he put it, "and found myself famous."
His *Childe Harold's Pilgrimage* was a sensation when it was first
published, in 1812. She was fourteen then, on an extended visit
to a remote corner of Scotland, and even there they were talking about Byron.

And to call down these beautiful, poetic outpourings, Byron
had only to sit at his table and pick up his pen. Unlike Shelley,
who had to wander into the woods with a half-torn old notebook and lie on his back looking up at the clouds if it was day-
light, and the stars and moon if it was night, and get cold, get
hot, get sick, and scribble his inspiration on ink-blotted pages
that as often as not had to be collected from over and under the
fallen leaves.

Had she ever seen him sitting at a desk to write a poem? She
didn't think so. He sat to read, to study, she often with him—
especially in the beginning. Sometimes now. But to write? No.
His poetry was a magick spell to him, brought by the faeries.
Queen Mab. A muse. Often in human form.


A nd now by boat. Because what this boat was to him this
summer was more magic carpet than canvas and wood,
whose sails were the very "wings of poesy," as their friend Keats
had written. Their dead friend Keats. "Already with thee, tender is the night," and it was for Shelley, the night tender, in his
boat. The *Don Juan*, as it had been christened—a bad joke, that.

Shelley's boat named after Byron's poem, though it turned
out to have been Trelawny, not Byron, who'd had the name
painted on the sails. Trelawny, who claimed to have come to
Italy straight out of adventuring in deepest India, or the wilds
of America, or both, and looked the part. "Six feet high," she'd
written in her journal, "with raven black hair." And it was his

pirate spirit that had inspired first Shelley and then Byron to build boats this summer in the first place.

Trelawny had pitched up one night that spring at their house in Pisa with a model of an American schooner, and she and Jane Williams, also a new acquaintance, had sat and laughed as their husbands "caught fire." Trelawny said he knew a man living in Genoa, a retired naval commander, who could build them just this kind of "demon" of a boat. A two-masted schooner, "fore & aft rigged," with sails in line with the keel, about thirty feet long, which, according to Trelawny, would fly through the calm Mediterranean bays around here.

"The Corsair Crew," she had playfully dubbed them. Byron wasn't there that night, but jumped in afterward, and, as always, raised the stakes. Since, when he heard about Shelley's boat, he wanted one, too, only bigger—a three-masted square-rigger, and, unlike Shelley's open boat, decked, with guns, staterooms, even a library.

Which was what had caused Shelley to add the extra sail to his boat, and why she was worried this morning. Shelley had gotten it into his head that if Byron's boat would be bigger, his would be faster. To that end, Trelawny had got the boat builder, Roberts, to "pile on topmasts," as well as add a false bow and stern to stretch out the length.

"Tippy, under-ballasted," Shelley's cousin, Medwin, himself a former naval officer, had objected, but Shelley was beside himself with joy. When he caught his first sight of the boat, cutting across the bay here, it was so beautiful that he thought it must be Byron's. When he realized it was his, he fell into a trance of love.

And took his passion to the water—"Fast as a witch," proclaimed Williams, excited, too, at the speed, thanks to the extra rigging. And yes, the boat was beautiful, swift and sleek, more so without a deck, and who would want a deck on calm days, as they raced across the glassy bay that May and June?

Though once when she was out with them, the light blue sky had suddenly darkened in the first of those summer squalls—the *temporales*, as the fishermen call them—and the waves had started to splash in and fill the open hull. Then they'd all had to bail madly, and she saw how easy it would be for the boat to not only to "tip," but to fill with water. Founder and sink.

She'd been alarmed then, especially for Shelley, who'd somehow never learned to swim. But they were near enough to shore for Williams and the boat boy to fetch them in, wet, chilled, but none the worse. Still, she could see how it could have been trouble, if they'd been farther out.

She scanned the horizon, as much as she could see through the arches—nothing yet. But it was clear and calm today so far, with the kind of still bright waters the *Don Juan* was built and over-rigged and under-ballasted to sail through. The weather he must have been waiting for. The perfect day for Shelley to sail home.

She closed her eyes, drifted for a moment, and heard someone call her name low.

"Mary!" Low but beautful.

"Shelley!" she said in her dream.

# II.

Those first words, how it had started. "Mary!" "Shelley!" Eight years ago—though there were days now when she would believe it if an elf came to tell her that a hundred years had passed.

She was sixteen then, he was twenty-one. She knew little of life, and nothing of love. He knew everything, or so it seemed to her—proof of how little she knew. She was just back from Scotland, where she'd spent almost two years. Not long enough, she felt once she had landed back in her father's miserable house on Skinner Street, near the butcher shops in a mean part of London.

You could hear the animals crying in the night there, but it wasn't just the surroundings that made her long for the sullen rocks and skies of Scotland. She hated the house, hated the people, except for her father and her older sister Fanny. Half-sister. The child of her mother's impetuous love affair with Gilbert Imlay, an American bounder she'd met in Paris during the Revolution. Her mother! So brave, so strong, so dead.

Eleven days after she herself was born. "You didn't kill her," she was told more than once, a variation of "You killed her," to a child. But what was that to the fact that she was dead, gone, and even if the two little girls she left behind could sit by her gravestone and read her books, worship her words, there would never be that touch, that smile, in their lives.

Fanny had had her for a few years, but Fanny could remember nothing. You would think, since she'd been nearly four when their mother Mary Wollstonecraft had died, that there would have remained something she could have told her sister, but Fanny could only shake her head and look down. Poor Fanny. She had thought herself Godwin's daughter, too, like her sister, Mary, though when she was twelve or so Godwin apparently had a "conversation" with her.

But why? she herself had always wondered. Was it just meanness? A warning to poor Fanny that though she'd been kept through her childhood, she was not to expect much beyond?

But Fanny had no expectations of anything, even when she'd thought she was a legitimate child of the house, had always gone around with a timid second glance over her shoulder. And after that so-called conversation, she became increasingly reluctant to sign her own name. Wasn't sure if she was meant to keep using Fanny Godwin, after the man who'd taken her as his till then, or Fanny Imlay, after the man, hateful to them all, who'd refused to support or even acknowledge her birth. The man who'd driven the bold, valiant Mary Wollstonecraft, their mother, to weight her clothes with stones and throw herself into the Thames in despair.

By great good luck, she was fished out, unconscious but alive, and she lived on after that to meet William Godwin, the passionate, radical philosopher, fighting the same war against injustice and repressive social institutions as she was. "Resolve to be happy," Godwin wrote to Wollstonecraft, proposing that they move in together, and she did. And she was happy, they were happy, though they didn't marry at first, as they both disdained marriage, and had said as much, in their published writings.

But when Mary Wollstonecraft found herself pregnant, they both assumed it was a boy, and, seeing a brilliant future for their child, resolved to legitimize him. On March 29, 1797, they were married in a church, and five months later, on the thirtieth of August, she was born.

"William," they had called her before her birth, and who knows what they made of a Mary? Her father, though never warm, had always made her feel like a favorite. She was the one he called upon to meet the guests who still made pilgrimages then to visit him as the preeminent political philosopher of his day. Radical, but optimistic: "What the heart of man is able to conceive, the hand of man is strong enough to perform"; "The institutions which limit the human mind and acquisition of knowledge—the government, systems of punishment, religion, marriage—all evils to be eradicated."

This was written in the 1790s, before she was born, and this was the man her mother had loved and married. The man her future husband Shelley had read as a prophet when he was young, and whose optimistic vision of progressive social justice had formed his own.

Though by the time Shelley came into their lives, fifteen years later, the French Revolution had gone bad, and Godwin's dream had lost much of its currency. But when she was young, their house was still a point on the compass for forward-thinkers, politicians, poets, passing through London. She remembered her father laughing over a letter written by the American exile Aaron Burr, who'd come to tea one afternoon. She herself was twelve then, her half-sister Fanny sixteen, stepsister Jane, as Claire was still called, about eleven. The children had given a speech and served the tea. As Burr described the scene in his letter, "Mary wrote it, Fanny made tea, and Jane spoiled it by an overdose of tea leaves."

True, her father had laughed, a perfect portrait. And then there were the poets, starting with Coleridge. He was kind to her, to them all, Fanny, too, which wasn't always the case. But to her, Mary, especially—called her hair "a golden cloud." Allowed them to hide under the sofa while he read aloud, in his trance-like chant, *The Rime of the Ancient Mariner*. She was small then, nine or so, and could barely understand most of it, though some lines proved unforgettable.

> *The ice was here, the ice was there,*
> *The ice was all around:*
> *It cracked and growled, and roared and howled . . .*

She'd woken that night shaking, her blanket on the floor, but years later, when she picked up her own pen to write *Frankenstein*, there was Coleridge's ice. "All around."

"Kisses for Mary and Fanny," he wrote to her father in his long, long letters. "Dear little Fanny and Mary!" He said that his own little son, Hartley, sent his love to Mary. "What? & not to Fanny?" "Yes, and to Fanny—but I'll have Mary."

They still lived in the Polygon House then, on the edge of London, surrounded by fields and nursery gardens. She'd loved it there, though it was also there that her father had chanced to meet the person whom he made his second wife. She had, by terrible luck, moved in next door, and seized her opportunity.

"Call her mother," Godwin told his girls, and Fanny, good Fanny, obeyed, but Mary herself was hard-pressed to bring that word from her mouth. She hated the woman as much as her true mother would have. "Mrs. Godwin," she called her, though not to her face. To her face she mostly called her nothing. The woman was soft, common, stupid, though not illiterate—that is, she could read, but she didn't, much. Preferred to cook, which was probably how women like her get men like Godwin, especially on the second round.

Plus there was bed. Their son. Those $X$'s in her father's journals, which signified, she realized later, precisely that. The first $X$, after the woman's name, Mary Jane, was oversized, wavy. An exclamation. It had been years, after all, since Mary Wollstonecraft had died.

Nor did the woman come unencumbered. She brought children of her own, whose father was supposedly Swiss, as well as supposedly dead, both of which dealt neatly with their mother's claim to her widowed state—as opposed to unwed adventuress, which was the general conclusion among Godwin's friends.

It wasn't a happy childhood after Godwin's marriage. She still had her father, but fathers don't always answer—she felt a shock of recognition, alongside the horror, when years later, she first read "Hansel and Gretel." Coleridge wrote a worried letter about "the cadaverous silence of Godwin's children," but not all of that could be blamed on the new Mrs. Godwin. Godwin was at that point beginning the spiral down into the debt from which he would never again free himself. His work was no longer relevant to the general public. England was at war with France, whose Revolution—liberty, equality—Godwin had dedicated his life and work to advancing. Now no one in England was buying his books. Nor did anyone in the increasingly repressive war government see fit to extend to a radical, not to say outdated, philosopher the kind of stipend customarily offered to such figures, leaving him no clear path to supporting himself.

When she was thirteen, they were compelled to move to smaller, less expensive lodgings, on Skinner Street, near the butchers' quarter. Mrs. Godwin had the idea of opening a children's bookstore in the space below their apartment. Her father contributed some of the books, and she, Mary, wrote a funny poem that sold out. It seemed then like this bookstore might be the way forward. To this day she still wasn't sure why it hadn't worked out.

She wasn't sent to school—being a girl—but her father hired a Latin tutor and taught her to read, and she read all the time, what everyone was reading. *The Lady of the Lake*, *The Sorrows of Young Werther*, Madame de Staël's *Corinne*, and her mother's books—*A Vindication of the Rights of Woman. Letters Written During a Short Residence in Sweden, Norway, and Denmark*. Those she would take to the churchyard at St. Pancras, and sit beside her mother's grave, as close as she could get. She knew her from the beautiful portrait that her father still kept in his study. The intelligent, interesting face, the auburn hair, the simple flowing gown—her mother was pregnant with her when the portrait was painted. With three months to live.

No, no, she didn't blame herself. Still, it was hard to keep from whispering, "I'm sorry." But her mother knew, had to know, had to love her, not blame her. She had lived for eleven days after the birth, long enough to have kissed her daughter's head, surely. Breathed in that lovely scent all newborn babies had in their soft hair.

Still, her mother never really came to her in those days, there was never the feeling that maybe a dragonfly alighting on the gravestone or a robin hopping nearby might be a visitation. Fanny would never talk about her at all, refused to come to St. Pancras. "Mamma" wouldn't like it, she said, in her nervous way. Rather than growing, Fanny seemed to be getting smaller,

as if she were trying to disappear. Take up less space, lest someone notice her one day, and put her out.

But why would they, when she ate little and ruffled no
feathers in the household? She had overheard Godwin
describe Fanny as "modest, and by no means handsome," as
opposed to "Mary," who was "invincible," "very pretty," and,
according to Mrs. Godwin, "getting worse." She'd already
been sent away once, at twelve, for a few months, to a stifling
boarding school at the seaside, allegedly for her health. She'd
begged to come home, but once returned, had fallen back into
continual strife with Mrs. Godwin. To the point that when
she turned fourteen, her father informed her that she was to
be sent to Scotland on an extended visit to his acquaintances,
the Baxters.

The Baxters were vegetarians, and took hikes together, and
trips to the sea around Dundee. Their daughter, Isabella, was
obsessed with Charlotte Corday and Lady Jane Grey. The talk,
when she first arrived, was of an Arctic explorer ship lost somewhere in the ice. The "excessive reserve" of which Godwin had
warned the Baxters fell away as she became an enthusiast—of
Scotland, of Isabella Baxter, Charlotte Corday, even the boat
in the ice. Arctic exploration. They talked of it for hours. And
it was here, as she would write later, that "my imagination
was born."

She barely skimmed her father's letters from home, some
of which told of a rich young poet, Percy Bysshe Shelley, who
had appeared as "our Saviour," with an offer to solve Godwin's
money troubles. Shelley was said to greatly admire her father's
work, and had pledged to be "a lasting friend" who would give
Godwin money for the rest of his life. Pay his debts. Free him
from all cares and woes. Godwin had told Shelley about her, he
mentioned, at the end of his letter. Boasted that he had planted

in her the "seeds of intellect" that had already "unfolded to the delight of every beholder."

That was in 1812. Fanny wrote, too. Shelley had come to dine with his wife, Harriet, who was "a fine lady" with a beautiful complexion. The young poet himself was beautiful, too, if very thin, with blue eyes and long wavy hair, and had just published a book called *Queen Mab*, named for the fairy in *Romeo and Juliet*. Fanny quoted Mary some of her favorite lines:

> *War is the statesman's game, the priest's delight,*
> *The lawyer's jest, the hired assassin's trade.*

Which Mary liked well enough, but the point here seemed to be that her father had miraculously found a way out of his money troubles. When she paid a visit to London with one of the Baxter girls around Christmas of that year, she met the so-called "Saviour" when he came to supper one night, though for some reason without his wife.

Or no reason—it was still all the same to her. He wasn't the one she and Christy Baxter were talking about on the long boat trip back to Scotland a few weeks later. Godwin had taken them to one of Coleridge's lectures on Shakespeare that were a sensation in London that season, and Lord Byron was said to have been in the audience. They had both read, reread, half memorized Canto I of his *Childe Harold's Pilgrimage*. They, too, were "sore sick at heart" with their lives of "revel and ungodly glee," or were hoping one day to be. Longing, dreaming, to know enough of the world to be, like Byron's hero, weary of it.

The sun was rising higher. Soon it would be hot. She shifted a bit on the sofa—carefully. Cautiously. Yesterday evening, when Jane Williams and Claire were preparing to go out for a walk in the hills behind the house, she'd gotten up as well. "No, don't, be careful!" they'd come running to her. Tried to keep her in bed, but she couldn't stand it, said she'd just come out to watch the light change color over the water, she'd sit still out here, she told them. But once she got out, she found she couldn't sit still here, either, found herself pacing back and forth, one-two, pacing and, yes, bleeding.

But somehow the back-and-forth, the counting of her steps, had floated her back to that time, that interlude, when she'd met Shelley but he was nothing to her. When she was still free, her own sovereign self—she had gone back to Scotland wholly free from Shelley, any thought of Shelley, and turned fifteen and then sixteen. As for love, the closest thing she knew of that was her attachment to the older Baxter girl, Isabella.

She tried to remember if Fanny's letters from those days had mentioned Shelley. They might have—she had somehow gotten the idea that Fanny was taken with him. Maybe her father had mentioned it in passing, joked about Fanny having a "chaste infatuation." Or maybe Fanny had said something, but either way, the only feeling she herself had about Shelley then was that he was Fanny's subject, not hers.

It was hard now to truly recall that detachment. She would try, sometimes, to conjure it again, grasp that golden bough of her girlhood, her own autonomy, that last early spring in Scotland that had somehow reflected it back to her. She'd climbed mountains, read Shakespeare, eaten vegetables, and some-times found herself alone with Robert Baxter, Isabella's older brother—who meant little to her, compared to Isabella. She played chess with him, and they went walking, sometimes even read plays together, nothing more. Though when she finally went back, reluctantly, to London, he eventually followed and asked her father for her hand. She was sixteen then, but might have accepted him, just to get back to the Baxter family—if he'd come a month earlier.

But he hadn't.

S he arrived in London in March, to the same Mrs. Godwin, the same dreary Skinner Street and butchery of animals, the same not-quite sisters and brothers and no money, as before, only more oppressive to her now, for knowing another way of living. Her time was divided between working in the bookshop under Mrs. Godwin's mean little eye, and studying upstairs in what they called the schoolroom. She was working on her Latin, and resolved to save her own life by making a new translation of Virgil. That was all the light there was for her in that house that spring, until the fifth day of the merry month of May 1814, when Shelley came again.

Apparently his finances were too entangled for him to simply write her father the check he'd promised, so he'd come to London to sign off on an extortionate loan against his future assets in exchange for ready cash for Godwin. Who was avid for the thing to go through, despite the eventual loss to Shelley, since, as Godwin would argue all his life, he needed money, and it was the role of those who had it to provide it. His "saviours."

Which was how he saw Shelley—but that wasn't what she saw, that day when he slipped into the schoolroom, where she was working. She hadn't heard him come in, and when she looked up, it was straight into two large blue eyes and a gaze that didn't waver. She was taken aback, stammered hello and maybe something about her work. He didn't answer, just kept looking at her intently, as if studying her, until she felt her cheeks grow hot. Finally he smiled, and asked what she was reading. She mentioned the translation, they exchanged a few more words, and then he left and it was over, she told herself. Nothing.

But that evening she asked Fanny to loan her her copy of *Queen Mab*. She wanted to read it straight through this time.

Fanny wouldn't loan it, though. She was being sent to Wales in the morning, she said, to visit their mother's cross old sisters. Mrs. Godwin was insisting.

She was surprised. Fanny clearly didn't want to go, why send her? She was always so helpful, worked in the bookshop, served as Godwin's scribe, copied his manuscripts, his letters. Why? she asked Fanny.

"To get me away from Shelley!" Fanny said low to her.

Fanny's face was an unaccustomed pink. Was she in love with Shelley? Had he come to the schoolroom to see her rather than Mary? That made sense. Fanny was older, Fanny had known him longer, he'd come to see Fanny. Of course.

They didn't say anything further on the subject, and Fanny left on the mail coach the next morning, Shelley's *Queen Mab* clutched in her hand.

# III.

He came again, ten days later, into the schoolroom, and this time Fanny wasn't there. He didn't ask for Fanny, though. He had brought her a present, he said, a notebook for her Virgil translation. That was May 16. She marked the day in her journal, not that she had to. All these years later she could still call back those days in May, when Shelley began to replace Virgil as the sun in her sky.

The next time, he brought his friend Hogg to the house, and led him up the stairs into Godwin's library, on the pretext of introducing him to the famous man. But when they were informed that Godwin wasn't home, Shelley still lingered, pacing the floor.

She was in the schoolroom, on the other side of the wall, holding her breath—she knew his steps by then. She wasn't sure then if she should, wasn't even sure if she would, until she stepped, trembling, out into the hall.

As Hogg would tell it later, "A thrilling voice cried 'Shelley!' A thrilling voice answered 'Mary!' A very young female, fair and fair-haired, pale indeed, and with a piercing look, wearing a frock of tartan, unusual dress in London at that time, had called him." He went to her like "an arrow from the bow of the far-shooting king."

Yes, that tartan dress. From Scotland—Hogg was right, no one else in London had one then. It fit her like a glove, she was sixteen, with clear gray eyes and gold-red hair, even more beautiful, people told her, than her mother's. "Titian hair," the Baxters called it. It danced around her head, Coleridge had written, "in a cloud of light."

And as for the arrow from the far-shooting king, it must have struck her that day as she rose from her books, and that was that. They started meeting secretly, first in the sunny garden of Charterhouse School, down the street. To evade Mrs. Godwin's suspicion, she took her stepsister with her—fatally, fatally—to walk down to the schoolyard, where Shelley would be waiting. In those first days, he would invite her to sit on a bench with him to discuss "philosophy," and suggest to Claire that she walk to the corner. Then beyond the corner, farther each day. Never far enough.

Shelley brought to those meetings his own copies of her mother's stirring books. "Prudence," they read aloud to each other, was "the resort of weak people"; "Passions are spurs to action and open the mind."

Hardly idle writing—her mother had lived by her words. Her first lover was the Romantic painter Fuseli, who had loved her for her red hair and then left her for a younger woman, with redder hair.

She'd then fled to Paris to forget him in the Revolution. She'd gone as a journalist and a partisan, one of the women marching through the streets behind the Tricolore, though she found herself in tears as she glimpsed Louis XVI, by then just a man, rolling past in his cart, on his way to the guillotine. And then came the Terror, with blood running through the streets around the Place de la Revolution—carrying away with it the hopes of a whole generation. But she'd stayed on, even after

England and France went to war, since she'd met and fallen in
love there with Gilbert Imlay, Fanny's father, the same sort of
cad as Fuseli, it turned out.

To his credit, Imlay, an American, saved her life by claim-
ing her as his wife on his passport, which got her out of France.
But he refused to live with her in London, refused to take any
responsibility for Fanny, and Mary Wollstonecraft, the strong,
brilliant author of *A Vindication of the Rights of Woman*, threw
herself into the river for him.

But once saved, she found the courage to live on and "be
happy," even Fanny had been happy, and then she, Mary,
was born a year later, and Mary Wollstonecraft, age thirty-
eight, was gone.

But as Shelley read her mother's words aloud on the bench
in the Charterhouse School garden, it seemed to her that she
and her mother had come together at last, now that she was
sixteen and in no danger of "resorting to prudence." Willing,
every day more, to "open her mind" to the passions her mother
wrote of, her whole life then "wrapt in excitement." Moving ever
further from her father's problematic world; living wholly, radi-
antly, in the world of her mother.

Before long, she and Shelley graduated from the school garden to the tangled privacy of the St. Pancras churchyard. The
place was overgrown, poorly kept, barely frequented, perfect for
them. They sat among the weeds beside her mother's grave and
continued to read her books to each other.

"The man who can be contented to live with a pretty companion who has no mind . . . has never felt the satisfaction . . .
of being loved by someone who could understand him." At
this, Shelley's eyes filled with tears. He had married Harriet
Westbrook impulsively, he explained, when she was sixteen and
he nineteen, in a romantic escapade to rescue her from the school

she hated. She was pretty, pink and white, and he thought he could educate her into a soul mate. They had trekked to Ireland and handed out leaflets favoring emancipation; to Wales, where they tried to instigate an uprising of the poor. He wasn't sure in those days if he was a political activist or a poet, but then he wrote *Queen Mab*, and saw that he could be both.

Though no longer with Harriet. Soon after Wales, they had a child, and Harriet's older sister showed up and reeled her back in, away from Shelley. Stopped her from nursing the baby, which Shelley ardently desired, and opposed their return to Wales to continue their political activism there. A diametric opposition took hold, with the sister prevailing and the husband leaving home.

Though not before "getting," as they said, another baby, still to be born, in 1814, when she and Shelley met. This was a knot that she, Mary, couldn't untie.

But there was her mother again, urging her "very early in life to form your grand principle of action, to save you from vain regret, of having, through irresolution, let the springtime of existence pass away unenjoyed. Gain experience—ah! gain it—while experience is worth having, and acquire sufficient fortitude to pursue your own happiness . . ."

"The springtime of existence"—where was she but there? In the heart of it, with her own mother's words that she'd never heard so directly, so clearly, urging her not to let this moment "pass away unenjoyed." And what were those words to a sixteen-year-old girl sitting breathless on her mother's grave, face-to-face with a twenty-one-year-old boy, a poet and beautiful, if married—but a resounding yes?

On Sunday, the twenty-sixth of June, the Godwins went to tea, and she slipped out alone. Shelley was waiting in the graveyard. They pledged their love. He blessed her "beloved name."

For the first time, she felt the truth of what she'd been told: that she'd been born under a lucky star. A comet had blazed at her birth. It was auspicious after all.

Later Shelley would write how it was that day, how she looked to him as she stepped from the shadow of the old church, into the light.

> *How beautiful and calm and free thou wert*
> *In thy young wisdom, when the mortal chain*
> *Of custom thou didst burst and rend in twain,*
> *And walked as free as light the clouds among . . .*

And he was right, she was both ecstatic and calm. Proud, too, that she had, like her mother, "burst custom" and "walked free." Shelley called it his "real birthday." His plan now was to ask Godwin for her hand, not in matrimony, given his entangled status, but ceremonially, nonetheless. As he foresaw it:

> *We will have rites our faith to bind,*
> *But our church shall be the starry night,*
> *Our altar the grassy earth outspread,*
> *And our priest the muttering wind.*

And she, too, had expected it to be like that. Expected her father to bless their love, their union, and Harriet to agree to a legal separation or, if she preferred, to come to live with them "as a sister." She'd actually envisioned it this way—that was when? Eight years ago, in those light sunny days of that summer of 1814. Looking back now, she wondered if she was already pregnant.

# IV.

July is never what June is. It's high summer, true, but without that promise. No longer offering infinite, lengthening days. Shelley approached Godwin on the sixth of July. He offered him £1,000, which, God knew, her father needed, but also asked for her hand. Godwin, shocked and incensed, barred him from the house and ordered her to her room. He did not, however, refuse—was incapable of refusing—Shelley's money.

Two days later, Godwin called her out and confronted her under her mother's portrait. Shelley was a "seducer," he told her. If he'd really loved her, he wouldn't have asked her to become "an outcast."

She had given herself freely, she answered.

If so, countered Godwin, then she had encouraged him to do what the unspeakable Imlay had done to her mother. She, Mary, his pride, his great hope, was bringing infamy on the family— Godwin was shouting now. Infamy, and would she send her own father to debtors' prison as well? Since how could he continue to take money from a blackguard who was ruining his daughter?

That was the only argument that could have succeeded with her, and it did. She had read her *Corinne*—she knew about romantic letters of renunciation. She would write Shelley, give him up, she told her father, and retreated to her room, ill and in tears.

Shelley was forbidden access to the household. But a few days later, a porter from the street came into Godwin's bookshop and slipped her a copy of *Queen Mab*, with a letter, written hastily in pencil: "You see, Mary, I have not forgotten you."

She slid the book under her clothes, next to her skin, and took the first chance to escape back to her room. "This book is sacred to me," she wrote inside. On July 13, Shelley went to Harriet, to put his situation to her in plain English. He was still her friend, he told her, but no longer her lover. There had never been between them, as she must agree, the "all-sufficing passion" to which he was now subject. He could never live with someone who didn't "feel poetry and understand philosophy," as Mary did. Surely she could see the logic of that?

Harriet was silent, and Shelley left, thinking that she was reconciled. Whereas, she was simply stunned, and once she caught her breath, she went to the Godwins in tears and begged them to keep Mary from Shelley. To this they agreed wholeheartedly, but what it turned out they couldn't do was keep Shelley from Mary. On July 19, when Godwin was out, Shelley pushed past Mrs. Godwin, rushed upstairs, and burst into the schoolroom with a pistol and a bottle of laudanum. Mary could take the poison, he told her, and he would shoot himself then and there, and they would be together in death, where no one could part them.

She ran to him in horror, and begged him to be calm, to wait, she was his, she would always be his, she swore to him, tears running down her cheeks. He finally left but—but then what, exactly? It was hard now to sort through the chaos of the next few days. Did they see each other in that eternal stretch, that interim, or live through go-betweens, secret messages? All she could remember was that he somehow got word to her: if she could slip out of the house at four in the morning on the twenty-eighth of July, he would be waiting at the corner with a coach to speed them to Dover, where they would catch the first boat across the Channel and be free.

And then—even now, she found herself drawing her hand across her eyes so she didn't have to see it, though she did see it, clearly. One of those Maniac's moments, as Shelley would call it in his poem "Julian and Maddalo," when mischief is set inexorably afoot. As she was slipping into her black silk dress that dawn, her stepsister awoke and begged to come along. One definitive *No!* or, better, knowing her capacity for "spoiling the tea," some temporizing—*We'll send for you*—and her own life would have, could have, had more of the dream that shone before her eyes that morning.

But she didn't say no—why? Because she was trembling and thought she might not mind the company of the girl who had been helpful to them, lied for them, covered for them? Because she was distracted, overexcited, in love with all the world? *Quidquid id est*, as Virgil was saying the very day Shelley first came to her schoolroom, for whatever reason, instead of no she had said yes—one small word whispered in a dark hour, and never to be unsaid. No matter how many "If only's" she'd thrown up against it since that day.

If only she'd slipped out of her father's door alone—but she didn't, she slipped out with Jane Clairmont, who soon changed her name to the more romantic "Claire." As if a change of name could change a fate, or a fateful slash through her own life. Though that morning she had no sense of what it boded, to have her fifteen-year-old, black-haired, black-eyed anti-double running by her side down the still-dark street to the corner, where Shelley was waiting with his carriage. If he was surprised to see two girls instead of one, he made no objection. On the contrary, community had been part of his greater quest all along, ever since his father had barred him from his own home for "atheism," when he was just eighteen.

So perhaps in one more girl, he saw the sisters he'd lost. He helped them in, the driver whipped the horses, and they started off on a seemingly endless drive to Dover, eleven hours on the hottest day of the year.

She was sick along the way. Despite fearing pursuit by Godwin, they had to stop a few times for her to rest in the shade. Was she already pregnant? The baby was born—early— in February. So probably yes, though she had no idea then of that. Just knew she was sick enough when they finally arrived at Dover to need a swim, to seek relief for her aching head and heaving stomach in the icy water there.

And then there was no proper ship in the harbor to take them across, so Shelley hired an open boat. It was a terrible crossing—a storm came up, she was sick, and lay with her head on Shelley's knees, falling in and out of sleep, of dreams, until, finally, he kissed her.

"Mary, look," he said. "The sun rises over France!"

# V.

Someone had come out onto the terrace—she opened her eyes. Jane Williams, though not really "Williams." That is, not really married to Ned. She was married, though, but to another English officer whom she'd left behind in India, when she ran off with Ned. She and Shelley had found them "very soft society," as he'd put it, when they'd first met, in Pisa. But the Williamses had brought some fabulous costumes with them from India, which they'd put on for Carnival, and that's when she started to like Jane, when she saw her in a brilliant turquoise sari, eyes lined with kohl. A red dot on her forehead— the East.

She, too, had caught the spirit and got up a Turkish rig, all silks and veils, and went out into the night with them, for the first time in a long time. And life in Pisa took on a lightness, a charm with the Williamses as neighbors, not that one would have thought to share a house with them.

But then Shelley had found Ned Williams an ideal sailing partner. He brought a bit more experience, a level of expertise beyond Shelley's own, and a sort of calm on the waters that suited. No poetry—unlike with Byron, with Williams Shelley was the poet, and Williams the clear-eyed navigator. And it was this sailing partnership—more than partnership, this linking of passions—that had tumbled them all together here this summer.

Which had been fine, even key, for Shelley, and not all bad for her, especially at first, since she liked Jane well enough, and often enjoyed her company. Until she realized that, over the summer, as she found herself increasingly laid up and helpless with a troublesome pregnancy, Shelley was becoming smitten with Jane.

Or rather, with her music—the way it often was with him. Love coming in through the ear. He'd even bought her a small guitar, beautiful, inlaid, which she took out in his boat on gentle evenings, and, propped picturesquely—again, those Indian costumes—against some pillows, sat playing languidly, sweetly, the music wafting into the very room where she herself lay bleeding in bed. One stupid song after another.

Which Shelley seemed to love. The good news being that Ned was always out there, too.

Now Jane Williams came out on the terrace, cheeks pale with two bright spots of red, as if she had a fever. Maybe she did. "I'm going to Livorno to find out—"

She, Mary, pulled herself up now, straighter. She didn't want her to go, wanted to be left to drift here a bit longer. As it was, the mail would come in an hour or so—there was no stopping that. "We're bound to get a letter," she said to Jane.

But Jane insisted she could wait no longer. It had been five days—"Too long!" Jane Williams cried.

But wasn't this limbo better than the worst of all news? And how could dumb Jane Williams not know that? Because, *alla fine del giorno*, as they say here, at the end of the day, despite looking exotic as a Hindu princess and playing to Shelley's small guitar, Jane Williams was dumb.

"I'm going!" cried Jane Williams.

She, Mary, considered. There was, of course, the chance that the news might not be bad, might even be good. Jane could arrive in Pisa to find that both Shelley and Williams were fine, had been fine all along, had simply been delayed—there was much to keep them there. For starters, the *Liberal*, the magazine that Leigh Hunt had come to Italy to publish—and which Byron had promised to fund. Had even agreed, at one of their midnight suppers, to house Hunt and his family in his grand, half-empty Palazzo Lanfranchi.

But Byron, being Byron, was starting to pull back at the very moment that Hunt and his wife and too many children had landed on their shores at long last, which left Shelley to mediate between "the eagle and the wren," as he called them. He being the only one who could keep Byron—the eagle—both engaged and "vegetarian," so as not to devour Hunt, Shelley's beloved wren.

So there was that in Pisa, as well as her own sense that had something happened, something dire, she would have known it, dreamed it, felt it.

So, "Fine," she said to Jane Williams, "go," and Jane went back inside and bustled around, then rushed down to the beach to get someone to row her across the bay to Lerici, to catch the coach to Livorno. But the sea was coming up again—she could hear it, pounding on the rocks, starting its rush in, under the house—and no one would take her across.

"*Dopo*," they told her, later, and Jane Williams limped back, bedraggled, wilted—but couldn't this also explain why Shelley and Williams hadn't come back this morning? First detained by something, Byron and Hunt. And now the impassable seas. A high swell.

And the fact that she would have known.

. . .

Though would she have? Was there still that connection? There was much that had come between them since those first euphoric days, when they fled England, and walked across war-torn France, all the way to Switzerland. It seemed incredible now, but they were young then—Shelley was twenty-one, she sixteen, Claire fifteen—and powered by the elation of their defiance. "With my heart full of youth and my beloved by my side," as he would put it, they read her mother's books, and started work together on a story called "The Assassins," set in their idea of Beirut. They even kept a joint journal in those days.

But by the time the August winds had started blowing chill off the Alps, Shelley had run out of money, and they had to retreat back to England the cheapest way possible. This entailed first a crowded slow boat down the Rhine, which took them past a crumbling old castle said to have belonged to an aristocratic alchemist called Frankenstein. She didn't note this in her journal, but it clearly stayed with her.

Once they got to the Channel, Shelley had to beg passage across, promising to pay immediately upon arrival in London. The ship's captain agreed, but sent a man, armed with a cudgel, to dog them all the way to the bank in London. Almost comical at first, though when they got there, Shelley discovered that Harriet had withdrawn all his money, and the man wanted to haul him to prison, then and there. But he begged for time, and then led them from one friend to the next, with no results and the captain's man close behind them with his stick. Finally, Shelley had the carriage pull up at Harriet's father's house.

With the man stationed outside the front door, and her and Claire huddled in the carriage down the street, blinds drawn, Shelley went inside, for what seemed a very long time—too long, she remembered thinking. If Harriet denied him, he would go to prison—but how could Harriet not deny him? What answer could there be for him from Harriet, except a well-deserved no?

She'd never brought herself to ask him about the scene inside the house that day, what he could possibly have dredged up to say to his pregnant, deserted wife. When he finally came out with the money, all she'd felt was a vast relief, but later came to see that it told of Harriet's hopes.

Of which Shelley had to disabuse her once again—his and Mary's "spirits," he wrote to Harriet soon after, "are united. We met with passion, she has resigned all for me."

W hich proved to be truer than she had expected. "Mary has committed a crime," her own father wrote to them. Though still willing to hound Shelley for money, he adamantly refused to see her. Her old friends shunned her as well, even her beloved Isabella Baxter. She had married, and her husband judged Mary unfit company. Her letters to Isabella were sent back unopened.

Painful, that, but it was the rejection by her father that caught her off guard, he being the man who had famously written that "the institution of marriage is a system of fraud, the worst of all laws." Who'd gone so far as to assert that in his vision of utopia, "it will [not] be known . . . who is the father of each individual child," because "such knowledge will be of no importance."

She'd grown up on those words, and now? Just words, easy enough to write? She found the position he'd taken against her irreconcilable with the father she knew, or at least had read. She wrote out her argument, citing his texts, the texts of her mother. Even went and cried out to him, under his window. He sent down Fanny, who wouldn't even look at her. Kept her eyes on the ground—she must have been instructed.

She herself turned and walked away from much that day. Couldn't stop her heart from bleeding over the man who'd been everything to her till Shelley, father and mother, teacher, guiding light. But in place of the man, she put his books, and all the books she and Shelley were reading then—Wordsworth, Coleridge, Diogenes. She was learning Greek and was distracted, too, by life itself—money, for starters. When Shelley's father learned of their elopement, he took steps to cut him off completely, and now they found themselves unable to pay any of the bills that started falling due, one after another, till they could get no further credit anywhere in London, not even for a bag of tea.

In the lunatic days that followed, Shelley left her and Claire lodged in dark little rooms, while he hid out with various friends, barely sleeping, with a string of bailiffs and bill collectors on his trail. Sundays were the only time he could stay with her without fear of arrest, it being illegal to haul in debtors on the Lord's Day. During the rest of the week, they were forced to snatch moments, passing notes at prearranged spots—dingy inns, the steps of St. Paul's. "Adieu," read one she still kept, "remember love at vespers."

And she did remember, making love on a Sunday as the evening sun came through a small window in the dark room where she was staying. But what she remembered, too, was the first inkling of the despair creeping in, a dawning of the uncertainty that would stalk the background of her life with him from then on. The question she was asking to this day: When is Shelley coming back?

Although then, that fall in London, 1814, it was more straightforward, but nonetheless hard: he was in hiding, and she was indeed the outcast her father had predicted, which had, at the time, evoked boldness and freedom, but meant in practice no friends. No one to talk to, or write to, or visit. She conjured courage, ironically, from her father's memoir of her mother, which told of Mary Wollstonecraft's fortitude in the face of social ostracism over her affair with Imlay.

But her mother was in her thirties by then, and had cultivated an inner strength, slowly and surely, in the process of living her life, the sort of fortitude that she, her daughter, had to summon out of the air, off the printed page. She was seventeen then. Pregnant.

And sick in bed much of the time, though at least with Cicero for company. Shelley had given her a copy of *Paradoxa Stoicorum*, a quaint defense of the Stoics' so-called laws, like "All fools are mad." Sometimes she laughed out loud, and wondered if Shelley had possibly laughed right then as well, since he was reading it "with her," he wrote.

His letters always buoyed her, but there came a day when she and Claire had to sell a watch Shelley had left them, for food. They both were starting to grow desperate during those weeks of real poverty in London, and Claire was about to peel off, go back to Skinner Street. She told her mother she'd had enough of the adventure by then, and her mother, greatly relieved, was helping her to rent some rooms where she could teach music, or was it French?

Both, maybe, and there was that moment when Claire almost set her own life aright, when she still could have escaped relatively unscathed. Tarnished a bit by a madcap adventure, but always under the influence of her older stepsister, Mary, on whom the blame could be, and was, firmly placed.

But it was then, too, right then, that Shelley managed a détente with his father, who agreed to pay his debts and even advance him some funds. This allowed him to come back and live with her—and Claire, who, though about to leave, hadn't left. Claire, who was not pregnant, not sick.

And that's when it started, Claire's first push for Shelley. Her stepsister didn't touch his face or kiss his lips, but she saw her eyes on his face and his lips, and when she herself fell helplessly into bed, early, exhausted, Claire would sit up late at night with Shelley. Listening to ghost stories, giving herself "hysterics," only to rush screaming into their room in the middle of the night.

And that's when she started hating Claire, recognizing her "horror" tricks for the escapades that they were. Claire was sixteen then, and excited, even fevered, to be in Shelley's constant company, his magnetic field, one might say. She herself was sleeping so much they called her "the Dormouse," but still she saw, or rather felt, the electric excitement of a growing familiarity between them, waking up in the same house, down the hall from each other—not in the same bed, but still too close. And then would come the daily rounds, all that had to be seen to and done in the city, and though Shelley would kiss her and call her his sweet Dormouse, his great love, what was that compared to what fell to the unpregnant, unsleepy Claire, ready and waiting each day, to head out, "hopping about the town with Shelley"?

And on top of that, those "horror scenes" at night, when Claire just wouldn't leave well enough alone. That's what she hated most. That she conceded to her stepsister the days, but she took the nights—tried to, wanted to. Wanted Shelley.

Who was hers, he swore, and she was his "beloved," but that didn't keep the days from darkening that autumn. They saw practically no one but Shelley's few loyal old friends. No one else would receive them: she was pregnant with his child, Harriet was pregnant with his child—unanswerable, indefensible. Brought to a close only with the birth of Harriet's baby in October, a boy they'd named Charles, Harriet's sister wrote to Shelley, his "son and heir." A freighted word, given her own status as interloper, with a child soon to come into the world heir to no one and nothing.

Nor was there any way out for any of them, Harriet, either, divorce being close to impossible. And then there was their shared and adamant philosophical stance, hers and Shelley's, against marriage, against allowing church and state into one's private life.

Which was what kept her warm that winter, that resistance, them against the world. Godwin maintained his stony silence, and prohibited Fanny from coming around as well. Looking back, she could almost forgive him. When the word had gotten out—the married atheist Shelley had run off with both of Godwin's "daughters," leaving a pregnant wife behind—Godwin, too, had been dragged through the mud, along with his whole life's work. Which was seen as leading directly to the calamity that had befallen both girls, in one fell swoop. Logical, the Tory press pointed out, if you read Godwin.

Not that anyone was reading Godwin anymore. This, too, was remarked upon in the press.

Her own baby, a girl, was born on February 22, 1815—a "six-months baby," the doctor called her. Said she wouldn't live, and packed up his bag. Still, they tried. Didn't name her, but they fed her, even started loving her, and she hung on for ten days, but on the eleventh, they woke to find her twisted up and dead in her cot.

Fanny broke Godwin protocol then and came to see them in the rain. Kind and sisterly, but then she turned and caught Fanny gazing with longing on Shelley. So—Fanny, too. Not just Claire.

Not that Fanny was another Claire. Fanny was shy and loyal, she would never come screaming through the house in the night for Shelley like Claire did. But still, she kept him up talking till three that morning. Till finally he mumbled an excuse and fled to bed.

She tried to remember if Fanny slept there that night. Or was she left to slip out alone, with no one to notice, or even wonder, if she got home safely or not?

Fanny.


That April, she, Mary, and Shelley determined to move away from London, some place by a river, or in the woods, it didn't matter where, so long as it was, in her words, "*absentia Clariae*." She wrote it in Latin—it had come to her that way. More authoritative, closer to neutral, though to her it was nothing close to neutral, and Shelley seemed to agree. Then.

They took a house in Bishopsgate, near Shelley's friend Thomas Love Peacock, close enough to the Thames so they could keep a small boat. She wrote of "regeneration," took it as the start of the life they would live now, the two of them, boating, reading, studying. They even ventured into London to visit an animal show, where they fell in love with a "very pretty antelope"—and glimpsed her father across the park. He pointedly turned away, but wrote to a friend that he found Shelley "so beautiful, it was a pity he was so wicked." Fanny said that her hand shook when he had her copy out the letter for him.

Cruel of Godwin, really, to make her copy it. Both parts—

the "wicked," which Fanny knew to be false, and "so beautiful," which she knew to be true.

So true—because he was beautiful that summer, everything was beautiful then. Claire had gone to Ireland, where with any luck she would stay forever. Longer.

And then came the further great news that Shelley had gotten a windfall—his grandfather had died and left him some money. He had to go down to London to see to that. He would be back shortly, he promised as he kissed her and left.

She was pregnant again. Had not yet turned eighteen.

Days passed, one and then another, until it was the twenty-eighth of July. One year to the day since they'd run off together. Their "anniversary," they both called it, him, too, not just her. She was sure that Shelley would come back to mark the day. She waited, kept watch, jumped up at every noise outside, every possible sound of arrival.

But the clock chimed heartlessly on, noon, afternoon, dusk. At midnight, she picked up her pen in tears.

"Dearest best Shelley, pray come to me—pray pray do not stay away from me," she found herself writing. Knew she shouldn't, but what was keeping him? Claire wasn't answering her either, there'd been no response all week to the letters she'd sent to Ireland. Was she in Ireland? If not, where was she?

Shelley had just written a beautiful homage to Coleridge:

> *Ah! wherefore didst thou build thine hope*
> *On the false earth's inconstancy?*

"Pray," she couldn't stop herself from writing at the end. Using a nickname, to lighten.

"Pray," she wrote, "is Clary with you?"

# VI.

And, looking back, she realized that she still didn't know. When he came home that time, she didn't ask, and he didn't say. And it was still unspoken between them, which was better—her dignity—though sometimes she wanted to break those chains, too. Beg him to swear, to tell her there was nothing, ever. That he hated Claire, too.

Though he didn't—hate Claire. She glanced out, sat up—there was something on the horizon. Sails, and she had a moment of thinking, *Yes!* but they weren't his, they were too big, the triangular rigs of one of the local *feluccas*. Some fishermen coming home early, before the storms blew in.

The way they did around this bay, out of nowhere. These seas were always changing, hard to read—a local girl who came yesterday with the laundry told her that July was always "*difficile*," meaning, she thought, more "complicated" than "difficult," though neither was good on the water. Especially since she wasn't convinced that Shelley quite understood how *difficile* it could be.

She wanted some tea—there was a bell. She picked it up to ring, but then stopped, in case it would bring Claire out onto the terrace. She didn't think she could stand the sight of her just now.

Though Claire seemed to be history these days to Shelley. Now it was Jane Williams, whom she had to put up with living right here, under her nose, though she'd come to terms with the phenomenon. Saw how his infatuations led to poetry, and came to regard his muses as little more than sequential midwives to his best poems.

First Claire:

> *Even while I write, my burning cheeks are wet.*
> *Alas, that the torn heart can bleed, but not forget!*

And then Sophia Stacey, an Englishwoman who played the harp and chanced into their pension in Florence:

> *Thy deep eyes, a double Planet,*
> *Gaze the wisest into madness.*

Next, the beautiful Italian girl whom they called "Emlia" and had both half loved for a while:

> *The merry mariners are bold and free:*
> *Say, my heart's sister, wilt thou sail with me?*

And now Jane Williams:

> *Forget lost health, and the divine*
> *Feelings which died in youth's brief morn;*
> *And forget me, for I can never*
> *Be thine.*

Poems of longing, but unconsummated, if one read closely. "Unheard melodies," as Keats had put it, but there was another poem, with nothing unconsummated. On the contrary.

> *His strong heart sunk and sickened with excess*
> *Of love. He reared his shuddering limbs and quelled*
> *His gasping breath, and spread his arms to meet*
> *Her panting bosom;—she drew back awhile,*
> *Then, yielding to the irresistible joy,*
> *With frantic gesture and short breathless cry*
> *Folded his frame in her dissolving arms.*

His poem to her, which the English critics read as pornography, but which she took as an expression of pure love, written in the fall of 1815, that moment when the two of them were finally living together with no Claire. They'd spent the fall taking long and delirious boat rides on the Thames, which seemed to set something alive in Shelley. He was writing such beautiful poetry amid the calm that they'd cultivated between them, the stillness.

She, too, was happy then, even well, though pregnant again. Reading Locke and Voltaire, studying Greek with Shelley, who was reading Aeschylus and Euripides. He would lie in the grass, books open, as the autumn wind tossed leaves and blew around his pages. Claire was back in London from Ireland, but living at Skinner Street, so not with them. She knew Shelley was giving her money, he felt responsible, but was he—responsible? Again, she refrained from asking. Not wanting him to put in searing words why he might be responsible, or for what.

And then, too, it seemed less to matter. First, because in January their second baby was born, a son, William, strong, healthy, and beautiful. A full nine-months child who would live this time.

"Willmouse," they called him. He was their hearts' delight. Their heads together, they would watch him, gazing into their eyes, looking from one to the other, the smiles bouncing back and forth between them. Still *absentia Clariae*. Because that spring of 1816, Claire had found another poet to chase.

L ooking back, she wondered if she would have stopped it, given the chance, the way one stops a child from wandering into a pond. Not that she could have foreseen how badly it would end, with what degree of casualty. Nor had she been given any hint of what was afoot at first, when it might still have been deflected. Though even if she had caught wind of Claire's scheme to seduce Lord Byron, she probably wouldn't have given it a second thought.

Since who could have imagined Claire getting into Byron's presence, let alone his bed? He was the most popular poet in England, as well as handsome, noble, and rich, and Claire had neither the beauty nor the standing that Byron usually took as his starting point. But timing was on Claire's side that spring, because at the very moment that she came "prancing," as he would later call it, into his life, Byron found himself the object of the kind of scandal that the generally permissive, fashionable London ladies of his acquaintance decided not to forgive.

He blamed himself—not for his so-called crime, but, on the contrary, for his one attempt at conformity. He had allowed himself to be persuaded to marry an eligible young woman whom he barely knew, in an attempt to divert his real love from a woman he knew too well—his own sister, Augusta. Half-sister, to be fair, and they hadn't been raised as siblings. She was older, the daughter of his father's first marriage, and they hadn't met until he was almost grown. He had no siblings—neither did she—and they'd found a sympathy, a familiarity, that neither had known till then. He asked to be "more than a brother" to her, and she, too, must have felt more than a sister.

As the whispers grew around them, Byron took refuge in an arranged marriage, which lasted only a few bad nights. Word got out that Byron had left his new wife to spend the summer with his sister at the family place in Nottinghamshire. After which she retired to give birth to a baby, a girl she named Medora, after the heroine in Byron's *The Corsair*.

His baby, it was whispered from drawing room to drawing room. His wife moved home and filed for separation—her specific grounds were "attempted sodomy," a serious crime in Regency England—and her father went to court, demanding that Byron be either jailed or thrown into the madhouse, or both. Mayfair and Piccadilly were outraged. Women whose love notes he'd burned without reading now could wheel their silken backs to him in the street.

And in the midst of this, he received Claire's letter.

"I place my happiness in your hands. . . . If a woman whose reputation has yet remained unstained, if without either guardian or husband to control she shd throw herself upon your mercy, if with a beating heart she could confess the love she has borne you these many yrs., if she shd secure to you secrisy & safety, if she shd return your kindness w fond affection & unbounded devotion cd you betray her or wd you be silent as the grave?"

No reply.

She tried a different tack: "I am now wavering between adoption of a literary life or of a theatrical career." Could she come to him for advice? Hoping to dazzle with some basic Dante: "*Lasciate ogni speranza, voi ch'entrate,*" to which she appended, "A most admirable description of marriage." Her Godwinian credentials.

Not that she needed to produce that reference—their scandal had rivaled his, and Byron would have known of Claire's role in the Godwin/Shelley affair by then, which is probably why he agreed to see her in the first place. But lest he doubt, she brought some of Shelley's unpublished poems along to her first meeting with him. Which was followed by an invitation that extended to her, Mary.

"Come!" Claire had begged her, "he wants to meet you," and she went—who wouldn't?—to his grand house at Piccadilly Terrace one afternoon, her favorite lines from his *Childe Harold's Pilgrimage* echoing in her ears.

> *Whilome in Albion's isle there dwelt a youth,*
> *Who ne in virtue's ways did take delight . . .*

True, there must be a boy like that! she had cried to the Baxter girls, at fifteen. And it occurred to her, walking to Piccadilly that day, that reading Byron had prepared her for meeting Shelley. She had recognized him at once as a Byronic hero, more even than Byron, she felt, especially after meeting Byron in the flesh. A sweet Byron, a much-subdued Byron, reduced from his usual duchesses to serving tea to an obscure poet's outcast lover, brought his way by their own third wheel.

Claire had led her into Byron's sitting room that day, tossing her black hair and moving to his pianoforte as if she had played it before—had she? She touched the keys, lightly but not tentatively, and then, sitting straight and concentrated, began to play better than she'd ever played before.

Shelley had been paying for lessons, expensive lessons, much begrudged by her, Mary, but on the other hand, here they were, on parade, and the result was—well, "witchcraft," as Shelley would write. She didn't usually succumb to the music,

Claire's chief weapon in the Shelley wars, but Shelley wasn't there to be won or lost that day, Byron was. And he was leaning in slightly toward the music, which meant toward Claire, with a half smile on his beautiful face.

Claire had called him "hardly a man, a god. His beauty haunting," which was true, she, too, thought, watching him that day, calm, relaxed, listening. She tried to remember what Claire had played—one of her French songs? Her mother had sent her to school to learn French, and she sang it well, and German, too—had she learned the Schubert yet? "The Elf King"? Anyway, it was something like that, romantic and exciting, and Byron was moved, she could see. Beyond that, she had no idea how far things had gone between them.

But as for her, she'd been expecting a fire-breather, a wild satyr, and she couldn't believe "how mild he is, how gentle!" He told her that he'd read and greatly admired her father, and also how much he liked the Shelley poems that Claire had brought for his "advice." She was thrilled—he liked the poetry—though sharply annoyed by Claire's presumption. Riding in on Shelley's poems, as if she had the right. Presuming to ask for advice.

And yet, it had brought them closer to the next step—to Shelley meeting Byron. The closest Shelley had come thus far was to meet Byron's publisher, John Murray, who'd turned his work down flat. It shouldn't have come as a surprise, though—Murray wasn't a publisher of poetry, he was a publisher of Byron. *The Corsair* had sold ten thousand copies in one day in February. Shelley's only published work had been suppressed under the libel laws, his publisher threatened with prison.

Still, Byron was "impressed," he told her, by Shelley's poetry, and what might a word from Murray's shining star not do for a fellow poet? Which had been her own secret agenda in coming that day. Though as she sat listening to Claire and looking at the curve of Byron's mouth—cruel, possibly; selfish, no doubt—she saw that even that small favor, a word to Murray, would require some playing. Only a fool with ass's ears would ask early and risk a no.

Anyway, Byron was Claire's that day, and she was content to stay back in the shadows, wishing her stepsister well. Since one way to get Claire out of her own life was to get her into Byron's. She knew Claire's plan was to play Mary to Byron's Shelley, to follow in her footsteps, and then leave her in the dust, Byron being more famous than Shelley.

There was, however, one detail that Claire had overlooked— the overwhelming passion that had swept Shelley to her in the first place. And there was none of that at Byron's house that day, nothing close to passion, except at the piano, in the music itself. For as she sat there under Byron's gaze, listening to Claire's heartrending Schubert, she had sensed in him an emotion that was far from scandal. That was closer to love.

Though probably not for Claire—but he seemed to like her, to be amused by the "worldly ingénue" role she was playing. There was bit more teasing, laughter, and then he showed them to the door, and the two of them went off into the blue evening, Claire talking nothing but Byron.

Though Claire apparently didn't see him again after that for a while. He was never home when she went by, nor did he answer her letters. Still, with nothing but him between herself and the deep blue sea of insignificance, she continued her pursuit. Relentlessly: "I have called twice on you, but your servants declare you to be out of town." Coyly: "Do you know I cannot talk to you when I see you? I am so awkward and only feel inclined to take a little stool and sit at your feet." Chummily: "I had ten times rather be your male friend than your mistress."

Politically: "Numerous vagrants lie about the Streets of London, naked and starving . . . the price of bread is extremely high." Seductively, proffering not just the "sparkling cup . . . but the silent and capacious bowl . . . unloosed" from the "trammels of custom & opinion."

And finally with coordinates: "On Thursday Evening we may go out of town together by some stage or mail about the distance of 10 or 12 miles. there we shall be free & unknown; we can return early the next morning. I have arranged every thing here so that the slightest suspicion may not be excited."

To Byron, there was no "no" to this. "A man is a man," as he defended himself afterward, "& if a girl of eighteen comes prancing to you at all hours of the night—there is but one way."

But Claire wasn't eighteen yet, she was seventeen, and he had recently written her what could be fairly called a love poem.

> *There be none of Beauty's daughters*
> *With a magic like thee;*
> *And like music on the waters*
> *Is thy sweet voice to me.*

Claire put it to music, and had some reason to believe that spring of 1816 that she was finally moving onto the stage of her own life, a leading role this time, especially when Byron went along with her plan for the country inn, more than once. She confessed that she'd been worried the first time she went to bed with him—not of losing her virginity, but because she'd implied a greater worldliness and was afraid that Byron might take her for a fraud.

She even wrote nervously before their first encounter: "On Saturday, a few moments may tell you more than you yet know. Till then I am content that you believe me vicious and depraved."

Cute, she'd thought, when Claire showed her that note. Maybe Byron, too, would appreciate the wit of it, the geste, high spirits. And it must have gone well, since the next day Claire wrote him again: "I was never so happy."

And there seemed to have been several more nights at the inn after that. But when Claire went by Piccadilly Terrace a week or so later with another note, she found the house in shambles, in the process of being torn apart by Byron's creditors, who were even ripping the molding from his walls for money owed.

As for milord himself, he had, Claire was informed, decamped in the dead of night, fleeing bailiffs and a pending arrest on morals charges. He'd left no word for her, but at least she knew where he was headed. She'd been there when his new traveling carriage arrived, a replica of Napoleon's, with his crest—"*Crede Byron*," "Trust Byron"—on the doors. He'd ordered it for his trip to Lake Geneva, he let slip, though when she offered to accompany him as "traveling mistress," he nixed that at once. When she suggested that the world was wide, and she might come anyway, he'd called her a "little fiend." The only address he gave her was *poste restante*. General delivery.

What did that mean? Claire asked her.

*That it's over*, she didn't say, but it was, for him if not for Claire. "God bless you," Claire was writing, almost daily, to Geneva. "I never was so happy." Which was probably true. Those few weeks when she could still "*Crede* Byron" were probably the only unalloyed happiness in her life.

"Ten minutes," she heard Claire telling Jane Williams recently, scorn and sorrow mixed. "But those ten minutes have discomposed the rest of my life." True enough in retrospect, but at the time, Claire was walking around with stars in her eyes. Plotting how to get to Geneva.

. . .

As for the two of them, Shelley had just lost a court case in London, in an attempt to break up his father's estate for ready money—which turned out to be a blessing. Since much of that money would have gone to the bottomless pit that was Godwin.

But what it meant at the time was that they had no idea where they'd get the cash they needed to live on. Then Shelley's father offered—through his lawyer; he refused to speak to his son—to pay their debts and provide an annual allowance of £1,000. Given that a portion of this had to go to Shelley's wife Harriet and the two children, it didn't leave enough for them to live in England. But on the Continent, where the cost of living was depressed by twenty years of war, it might just do. There was also the allure of putting a body of water between themselves and Godwin.

To whom neither of them had learned to say a proper no. But to go far away, beyond the reach of Godwin's messengers—as often as not poor Fanny, since he never came himself—seemed suddenly and obviously the solution. Let the English Channel keep him from their door. He would send letters, but letters could be lost, letters could be answered slowly, with deliberation, consultation between them. As opposed to her sister Fanny standing at their gate, pleading that if Shelley didn't come up with more money, Godwin would be hauled to debtors' prison that afternoon.

The chance to get beyond his reach seemed not only attractive but key to their survival. Shelley's health was problematic as well—one doctor thought consumption, another kidney disease. Both recommended somewhere warm and sunny. Italy, they were thinking.

But why Italy, argued Claire, when they could go to Switzerland, equally healthful, and meet Byron? Byron would help Shelley, recommend his poems to Murray, get him published, if only they could meet. And this would be the perfect time, and lovely, sunny Lake Geneva the perfect place.

# VII.

She could still see them all as they set out from England—
happy, hopeful, she, Shelley, baby William, the English
nursemaid, and Claire, barely contained, leaning forward in her
seat, striking sparks with her impatience. They left on the second day of May, and this time, the crossing was easy—Hermes,
not Aphrodite, guiding their star, they joked. They took a carriage rather than walking across France to Switzerland this
time. They had brought clothes, books, the baby, and they were
older—she, eighteen; Shelley, twenty-three.

France was still desolate from the Napoleonic wars, and both
Shelley and Claire were pushing for Geneva. Shelley insisted on
crossing a steep pass over the Jura at dusk, the snow had come
up over the wheels of the carriage, and they found themselves
stuck and nearly trapped overnight. But in the end, some moun-
taineers heaved them through, and they pulled up at the Hotel
d'Angleterre on Lake Geneva on the fourteenth of May, 1816,
where they took the least expensive rooms, on the top floor of
the hotel.

Byron wasn't there yet. It turned out that he'd stopped at
Waterloo to tour the battlefield, a melancholic exercise, he
told Shelley. The defeat of Napoleon was also the death of the

French Revolution. Byron said that as he'd walked through the mud there—his carriage, too, had gotten stuck up to the top of the wheels—he'd been overcome with the memory, the feeling, of that time when Napoleon was still their hero. A beautiful dreamer, almost a Werther, but a fighting version, the liberator come to carry freedom and equality to the world. Before it all turned to nightmare, first on the plains of Spain, then through Italy, all the way to Russia, with the dead stretching across the Continent from end to end.

And now Napoleon paced alone in the middle of the South Atlantic, France was in tatters, and Byron's carriage, still splattered with mud, pulled up at the Hotel d'Angleterre. It was the twenty-fifth of May. His trip hadn't been easy—he entered his age as "100" in the hotel register and went straight to his rooms.

"I am sorry you are grown so old," Claire wrote that afternoon. "Indeed I suspected you were 200, from the slowness of your journey. . . . I am so happy."

She'd been waiting for him, watching, patrolling the gardens, *Childe Harold's Pilgrimage* in her hand—though what she should have been reading was *Glenarvon*, Lady Caroline Lamb's explosive best seller that gave a lightly disguised version of her disastrous affair with him. "Mad, bad, and dangerous to know," Lady Caroline had called him.

Or even if Claire had just taken heed of the epigraph from his own *The Corsair*:

> *He left a name to all succeeding times,*
> *Link'd with one virtue and a thousand crimes.*

But she didn't, just kept writing witty little note after note that he didn't bother to answer, nor did he emerge from his rooms. Maybe he was writing his beautiful, melancholic "Epistle to Augusta": "My sister! my sweet sister!" It was true that Byron's sister was one of his "thousand crimes," but when she, Mary, read this poem, she felt again the sweetness that she'd glimpsed at his house in London that day.

"My whole life was a contest," he wrote. Spoke of his "inheritance of storms." She knew some of them: Born with a clubbed foot. Father, "Mad Jack," first crazy, then dead. Mother banned from his school for her outbursts. Title inherited from "Wicked Lord William." No brothers, no games at home, no one to turn to, with whom to say "us," "our."

Until Augusta:

> *I did remind thee of our own dear Lake,*
> *By the old Hall which may be mine no more.*

"Our own dear Lake." Augusta's, too. No explanation required. The only one in the world who could see it as he did. The only place,

> *. . . my own sweet sister, in thy heart*
> *I know myself secure, as thou in mine.*

And how could Claire compete with that? Claire, whose infatuation Byron would have scented from afar for what it was, both garden-variety and essentially impersonal. Cold. Little to do with him as a man with a "dear Lake," and all to do with his "Fame . . . unsought."

Though if Claire had once understood this deep need in his soul, or even read this poem instead of his outgrown *Childe Harold*, she might have turned out to be interesting to Byron after all. But Claire didn't read much poetry, and, in her defense, was just seventeen.

. . .

When Byron finally emerged for a sail on Lake Geneva, Claire, on full alert, caught sight of him at once, and begged them to accompany her on a stroll down to the quay. When Byron saw them, he hopped gallantly out of his boat and limped toward shore. He'd managed to disguise his bad foot when she and Claire had visited him in London, and now she could see his frown as he struggled through the shallow water. He nodded briefly to her and Claire, and shook hands with much reserve with Shelley, who was equally ill-at-ease with his own role in this charade. It fell to her, Mary, to produce the small conversation—his journey, the hotel, the weather, which had been "rather bad." It was the first nice day, they all agreed. That settled, Byron invited Shelley—pointedly, only—to dine with him that evening and then made his way back to his companion, the young doctor John Polidori, to help him bring in the boat.

That night, Shelley reported, things went better with the poets. Female distraction at bay, they relaxed in each other's company and talked till dawn. Claire considered this a personal victory. It was she, after all, who'd produced Shelley. Byron would clearly take him as an extension of herself.

Though what Byron took Shelley for was a shield against her. She, Mary, was already noting how Byron stiffened whenever Claire came onto the scene. He rebuffed her various attempts at establishing herself as his public companion—a stroll by the lake, a cup of tea in the hotel dining room. Claire then sent him another note: "I have been in this weary hotel this fortnight & it seems so unkind, so cruel of you to treat me with such marked indifference. Will you go straight up to the top of the house this evening at half-past seven & I will infallibly be on the landing place & show you the room."

He would, he did. It was still essentially lighthearted for him at that point. As he confessed to his sister, his confidante, Augusta, "Now—don't scold—but what cd I do?—a foolish girl—in spite of all I cd say or do—wd come after me—or rather went before me—for I found her here . . . I cd not exactly play the Stoic w a woman—who had scrambled 800 miles to unphilosophize me."

But though Byron was perfectly willing to accompany "a foolish girl"—his words—"to the top of the house"—hers—it was Shelley who'd captured his heart and mind that summer. They bought a small boat together, and moved out of the Hotel d'Angleterre, which, as May turned to June, was filling up with the kind of English tourists who both disapproved of the poets' lifestyles and were dying for a peek into their rooms.

They found places to rent across the lake, a nice cottage for the Shelley party, and the grand Villa Diodati for Byron, about a ten-minute walk away, through vineyards, up a gentle hill. They all loved the fact that Milton had once spent a summer there, with his school friend Diodati. Byron and Shelley took advantage of a break in the continuing bad weather to sail the boat around the lake, visiting the Castle of Chillon, where they climbed down into the dungeon and read the names of the prisoners scrawled in desperation on the walls, and gazed on "a beam, now black and rotten, on which the prisoners were hung in secret," as Shelley wrote to her. "I never saw a monument more terrible."

They continued around the lake, on a pilgrimage to the sites where their beloved Jean-Jacques Rousseau had set his novel *Julie, ou la Nouvelle Héloïse*. Shelley told her afterward that one afternoon a storm had come up and the boat nearly capsized. Byron had learned that Shelley couldn't swim—and "I knew [he] would have attempted to save me, and I was overcome with humiliation." Said he would have preferred to drown.

But his mood after the trip was anything but tragic. He'd

been struck mute at first by his proximity to Byron, daunted by the other's clear, far-ringing voice. Still he came back from their trip together with the only thing that could cure his various ailments, poetic inspiration. He wrote "Hymn to Intellectual Beauty":

> *I vow'd that I would dedicate my powers*
> *To thee and thine: have I not kept the vow?*

Followed by the "The Daemon of the World":

> *Floating on waves of music and of light,*
> *The chariot of the Daemon of the World*
> *Descends in silent power:*

And then "Mont Blanc":

> *—Is this the scene*
> *Where the old Earthquake-daemon taught her young*
> *Ruin? Were these their toys? or did a sea*
> *Of fire envelop once this silent snow?*

And as for Byron, he came back with "The Prisoner of Chillon":

> *My very chains and I grew friends,*
> *So much a long communion tends*
> *To make us what we are:—even I*
> *Regain'd my freedom with a sigh.*

—which Murray published and which sold out the first day.

# VIII.

As word went out among the English tourists that a "League of Incest" had sprung up across the lake, the Hotel d'Angleterre began offering cruises past Byron's villa, complete with a spyglass. One day some sheets were drying on the balcony—"women's petticoats," the scandalized tourists wrote home. "No person of respectability would visit," an English clergyman sniffed.

Which was fine with the "League" themselves, perfect—everything was perfect, except the weather. It turned out that 1816 would be called "the year without a summer." A volcanic eruption on the other side of the world caused temperatures to fall and crops to fail all across Europe. For the five of them, she, Shelley, Byron, Claire, and the young doctor, Polidori, it meant incessant rain that kept them from sailing, and spectacular storms that occasionally stranded them overnight at Villa Diodati.

They would sit on the balcony, watching as the storms "approach from the opposite side of the lake, observing the lightning dart in jagged figures upon the piny heights of the Jura." Storms "finer," she wrote, than she had "ever before beheld." Claire wasn't yet persona non grata at the villa, and on the nights when she played and sang, Byron took her to his room.

Sometimes they sat up till dawn talking, mostly about what they were reading that summer—Schiller, Dante, Ariosto, Shakespeare, and, always, Coleridge. And then there were the new Gothic tales they were passing back and forth, with the thunder rolling and the lightning flashing all around them.

Thrilling stories of the dark and primal that yet connected with the latest scientific inquiries into the "nature of the principles of life." Erasmus Darwin's famous piece of vermicelli that he'd gotten to jump around in a jar, with invisible electrical forces that no one quite understood. Luigi Galvani's "galvanism," which had produced muscular contractions in dead frogs during an electrical storm. His nephew was said to have taken it further, using the same electrical force to cause dead human bodies to sit up, move their arms and legs, even blow out candles.

They had all, even Byron, fallen silent at that—the vision of a corpse, seated upright, blowing out a candle. She herself saw it too well—she'd had to retreat out onto the balcony, into the rain, to get away from it, fill her eyes with lightning and storm clouds. When she came back inside, Byron was reading aloud from a new French translation of German ghost stories. One featured a dead twin who came back to life on her sister's wedding day, got to the church first, and tricked her sister's fiancé into marrying her—the dead girl instead of the live one.

Silence. A thunderclap outside, off the lake. Someone wondered aloud what would have happened next, between the ghost and the fiancé. The story ended prematurely, they agreed. The writer was afraid to go into the bedroom.

But would we? Byron asked.

It was late. The rain was pouring down. There was no light

on the horizon, no sign of it clearing the next day, or ever. They agreed to a challenge—they would each try to write a horror story. Byron turned to her—that's where his hopes were, he said. "Mary and I will publish ours together."

This caught her by surprise—did he mean it? Both parts—did he really think that she could do it? And was he serious about "publishing together"? To publish with Byron would be to publish indeed. But could she write something worth publishing, with or without Byron? She wasn't sure. She hadn't yet. Life had come between her and her pen, her birthright, as she and Shelley had both seen it. But there had been babies. Money trouble. Shelley himself. Byron. Claire.

But she was the daughter of Mary Wollstonecraft and William Godwin. Born for something, maybe even for this. To venture into the bedroom where men feared to tread.

She smiled at Byron, "sidelong," as they used to tease her, from under her lashes, without turning her head. "I take your challenge," she said.

They all did, but Shelley and Byron both soon lost interest—poetry and fiction must spring from different sources, she figured. Polidori started with a two-headed woman, but then picked up the tale that Byron had dropped, called "The Vampyre," which he later published in London, to some success. Not enough, though, to stop him from taking a fatal dose of prussic acid two years later. Poor "Polly-dolly," as Byron used to mock him. She had liked him almost in spite of himself. He'd been brought along that summer to oversee Byron's obsessive purges and fasts, his terror of getting fat, but Polidori was only nineteen, and, though already trained as a doctor, far too young for what one might call the cultural exigencies of the post. He'd lost patience with "milord" even before they'd gotten to the lake, and Byron, sensing rebellion, was merciless. "Polly-dolly."

But as for the challenge, she herself was the one, of all of them, who took it most seriously, took it as her great chance. Rise to it now and publish with Byron, or fade back into womanhood. Motherhood. The girl to the side, eternally pregnant, nursing, sleeping, sick. Her life the past two years, so utterly at odds with why she'd run off with Shelley. The freedom she'd envisioned, the passion that had carried her out her own door, Godwin's door, that midnight. She could cry now, weep bitter tears—or she could write.

She went to bed nights that summer, trying to "think of a story," woke up mornings, trying to "think of a story." It became a joke among them—"Have you thought of a story yet?" But she hadn't, couldn't, maybe wouldn't, she was starting to fear.

Look away from it, Shelley said to her one night, when the storms had come early and kept them at home. She picked up Virgil, and read aloud to him from Dido and Aeneas—"I will die unavenged, but let me die / Thus—thus—it is right that I go into the dark."

She broke down in tears at that and went to bed, shaken. Dreamed intensely, though not of the star-crossed lovers in their cave, but of a young scientist standing over a hideous oversized body pieced together from corpses. Very much like Galvani's, the one that blew out the candle, only this time the body sat up and came alive.

She screamed, and woke Shelley. It took some time for him to bring her back, to stop her shaking, but suddenly she became very still. Calm. Elated.

"I have my story," she said.

. . .

That was in June. In July, as she sought out settings for her tale, they decided to join Byron on an outing to Chamonix, and visit the famous Mer de Glace—though he backed out at the last minute when he saw that Claire was coming. His simple avoidance of Claire was turning to aversion—bad news indeed, she realized on this trip, when she caught sight of Claire's belly.

She'd turned, shocked, to Shelley, and saw in his eyes that he knew.

Claire must have already confided in him—how had he not told her? How had he held Claire's secret from her, held it over and above what was between the two of them? She would never have done that to him—she kept nothing from him in those days. And there was Claire, too, who'd trusted him, not her, but it wasn't Claire's betrayal that she minded. It was Shelley's.

She'd been happy on this trip—light of heart, almost care-free, both she and Shelley, or so she'd thought. In one of the hotel registers, as his profession, he'd written "atheist" in Greek, and for his next destination, "*l'enfer*," hell, in French. And they'd laughed, it was a joke, obviously, though a clergy-man who'd shown up later that summer had carried the tale back to England, where it created still more scandal. Further proof that they were lost.

But she hadn't felt lost there, among the highest peaks in the Alps. Everywhere she looked was the kind of drama she'd been seeking for her "story." The afternoon before, they had "heard a sound like the rolling of distant thunder" and seen an "ava-lenche rush down the ravine of the rock." She and Shelley had watched it together, both marveling, both entranced—or had he been worrying about Claire? All along?

She leveled her glance at them both then—"Does Albé

know?" she asked, using the nickname. Asserting her friendship with Byron to them both. Claire confessed that she hadn't had the nerve, or even the chance, to tell him—recently he hadn't let her near him. She'd been hoping that on this trip, but—

Yes, but. There'd been no Byron on this trip, since there was a Claire, and Byron could no longer abide her company. And would it remain that way? And if it did, what would become of the child? Though she knew exactly what: Shelley would have to take it on, and then the obvious assumption would attach— to them all, her, too. "The League of Incest." She took a deep breath and sat down, hard, on the grass, on the lovely Swiss hillside—or were they in France? It was beautiful there, but she insisted they go straight back, for Shelley to confront Byron with the news.

Byron's first reaction was to ask Shelley if the child might be his, Shelley's. She wished she'd been there to speak out, in her own defense more even than in Shelley's. How could Byron insinuate that she, whom he knew, whom he liked, who he believed would write a great story, would live as part of such a common mess as that? But Shelley, rather than taking offense, had simply sworn on his honor as a gentleman that there was no chance of this. The baby was Byron's.

And then Byron, to his credit, faced "the *suite*," as he put it, of his dalliance with Claire. He gave Shelley his terms: he would support the child, but have nothing further to do with Claire. The birth was to remain secret, and the child would be raised by a designee. Claire could visit occasionally as an aunt, but never as part of Byron's household. Claire, secretly reckoning that the baby, once born, would bring Byron back to her, agreed on all counts.

Not that she had any choice. The baby wasn't due till January, but the news had already cast its shadow over both houses. On August 4, they gathered to celebrate Shelley's twenty-fourth birthday, by launching a hot-air balloon out over the lake, but it burned up before rising, which she tried not to take as a sign.

Because for her, she was halfway through her outline. Her "story," Shelley told Byron, was becoming a book. Becoming more than that—her homicidal monster was dazzling her, illuminating her days. She was no longer wondering, as August came to a close, what further secrets Shelley and Claire might hold between them. She was thinking instead about the best way to tell her tale. She reread *Clarissa*—would letters work? An epistolary novel? There were several strands, several voices. So maybe letters?

They had to call her name twice, for Shelley's birthday toast. She hoped afterward that she'd said good night to Byron and Polidori. She barely noticed when she went in, early, that she'd left Shelley's birthday wine undrunk.

# IX.

At the end of August, Shelley and Byron went out for one last sail on the lake.

Shelley's money troubles were entangled again. They were obliged to go back to England to sort it out. Shelley agreed to carry Byron's latest work back to London, to Murray, his publisher, both as a favor and truly in the hopes that this would carry his own work along there as well. And hers, too, why not? Wasn't Murray whom Byron meant when he'd said they would "publish together"?

They left the beautiful lake in September of 1816. She had just turned nineteen. She and Shelley had passed two full years together by then. The passion that he'd pledged at St. Pancras, the pledge that she'd taken at sixteen as everlasting—there were still moments when she felt it. But trust in it, the way she did then? Maybe not. She might not then, by nineteen, have staked her whole life on that love, as she did that first summer.

Because what if it wasn't an entirely new kind of love that the two of them had discovered? What if it was just another one of those great romances that flames high and then turns to ash? This hadn't even crossed her mind till the time, a year later, when he hadn't come home to mark their anniversary. His "real birthday," he'd called it, but what did that mean to him, since he hadn't come home to spend it with her? What if he'd spent that day, or worse, night, in London with Claire? What was she supposed to do, weight her pockets like her mother and throw herself in the Thames?

She'd even considered it, briefly, that bleak night. But then, when he had come, they'd smiled into each other's eyes and fallen into bed with the same passion that had carried her to him in the first place—almost. Because that passion had been clear and pure, and from then on it was a bit clouded, like ether into which some tincture had been dropped. Fear, in her case.

Nor could she could walk quite so boldly as she had at St. Pancras, when she'd thought Shelley's love for her was infinite, revolutionary. The kind of love which had rendered her, in his words, "beautiful and calm and free." Hard, though, for "the mortal chain of custom" to "burst" while looking back over one's shoulder. Wondering, where is Shelley? Where is Claire?

Whose passage back to England that September was bought by Shelley, not Byron, for some reason—or all the reasons, the first being that Byron didn't, so Shelley did. But as for her, Mary, Claire wasn't as much on her mind those days as before. She was grappling instead with ideas, concepts—life forces, licit and illicit, and creators, creatures, the very meaning of life. If anything, she felt sorry for her stepsister. Before they left, she'd found a copy of a letter that Claire had written to Byron: "My dreadful fear is lest you quite forget me . . . now don't laugh or smile in your little proud way for it is very wrong for you to read this merrily which I write in tears . . . I shall love you to the end of my life."

To this Byron did not reply.

. . .

They decided to set up in Bath to sit out Claire's pregnancy, far enough from London to keep the affair from the Godwins. Shelley would go to London as needed to see to his finances. The seclusion of Bath, where they knew no one, would suit her as well. It would be nicer than London for little Willmouse, now nearly a year old, and a quiet place for her to work.

They rented a house with a study, and there she sat to outline — hard work on the surface, but the best part of her day. She was under the spell of the story, of a sort of pure inspiration that carried her to her desk first thing in the morning, and back to her desk at night. Woke her at dawn, when she would creep down with a candle and sit shivering, jotting notes that had come to her in dreams, sometimes sent, or so it seemed, by her mother. She had been trying to picture one of her monster's murders, and woke that morning with the painting *The Nightmare* by Henry Fuseli, her mother's Swiss lover, before her eyes, and then she had it. Her poor victim, Elisabeth, arms flung out, long red hair hanging down, as in the Fuseli, murdered by the monster on her wedding bed.

She had decided to call her scientist Frankenstein, after the crumbling German castle they'd passed on the Rhine two years earlier. To her poor motherless monster, her "creature," she gave no name — but, like her first child, that didn't mean she didn't know him. She even knew what he was reading, exactly what she was reading, or rereading, that fall — Plutarch's *Lives*, *Paradise Lost*, *Gulliver's Travels*. *The Sorrows of Young Werther*, which book, claimed her monster, taught him "gentle and domestic manners, and lofty sentiments," and served him, as it had served her, as a sort of Romantic conduct book. "I wept his extinction,"

her monster said of Werther, "without fully understanding it."
As she had, at fifteen.

Poor monster, poor parentless monster—she, too, found herself weeping, over him at that point, as she could look back over
her own young life and weep. Like him, she, too, had "entered
on life without a mother's care," as her mother had once written. Like him, she knew rejection. While her creature's "father"
had fled from his "watery eyes, his shriveled complexion, and
straight black lips," hadn't her own father reacted similarly
when she ran off with Shelley? When he could no longer see her
as the intelligent, innocent girl of sixteen that he'd been "creating"? Once she diverged from his vision, hadn't he, like Victor
Frankenstein, slammed the door and turned the key?

Not that she'd gone on her monster's murderous rampage,
but she knew why he'd done it. She'd felt his panic, and appreciated his despair. Of her father's behavior, she'd written to
Shelley, "I know not whether it is early habit or affection but
the idea of his silent quiet disapprobation makes me weep as
it did in the days of my childhood." And why this disapprobation, this wholesale rejection? Because she was pregnant and
unmarried?

But did that make her monstrous? And what about her
father? Hadn't he behaved monstrously? And Shelley's father,
too, Sir Timothy, who had banished his own son from the family home at eighteen. Shelley was his eldest son and legal heir.
He had been educated by Sir Timothy to inherit, not to work.
But when the result of his gentleman's education at Eton and
Oxford had led him beyond the established Church to an ongoing quest for social justice—his father had turned him out of his
house, as if he were a monster.

Though who really was the monster, now that she thought
about it? The creature with yellow skin and straight black lips,

or the creator who had made him that way? Godwin had educated her to be bold, to disdain social convention. Sir Timothy had somehow, must somehow, have opened a door or window for Shelley's mind to take flight. And yet he had cut Shelley off without a penny and banned him from the house when he married Harriet, and left him to, what? To starve to death? Kill himself out of remorse? What possible outcome could Shelley's father have been seeking? What that wasn't truly monstrous?

So who were the monsters? Her? Shelley? The monster or Frankenstein himself? She'd heard that when the play was produced in London last year, they'd called the monster "Frankenstein," and she'd written to correct it, but had come to think, *Yes, maybe.* They were mistaken, of course, mistaking the monster's name for that of his creator, but in the larger sense, yes, maybe he was the monster. Not the creature but the man.

B ut it had taken her time to come to this conclusion. She wasn't there yet, when she finally sat to write, on October 8, 1816. She remembered the date because it had proved so fateful, so tragic. When she wrote it in her journal, it had been hopefully, happily, even. Just to note that she had finished her outline and was planning that day to begin to write.

But she'd barely gotten to her desk when she got a letter. Her sister Fanny had written to say that she would be changing coaches in Bath on her way to Bristol, where she was planning to visit some Wollstonecraft relations. She was hoping that Mary and Shelley might like to come have a cup of tea with her at the coaching inn.

They didn't "like to," but they went—thank God they went. They hadn't seen her since their return to England, hadn't invited her down, their excuse being the need to keep Claire's

pregnancy strictly secret from the Godwin house. But, looking back, who better than Fanny to keep that kind of secret?
And in truth, it was more that they were annoyed with her—
and afraid that she would try to wheedle more money from
them for Godwin. Poor Fanny—even after she'd visited them
in London and seen their struggle, she'd still felt compelled
to write that "it is of utmost consequence for his own"—Godwin's—"and the world's sake that he should finish his novel,
and is it not your and Shelley's duty to consider these things?"

"Another stupid letter from Fanny," she wrote in her journal
that day. Blaming Fanny, and blinded, she feared, by the "stu-
pidity" to the cri de coeur that came toward the end. "I understand from Mamma"—only Fanny would persist in calling that
common, vindictive woman Mamma—"that I am your laughing-
stock and the constant beacon of your satire." When she, Mary,
reread it, after, she was stunned by the wanton cruelty of
Godwin's wife. To conjure that lie, and at Fanny's expense—
Fanny, "Mamma's" constant helper, there at her beck and call,
desperate to please.

But what about her, Mary? Had she rebutted that charge
at the time? Did she and Shelley disabuse poor Fanny sufficiently, or even at all, or had it all been lost in their angry
reaction to the endless importuning? In that same letter,
Fanny accused them of being "selfish," so it's not impossible
that her poor sad words at the end—"laughing-stock," "constant beacon of satire"—painful in the extreme to her, had
gone unaddressed by them, amid all the rest they were called
to defend that day.


When they met her at the coaching inn in Bath on the
eighth of October, Fanny hinted about the possibility

of leaving the Godwin house and coming to live with them. They'd probably exchanged glances—which Fanny would no doubt have caught. She had grown up with those glances, they comprised her earliest education. The prelude to, "No, Fanny. I'm afraid not."

Afterward, Shelley drew it plain enough:

> *Her voice did quiver as we parted,*
> *Yet knew I not that heart was broken*
> *From which it came, and I departed*
> *Heeding not the words then spoken.*
> *Misery—O misery,*
> *This world is all too wide for thee.*

The next day, the ninth, they got an urgent letter from Godwin, who enclosed a note from Fanny in a shaky hand: "I depart immediately to the spot from which I hope never to remove." She wrote that she was going to Bristol. Godwin was on his way down, but he urged Shelley to rush to Bristol, as they were much closer.

Shelley did, but Bristol turned out to be Fanny's smoke-screen. She had in fact traveled on to Swansea, on the Welsh coast, and taken a room at the Mackworth Arms, as the local paper would report. "A most respectable-looking female, who arrived late, took tea and retired to rest, telling the chambermaid she was exceedingly fatigued and would take care of the candle herself."

The next morning, her "non-appearance" caused the door to be forced, "where she was found a corpse with the remains of a bottle of laudanum on the table." She was wearing a blue striped skirt, a white blouse, the small gold watch that she and Shelley had brought her from France, stockings marked with

*G* for Godwin, and their mother's old stays with the letters MW, embroidered in red.

Her own first thought, as she stood swaying by her writing table, fingers turning white, pressed to the wood, was to wonder if Fanny was wearing their mother's undergarments because she liked them, or because they were all she had. Had no one ever thought to buy her stays of her own? But who would have? She, Mary, had gotten her first stays in Scotland, with Isabella and Christy Baxter. Their mother had taken her with the other girls. But who would have taken Fanny?

Her small leather purse, the paper reported, contained five shillings and a sixpenny piece. Had Fanny paid for the room in advance? She wondered this, too—anything to try to keep from seeing Fanny lying "a corpse," near the "remains" of the laudanum bottle. "Twenty-two," she found herself saying aloud, at her last birthday. The fourteenth of May. So nearly twenty-two and a half.

Fanny had left a note. "I have long determined that the best thing I could do was to put an end to the existence of a being whose birth was unfortunate, and whose life has only been a series of pain to those persons who hurt their health in endeavoring to promote her welfare. Perhaps to hear of my death will give you pain but you will soon have the blessing of forgetting that such a creature ever existed as—"

As whom? How did she sign it? Fanny Godwin? Fanny Imlay? Fanny Wollstonecraft? They never knew. The newspaper reported that the signature had been ripped off and burned to ash.

Fanny! Monstrous of them all to have left her with no settled name. Her birth "unfortunate," her life a "series of pain"—how could she herself not have seen that "that heart was broken"? She was Fanny's closest living relative, her sister, half-sister—

why had they all made such a point of that? Why had they kept that word, "half," between them, and why had she never once thought to slip out with her sister and buy her new stays?

Not that Fanny would have gone along with that. Even if they'd ever been able to afford it, rather than stays for herself, Fanny would have given the money to "Mamma." To Godwin, who returned the favor by begging Shelley not to claim the body, to "do nothing to destroy the obscurity she so much desired that now rests upon the event." In other words, to leave his name out of it. Better to let Fanny be thrown into an unmarked grave in a pauper's cemetery, wrote Godwin, rather than risk any further scandal to himself, and that is what they did.

A nd yet, sitting here now on the terrace, it came to her that the one person whose presence she could have wished for, or even stood, was Fanny's. That is, a Fanny free from Godwin, Fanny with her small smile. She hadn't appreciated it then, how Fanny had been left to pick up the pieces that she herself had left shattered behind her when she ran off with Shelley. She, in love, in France, had been oblivious to the way that Godwin had been savaged by the press. His very life's work blamed for her elopement with a married man who'd deserted a pregnant wife—criminal. And not only her, but her stepsister as well— called "both Godwin girls" in the press. Both willing to be seduced by the radical atheist Shelley. Precisely what was to be expected from children raised by Godwin.

Which left Fanny—known as the "third Godwin girl," at least in the press, if not at home. An outsider whose only connection to the household was the half-sister who'd disgraced them all and whose only justification thereafter was to atone for her sister's "crime," as best she could. She suddenly remembered a letter that Godwin had forwarded to her in Scotland, written by—painful to think of—Harriet, Shelley's wife, after coming to dinner at Skinner Street sometime in 1812.

Fanny would have been nineteen then. Harriet wrote that Fanny's beautiful mind "fully overbalances the plainness of her countenance." Yes, Fanny was plain. She had had smallpox. But Harriet was right, she did have a beautiful mind, though with no way to put it to use, no time or place to sit and write anything beyond those endless letters begging for money for Godwin. Which left Fanny, in the end, cast up on the shore, too discouraged to cut the ties that for most of her life had bound her, and that she could not, in the end, unloose.

"Misery." Fanny had sent her one last letter, which she barely read before she burned it. All she wrote in her journal was, "Fanny dies this night." There was no blame in the letter, if she remembered correctly, but she couldn't, quite. She'd been horrified at the time, guilty, at a loss, and there were still embers in the grate. She'd walked quickly over and thrown in the letter. Picked up the poker and pushed it into the hottest part of the fire. It flamed at once, and though she knew right then that it was a terrible mistake, it was too late to get it back.

Fanny.

It was a bad autumn after that, personal and general. She wore black for a while, but she threw herself into her work on *Frankenstein*, the horror on her pages, strangely enough, holding off her distress, at least at home. Outside, though, the talk was of bad harvests, food shortages, riots. Protests at Spa Fields, where revolution seemed almost at hand. The leaders were passing around pirated copies of Shelley's *Queen Mab*, for better or worse. Better, in that this was always Shelley's intention in the

writing it, to inspire a workers' movement. Worse, in that his
lawyer wrote that there was talk that he might be charged with
sedition. He should come to London to address that at once.

When he got there, he also got the news that Harriet had
been missing for over a month, and no one knew where she
was. This was in late November. Apparently she'd taken up with
a military man and had been living in Knightsbridge, under
the name of Smith. But she hadn't been seen there since the
ninth of November. According to her landlady, she was "in the
family way."

Her body floated up in the Serpentine on the tenth of
December. On the twelfth, there was a notice in the *Times*. "On
Tuesday a respectable female, far advanced in pregnancy, was
taken out of the Serpentine river and brought to her residence
in Queen Street, Brompton, having been missed for nearly six
weeks. She had a valuable ring on her finger."

Harriet, too, had left a note: "Too wretched to exert myself,
lowered in the opinion of everyone, why should I drag on a
miserable existence?" She bade a touching farewell to her sister, thanked her, loved her, and then addressed Shelley, whom
she called "Bysshe." His middle name. What she must have
called him.

"My dear Bysshe, let me conjure you by the remembrance of
our days of happiness to grant my last wish, Do not take your
innocent child from Eliza who has been more than I have, who
has watched over her with such unceasing care. Do not refuse
my last request. I never could refuse you. . . ."

But he did refuse her. To her own surprise, dismay, for
she'd been moved by Harriet's plea, he went straight to court to
fight for custody of the daughter Harriet wrote of and the son
he'd never met. He was quite sure of winning his case. He had
the whole of English common law ranged behind him, which

always stood firmly for fathers, as opposed to mothers, no matter the circumstances, his lawyers assured him. Though to further legitimize his claim, they advised him to take advantage of the fact that he was now free and "regularize" his current relationship. He agreed and urged her to come up to London right away to marry him.

This took her by surprise, and she hedged—she was working on her book, she had her principles, she scorned marriage, and didn't he? Rather than answer, he turned to Godwin, who was, he wrote to her at once, overjoyed at the prospect of seeing her "according to the vulgar ideas of the world . . . well married," to a "future ornament" of the English aristocracy. Though taken aback by his delight, even his choice of words, she could not in the end resist him. Thus it was that she found herself standing beside Shelley in St. Mildred's Church on a dark day at the close of a very bad year, pledging her troth in the eyes of a God she didn't believe in and men she for the most part despised.

All she told Byron of her marriage was that "another incident allows me to sign myself Mary W. Shelley." The "incident," Harriet's suicide, went unmentioned in the letter. Between themselves, she and Shelley blamed the seamy side of Harriet's life—her pregnancy, her officer—for the despair into which she had fallen, never once going near what lay beneath, their own part in it.

Which worked for a while. It was only as loss after loss struck her own life that it occurred to her that Harriet, in some demonic, avenging form, might have had a role. But that December 1816, she didn't mention Harriet to Byron. It was just as well that he was still abroad, she wrote. England was a disaster—failed harvests, regressive taxes, armed troops firing on the peaceably assembled people. Shelley's own father had spoken in Parliament in favor of the suspension of the ancient right of habeas corpus. So-called libel laws were tightened. Journalists opposed to the repressive government were either exiled or imprisoned. Shelley was tormented by all of this, and couldn't sleep at night.

But in the midst of all the turmoil, he received a brilliant notice in the "Young Poets" edition of the influential intellectual paper the *Examiner*. "Three young writers," wrote the editor Leigh Hunt, "appear to us to promise a considerable addition of strength to the new school"—Keats, John Reynolds, and Shelley, whom he singled out as "a very striking and original thinker."

He wrote separately to say that he'd like to publish Shelley's "Hymn to Intellectual Beauty":

> . . . *music by the night-wind sent*
> *Through strings of some still instrument,*
> *Or moonlight on a midnight stream,*
> *Gives grace and truth to life's unquiet dream.*

Shelley was overjoyed. He had felt till then, he wrote to Hunt, "an outcast from human society." And shortly after that, even the hated Tory *Blackwood's* called him "a scholar, a gentleman and a poet . . . strong and original . . . well entitled to take his place near to the great creative masters."

Thus the dark year closed for them on a hopeful note. To receive Harriet's two children, they took a twenty-year lease on a beautiful house, thirty miles from London, in Marlow on the Thames. They visited Hunt, and were taken into his circle. At his charming house in Hampstead, they dined with Keats and the critic William Hazlitt. Mary met Hunt's wife, Marianne, and her sister, Bessie—Marianne's "Claire," who lived with them, too, and was in love with Marianne's husband.

For the first time in two years, she had a woman she could talk to.

# X.

On the twelfth of January, 1817, Claire's baby, a girl, was born in Bath. Shelley wrote to Byron at once, telling him the baby was beautiful—but Byron didn't answer. Shelley wrote again—her hair was black, her eyes blue—but still no word. There was, they knew, the real possibility of desertion, of both mother and child. "Faithless Albé," as she called him in her journal.

The little fictions they invented—that the baby belonged to "a friend," one of the Hunts' cousins, and so on—had never worked, and the truth—that she was Byron's—was scarcely more credible. The whisperers, even in the Godwin house, accused Shelley.

He was, after all, supporting both Claire and the baby, and had even bought Claire a piano, which she herself didn't entirely begrudge her, until she came upon a poem on Shelley's desk:

> *Thus to be lost and thus to sink and die,*
> *Perchance were death indeed!—Constantia, turn!*
> *In thy dark eyes a power like light doth lie.*

Her own eyes weren't dark—though Claire's were.

*Her voice is hovering o'er my soul—it lingers*
  *O'ershadowing it with soft and lulling wings,*
*The blood and life within those snowy fingers*
  *Teach witchcraft to the instrumental strings.*

Whose "snowy fingers"? What "witchcraft"? Byron had called Claire a "prancer." Wrote that he'd "never loved or pretended to love her." Did Shelley really sit there, all those nights, "cheeks wet," unable to "forget," as the poem went on, as that unloved prancer pounded the piano they couldn't afford and still hadn't paid for?

She gazed at his face before getting into bed that night. He had a candle, he was reading. The worst part was that it was a beautiful poem, a love poem, though not to her. Did he still love her? He looked up—his eyes that clear blue, beautiful to her. Did she still love him? The answer was, "Yes, but." She loved him the way you love a man who writes of another woman's "snowy fingers," the "blood and life" in them. Who is prey to another woman's "witchcraft"—a woman who was lurking, even then, just a little way down her own hall.

The next morning, she went downstairs, and requested that Shelley write to Byron about the baby, and, with a searching glance at her face, he did. Your child, he told Byron, "continues to reside with us under a feigned name. But we are somewhat embarrassed about her . . . exposed to what remarks her existence is calculated to excite."

Byron was a gentleman—she was counting on that, and she was right. Call her Allegra, Byron wrote back, a Venetian name. He would take responsibility for her and raise her in Italy, though only without interference from Claire. His original offer.

And though she knew that Shelley shared Claire's hopes

that the child would inspire a rapprochement between the parents, she herself had few such expectations. But either way, her singular goal now was to get the child out of their house, both to quell the whispers that Shelley was the father, and to close the door on Claire.

And had it been unreasonable to expect that once Allegra left, Claire would follow? Move on with her life, as would she herself and Shelley. *Frankenstein* was finished, and though Byron's Murray had turned her down—"Faithless Albé"—George Lackington had agreed to publish it. And Ollier was publishing Shelley's new work, *The Revolt of Islam*, dedicated to her. "They say that thou wert lovely from thy birth." "Thou Child of light and love." The poem celebrated the triumph of good over evil—"an Eagle and a Serpent Wreathed in fight"—and nonviolent revolution through love and equality of the sexes. "Can man be free if woman be a slave?"

When she read that, she felt justified in having said nothing to him about "Constantia" and Claire. Let her strut and fret her moment. She and Shelley went up to London without her stepsister, that beautiful June of 1817. They visited Peacock in the great India House library, viewed the Elgin Marbles, newly installed in the British Museum, and went to the "Inventors' House" on St. Martin's Lane. Leigh Hunt saw them at the opera, Shelley "a thin patrician-looking young cosmopolite yearning out upon us," and her "a sedate-faced young lady . . . with her great tablet of a forehead & her white shoulders unconscious of a crimson gown."

Not altogether unconscious, she'd thought when she read that, but said nothing. There was, at that golden moment, nothing more to say. She was pregnant again, but still young, and there were still crimson gowns to fit low over shoulders that were still white.

．　．　．

Her baby was born three days after her twentieth birthday, a daughter, Clara Everina, her third child in as many years. This baby, too, was strong and healthy, and with any luck would live. They would stay in the house in Marlow, on the river, through the winter, and come April, take little Clara with Willmouse, now a year and a half, along with Shelley's other two children, whom he'd have certainly gotten by then, in the small boat through the gentle English sunshine, to pick daffodils and sniff violets. Byron would have come and taken Allegra to Italy, and Claire, like a mare with a foal, would presumably have followed. That would leave her with Shelley, to have an English spring.

But then, astoundingly, he lost his suit for his children. Harriet's father had gone to court and argued that Shelley, as both an atheist and a political radical, or either, was unfit as a father, and the court had agreed. This was almost unprecedented in English annals, and Shelley was shocked, shaken, and suddenly unsure of the legal ground on which the rest of his life stood. Could these same judges take his other children, should someone—his father—sue for them? In a panic, he took them all, Allegra, too, to a nearby church and had them baptized, to cover himself against those charges, at least.

But, damn it, he cried to his friends, and damn the judges, he *was* an atheist. So was Goethe, who lived in Germany not only unperturbed but lionized. Supported, even, by the court. What was wrong with England?

Though what wasn't? With habeas corpus suspended, the government was imprisoning protesting cotton workers at will, on no charges. Paying spies to betray reformers, who were hung to the cries of "Murder!" from the restive crowds. "Reform!" Shelley was writing, but there was no reform.

General or personal. The story of the "League of Incest"—
that she, Shelley, Claire, and Byron were living in a sort of
sexual melee—had become established in the prurient English imagination, and they found themselves subject to random
public abuse. Women she didn't know approached to turn their
backs. A man attacked Shelley in a post office, knocked him
down. Worse, his work, though praised, was suppressed. They
had become untouchables in their own land.

It was around this time that Byron wrote that he was
ensconced in Venice with his new love, Teresa Guiccioli, and
couldn't come for Allegra. He was still willing to give the child
his name and raise her, educate her, but she would have to be
brought to him.

Claire was crushed by this news, especially about Teresa,
and wavered about sending Allegra. "Poor little angel," she
wrote to Byron in tears, "in your great house, left perhaps to
servants while you are drowning sense and feeling in wine."

"Keep her," Shelley had started saying—but Claire, to her
own relief, wasn't about to let the Byron association go. With
him, Allegra was the daughter of a lord. How could Claire, an
obscure dependent, deprive the child of that? Not to mention
Byron's fortune, his fame—wouldn't Allegra benefit immensely
from the connection?

And wouldn't she, too, in the end? Somehow, sometime, if
not now, soon, eventually—to this illusion Claire clung. They
learned later that she had received a proposal of marriage
around then, from Shelley's friend Peacock. He was a writer,
too, but with a position at the India House, so could have supported her and Allegra. And there was his house in Marlow, on
the river, which could have been Claire's house, she could have

picked up Allegra right then, that spring, and walked the short distance out of their house and life, down a garden path into a life of her own.

But Claire refused to relinquish the Byron dream, and she turned Peacock down, without telling either her or Shelley, without giving them a chance to persuade her to what, in retrospect, would have saved her own life. Figuratively. Literally, in the case of others.

Or maybe Shelley knew and opposed it? "Constantia, turn!"

S helley was ill again, advised again by his doctors to seek the sun. He asked her—Italy or the English seacoast? They vacillated, tossed a coin. When it came up England, they turned to each other—"Italy." She was, at any rate, determined to get Allegra and the scandal around her out of their house and into Byron's. They would take her to Venice, since that was his demand. *Frankenstein* was about to be released—anonymously. There seemed no reason to wait for her own first copies. She had created her monster; now let him live or die on his own.

There was the problem of the twenty-year lease they'd taken on the house in Marlow, but when they managed to unload that, they booked passage on the next boat. She took it as a good sign that they sailed for the Continent on March 11, 1818, the day that *Frankenstein* was officially published.

T hey arrived in Milan a few weeks later, in "excellent spirits. Motion has always this effect on the blood," as Shelley wrote to the Hunts. Her own letters seconded his: "The sun shines bright and it is a kind of Paradise we have arrived at." The oxen pulling the carts were "most beautiful oxen I ever saw," and the bread they ate "the finest and whitest in the world . . . Shelley's health is infinitely improved."

Already. They were reading Molière, and attending the ballet and opera. It was April, Italy was heaven. Byron had sent instructions for turning over Allegra to an emissary he was sending for her. A stranger—this Shelley kept from Claire, as well as the way that he'd referred to the two, as "the bastard and its mother." Shelley wrote back by return post, to request that they be allowed to send the child with a nursemaid whom she at least knew. Byron assented, as long as Claire wasn't part of the group.

Claire had expected to go along and was dismayed to be excluded. The only way she'd been able to face the prospect of giving up Allegra had been to envision herself turning the child over to Byron, who would love her at first sight "once he sees how lovely she is." This would lead, then, Claire had convinced herself, to Byron's looking with new eyes on her as well, the mother. She was crushed to learn that this was not to be.

And maybe then, if Shelley had shown Claire Byron's let-ter—"the bastard and its mother"—but he didn't. And even if he had, could Claire have faced the prospect, then and there, of raising Allegra without Byron's support? Had Claire known—but one never knows. So, with hopes and dreams reconfigured but still tenable, Claire picked up her pen and wrote to Byron, "Yet dear friend, why should my presence tease you? Why can't the mother and father of a child whom both so tenderly love meet as friends?" This on April 28, the day after her twenti-eth birthday, when she kissed Allegra and sent her off to her father in tears.

And the first reports from Venice were in fact heartening. On May 1, Allegra's nursemaid wrote that Byron was charmed by the child, and "dressed her in trousers trimmed with lace and treated her like a little princess." Claire was thrilled—just so. Precisely why she'd sent the child to him, after all, to be raised as a princess, and she the princess's mother. She left it to Shelley to arrange for her visits, starting in a month or so, as "Auntie"—fine. Anything to see the child again.

They moved then to the beautiful spa town of Bagni di Lucca, and unpacked their books and sat at their desks. She herself was buoyed by the reviews of *Frankenstein*, even those of the "shocked" conservative critics, who were amazed, as word of its authorship slipped out, that a girl "not yet nineteen" at the time, had written such a story. The book was selling out. No less a luminary than Sir Walter Scott had loved it, praised it.

What next? people were writing to ask. Her father was convinced that she could support herself—him, too—as a writer. He suggested a history of Cromwell and the Commonwealth.

But it was hard in Italy to care much about Cromwell. Shelley had found a natural spring with a waterfall, in the hills behind their house, and made himself an open-air study, where he would "undress and sit on the rocks, reading Herodotus, and then leap from the edge of the rock into this fountain."

Like an ancient Greek, or their dream of one, and, rather than struggling with his own muse that summer, he had decided to put his elite education, the Greek he'd studied at Eton and Oxford, to work for those who'd had no such advantage. He started a translation of Plato's *Symposium*, which would give English readers the whole story for the first time—the love among the men, suppressed till then.

Thrilling work, half classical, half radical, and what she liked to do that summer, rather than "breaking her head," as the Italians put it, over another "story" was to sit in the shade and copy out Shelley's translation. "A most beautiful piece of writing," she wrote to Maria Gisborne, in Livorno. "It is true that . . . it shocks our present manners, but no one can be a reader of the works of antiquity unless they can transport themselves from these to other times."

This was Italy, not England, speaking. Italy of fountains and springs and clouds that came and went. A language they could speak well enough to rent the horses she and Shelley would ride, evenings, up into the hills. Occasionally they would wander down to the dances in the Casino on Sundays, where Shelley would waltz with the local girls when both she and Claire held back. Shy. Unpracticed.

She would dance, though, eventually, she told herself, in Italy. She was already braver on horseback. "We rode among chestnut woods hearing the noisy cicala. Not long ago we heard a cuckoo." This on a ride to "*il prato fiorito*," she wrote, in Italian—the flowering lawn.

It was beautiful there, she told Maria Gisborne. The children, Will and Clara, were playing beside her on the floor. Claire, obsessed with Allegra and Byron, was keeping herself to herself. Talking, even, of moving out, getting some work, as a singer, a teacher, whatever. Shelley's Plato translation was now inspiring his own poetry.

> *How beautiful is sunset, when the glow*
> *Of heaven descends upon a land like thee,*
> *Thou paradise of exiles, Italy!*

Which was how she saw it, too—paradise. Italy!

# XI.

That's how it was then. Though now—she'd started another, very different letter to Maria Gisborne just last week, stating that she found herself here "oppressed with wretchedness, yet gazing on the most beautiful scene in the world." She regretted having sent it, regretted the complaint, though it was true, both parts. It was beautiful here, the sunlight on the water, but it came to her through a harsh glare, as she sat shivering in the heat.

Hunt had called the year 1819 Shelley's *Annus Mirabilis*. And though through the lens of poetry, she would agree.

First his "Ode to the West Wind":

> *Wild Spirit, which art moving everywhere;*
> *Destroyer and preserver; hear, oh hear!*

Then "To a Skylark":

> *And singing still dost soar, and soaring ever singest.*

"Julian and Maddalo":

*This ride was my delight. I love all waste*
*And solitary places; where we taste*
*The pleasure of believing what we see*
*Is boundless, as we wish our souls to be.*

"Prometheus Unbound":

*Life may change, but it may fly not;*
*Hope may vanish, but can die not;*
*Truth be veiled, but still it burneth;*
*Love repulsed, — but it returneth.*

Miraculous poems, beautiful words, but were they true? Does love "returneth"? Does hope "die not"? Or does it die, and lie dead and buried forever, beneath a weight too great to ever rise again? Because as Shelley was writing "If winter comes, can spring be far behind?" her two children were dying, one by one.

Clara first, at a year and a half—smiling, teething, a bit feverish from that, but nothing to die from. It was late August, and she and the children were in Bagni di Lucca. Claire was elsewhere—Florence, she thought, or Venice. Shelley was away as well, though she wasn't quite sure where he was, either. He'd promised to be back for her birthday, on the thirtieth of August. She would be twenty-one.

Did she suspect that he was visiting Claire, intriguing with her? There must have been at least that suspicion—how else to explain her own part in what came next? She got a letter from him—"Pray come instantly," he'd written from Este, outside of Venice, where, he wrote, he awaited her.

She was stunned. She and the children were well situated where they were, in the hills, it was cool, Maria Gisborne was visiting. But Shelley's instructions were precise: "Get up at four o'clock & go post to Lucca where you will arrive at six. Then take Vetturino for Florence to arrive the same evening. From Florence to Este is three days."

In other words, pack up the children, take the night coach, travel without stopping for five days across a blazing-hot country in August—heartless on the face of it, but what haunted her now was her own role, going along with the scheme, putting him above the children. And why? How? Because he called her "my beloved Mary" in his letter, and he hadn't for a while? Because he said she could kiss him when she got there? Because she suspected he was there with Claire?

Looking back, she couldn't understand why she hadn't written, *We can't, Clara is teething, feverish*, or not written at all. *What letter?* That was perfectly plausible, in that time and place, though it would have entailed a lie to Shelley, a breaking of the faith between them. But that's precisely what she should have done, since when she discovered what lay at the heart of the matter—a ruse to get Byron to release Allegra for a visit with Claire—she realized that that faith had been broken, before she ever set out.

Because while Shelley and Claire and Allegra were strolling through cool, sunlit hills around Este, her own child was sickening unto death in a dusty coach, her fever rising in filthy roadside inns. And shortly after they arrived from the five days of frightful travel, baby Clara died in convulsions in her arms.

> *Oh! lift me as a wave, a leaf, a cloud!*
> *I fall upon the thorns of life! I bleed!*

This was what Shelley wrote then, but did he bleed? Her father, hearing that she had fallen into "a kind of despair," wrote her that only "persons of a very ordinary sort and pusillanimous disposition sink long under a calamity of this nature." But then what sort of calamity did brave and extraordinary people sink under? she wondered. Or do they never sink, just plow forward, writing poetry, marveling at sunsets, and the rest of it?

But she still had Will then, so she did try. That winter, they moved to Rome, where Shelley found inspiration again. And she picked herself up instead of sinking—even got back into bed with Shelley, and by spring she was reading the *Decameron* and expecting another child.

But then, in Rome that June, 1819, Will, her Willmouse, four years old and "all the hopes of my life," as she wrote to Maria Gisborne, got very sick.

"Roman fever," people called it. They had been warned to leave Rome, were planning to leave Rome—why had they lingered? Was it for Shelley to finish his epic *Prometheus*? Or just the fact that they were foreigners and didn't quite understand? That the Roman swamps were malarial at that time of year, you leave Rome in May or your children will die.

Mary is "cold, chaste," Shelley wrote in one of his poems soon after. And in another, unfinished, on a scrap of paper:

> *My dearest Mary, wherefore hast thou gone,*
> *And left me in this dreary world alone?*

Mary, he was saying, is no longer the lovely carefree girl he picked up five years before, at four in the morning in a muffled coach with curtains drawn. Now Mary is a black cloud, even in sunny Italy. Mary is "cold."

*Et tu*, Shelley? she had wanted to ask him. True, she couldn't put it in words the way he could. "Everything on earth has lost interest to me, I am not fit to live," was what she was writing those days. On August 4, they celebrated Shelley's twenty-seventh birthday. Not celebrated. Marked.

She hadn't been able to face her journal, but now she started a new one. "We have now lived 5 years together, and if all the events of the 5 years were blotted out, I might be happy." She'd had three children, all dead that day. Blot that out, and "I might be happy."

They made their way—somehow—to Livorno, and took refuge with the Gisbornes. In November of that year, Percy Florence was born, and after that, one might say that she came back from where she had "gone." They moved to Pisa, and she started work on *Valperga*, a historical novel. It wasn't *Frankenstein*, and Shelley mocked it as "raked out of fifty old books." But that's how you write historical fiction, and at least it was something, and maybe even some money. There had somehow been none from *Frankenstein*. Despite the reviews, the publicity, the stir around its publication, only five hundred copies had been printed, and there was no talk of a second edition, at least none that reached Italy. Her letters to the publisher went unanswered. Her sum total of earnings so far was £29.

So she would rake what she could out of old books, and Shelley could mock if he liked. At least she no longer spent half the day in bed, face to the wall. She had come back, with her red-gold hair and gray eyes, and went out and about in Pisa, had friends, even admirers, but Shelley was right, his "Child of light and love" was gone.

When could she last be glimpsed, she wondered, with what they'd called her "sidelong smile"? Because now that she thought about it, here on the terrace, as the sun rose higher and the five shadows of the arches receded back across the floor, she realized that that smile had stayed with her dead children. Not that she didn't smile—especially at baby Percy, she smiled at him and at her Greek admirer, Prince Alexander Mavrocordato, who had come every day in Pisa for "Italian lessons," and lingered to talk, to whisper, even. So, yes, she'd smiled at him, but not the way she'd smiled at Shelley, in St. Pancras, in Geneva, in London, in Bagni di Lucca, and even once or twice, after Clara, in Rome.

But not after Will. That smile was dead and buried with him in the Protestant Cemetery in Rome. And Shelley—had he changed, that way? He'd gotten older, there was gray in his long curling hair, noted his cousin Medwin, who had seen him recently, for the first time in seven years, "but his appearance was youthful" and there was "a freshness and purity in his complexion."

Which was true. He had remained untouched in some profound way, in some part of his soul. Not that he hadn't been desperate at Willmouse's bedside, his deathbed, but then he'd gone back to his desk and put it into words:

> *'Tis like a child's belovèd corse*
> *A father watches.*

"Time Long Past," he called the poem. Time Standing Still was how it seemed to her. It continued:

> *. . . till at last*
> *Beauty is like remembrance, cast*
> *From Time long past.*

"Beauty," he wrote—but what beauty? Where was the beauty, she'd wanted to cry, in all that death? But she no longer cried to him.

Partly because Claire had come back. She, Mary, had picked up his journal for the year 1820, and found her mark, her—what do you call it with animals? Scat? Droppings? On the inside of the back cover, she'd found written, "3 still/Clare." Right after Will had died. She'd had to keep herself from ripping the book apart when she saw it, tearing the triumphant declaration from the proximity of Shelley's words, his hand.

How dared Claire? And yet, wasn't it true? Weren't they "3 still," as late as that? And wasn't Shelley as much to blame as Claire? That was the real treachery, she could see now—his, not hers. For what was Claire's role, beyond the classic stepsister from all the old tales? The undead twin who slipped into church first, to marry her sister's bridegroom.

Or tried to, would have. And Shelley? The bridegroom who in a twist of his own had had them both? Funny, that. There'd been a rumor last year, about a baby, Claire's with Shelley, even blackmail around it. He'd denied it passionately, and she still believed him, especially since Claire, though increasingly on her own, living in Florence, had been around enough for her to have seen. Noticed.

They couldn't have hidden it—unless it was just a pregnancy, not a baby. An early miscarriage—Claire had been ill, she remembered. Still, she defended Shelley, in writing even, but then went to her desk in a rage, and wrote *Mathilda*, an incestuous love story, father-daughter. It wasn't true, of course—she had had no such dealings with Godwin, though she killed him off in the end, and rejected her poet-suitor, too, or, rather,

Mathilda did. Definitively. The "no" she hadn't given either of them in real life. And then she—Mathilda—retired from all society. No children to be born and lost to her.

She sent the manuscript to her father to publish—what had she been thinking? Just that it was good, authentic if not true, and could bring in some money. That people, women, in despair could turn to it for consolation, as she had, again and again, to Mme. de Staël's equally tragic *Corinne*. But Godwin had found it "detestable," and refused either to submit it for publication or send it back, claimed to have lost it.

Thinking what, that she hadn't made a copy? But she had, she loved that book. Loved writing it—sitting there, replaying it all, in an alternate version, and dealing them all their just deserts. It was at least some relief from the role she'd fallen into, of "other," almost of stranger in her own home.

"Heigh ho, the Claire and the Ma / find something to fight about every day," Claire had written in her journal then and left it open, for her to see. Another salvo. Along with the "3 still." "Mary is cold."

More than cold, freezing. Keats died around then—"Lost Angel of a ruin'd Paradise!" Shelley called him in his elegy, which rang only too true, not just for Keats but her own lost angels, too. As she read it, she suddenly saw them again, setting off from England that March day, praising the easy crossing. The "3 still," true, her, Shelley, and Claire, but three children as well. It was a beautiful day. If she'd heard the "herded wolves, bold only to pursue," or the "obscene ravens, clamorous o'er the dead," would she have turned back? Yes, of course—but she hadn't heard them, though she thought she knew death then. Her mother, Fanny, Harriet. But that was nothing like the death she knew now. The "deaf and viperous murderer" who "could crown Life's early cup with such a draught of woe." Clara and then Will.

Three children in that boat that day, crossing the Channel with a gentle tide, a good wind. She didn't want to see it anymore—she got up, slowly, trying not to see. Turned away from the sea, toward the hill, the tangle of chestnut and the scrub oaks, nothing noble or tall. Not her place.

She had been shocked when she heard that Byron had put Allegra in a convent outside of Ravenna. The child was only four years old. They knew it wasn't unusual for aristocratic Italian families to send girls of sixteen or seventeen to convents, to wait out their marriages—but a four-year-old? Unheard-of, certainly for an English child. Shelley went to Byron, to plead for an alternative.

But Byron had his reasons—it had gotten complicated to keep Allegra in his house, he explained. His lover, the Italian countess Teresa Guiccioli, was only nineteen, and of problematic status herself. Her rich, elderly husband was suing for her return. She hadn't risked all and left home to play Mama to Byron's love child.

Nor did he have time for Allegra. He was then deep into the writing of *Don Juan*—"My heart in passion, and my head on rhymes." A child had no place in his life, either, especially one who was proving headstrong, and reminding him more and more of Claire.

When Shelley had suggested an English boarding school instead of the convent, Byron replied that he had no intention of giving "a natural child an English education." And, given her illicit status, who in England would marry her, he asked, without the kind of dowry that he was in no way prepared to expend? But in Italy, someone would come out of the woodwork for much less, maybe even someone with a title, particularly if she was raised Roman Catholic. Hence the convent.

Which had its logic, Shelley had to admit, but Claire was

outraged and wrote bitterly to Byron that he was "condemning" the child "to a life of ignorance and degradation." Which turned out to be true—when Shelley visited a year later, Allegra no longer spoke English, just babbled in Italian, mostly about "Paradise and the *Bambino*." He gathered from the nuns that he was her first visitor all year. When he left, she begged him to bring "Mamina" to visit, and he realized, with sinking heart, that she meant Byron's lover, Teresa, and not Claire, whom the child had forgotten.

This he kept from Claire, but she knew, or knew something. She had moved, at long last, permanently to Florence, to make a stab at a life of her own, as a governess, but she was having recurrent nightmares, night after night, the same dreams. Sometimes it was the arrival of a letter, stating that Allegra was "ill, and not likely to recover," always that wording. Other times, it was that the child had been returned to her safe and well, "never to go back again." On those mornings, she'd wake up happy only to have to face the bitter reality once again, from scratch.

Claire began concocting plots to rescue the child. She would kidnap her, or, better, engage some local folk, shepherds, bricklayers, to slip over the convent wall in the dead of night. Or draw up some official-looking papers and forge Byron's signature. Then she could walk in and back out, with Allegra in her arms. To sleep in her bed with her and "never go back."

But Claire needed Shelley, to forge the letter, scale the wall, whatever it was, and then help them slip out of the country to Switzerland or Austria—she was studying German assiduously for this purpose, so she and Allegra could make their way, once they got there. Would Shelley help her? He had to—it was the only way. She was begging him, on her knees, she wrote.

Shelley put her off, and it was left to her, Mary, to lay out the

consequences of breaking Italian law. Italian prison, for starters, followed by the duel to which Byron, a crack marksman,
would certainly challenge Shelley for any part he might take
in the affair. But before she could send the letter, Teresa Guiccioli came to their door, one chill day in April, dressed in black.
Allegra had died in the convent of typhus. Filth and poverty.
She was five years old.

S helley wrote a poem not long after that, a sort of cosmic
wandering through the women in his life. Claire was
the "Comet":

> . . . *beautiful and fierce,*
> *Who drew the heart of this frail Universe*
> *Towards thine own; till, wrecked in that convulsion,*
> *Alternating attraction and repulsion,*
> *Thine went astray and that was rent in twain.*

"Astray," "rent in twain." They didn't tell Claire at first,
afraid that she would kill herself, or try to kill Byron, or both.
It was in fact why they'd rented this house in such haste—they
needed a place to bring her, away from Byron, where they could
break the news. Which, too, was why she'd agreed to move
into a house that didn't function, on a bay that had struck her
as bleak. To atone for her own part in ridding the world of an
inconvenient child. The child of a mother who had tried and
half succeeded in "spoiling the tea" of her life.

They managed to keep the news from Claire till they got
down here. But a few days into it, when they and the Williamses were huddled in a side room, debating how best to tell her,
she walked in on them and knew at once. She didn't collapse.

She didn't try to slip into Byron's palazzo with a poisoned knife. She wrote sadly of "hopelessly lingering on Italian soil for 5 years, waiting ever for a favorable change," yet "every hr has brought its misfortune, each worse than the other."

And as she herself ran over it now, impersonally, taking herself out of it, she was stricken with how tragic it all was, how disproportionate, punishment well beyond the crime.

For what had Claire done, besides be Claire and fifteen one fateful midnight? A regular young girl who, through sheer chance and no fault of her own, found herself in the Godwin household where, as she'd told Jane Williams recently, "if you cannot write an epic or novel, that by its originality knocks all other novels on the head, you are a despicable creature, not worth acknowledging."

Which had its grain of truth, and when Claire had tried to make a place for herself there, by bringing home the head of Lord Byron—was that a capital crime? To get life wrong at seventeen, and then be "rent in twain" at twenty-three?

It didn't seem justified, not that she would ever love Claire. But as she looked back on them all now—them and their three little children, all dead now—she could see that they'd been wrecked on the same shore.


And now Shelley—would he come back? Could he possibly not come back? And if he didn't, what would it all mean? That their Italian sojourn had been nothing but disaster? There'd been enough of that, true, but she'd recently picked up his searing "The Masque of Anarchy":

> As I lay asleep in Italy
> There came a voice from over the Sea.

And she realized that it had to be "from over the Sea." They'd had to come to Italy. You couldn't write a poem like this anymore in England. They'd call it libel.

> *I met Murder on the way —*
> *He had a mask like Castlereagh.*

Castlereagh was the Secretary of State for Foreign and Commonwealth Affairs of the United Kingdom. Leading the charge against liberty and reform, against workers and farmers, the people, the poor—Shelley's cause, justice, simple, fair, all his conscious life. People for whom he'd written what to her were his most stirring lines, the end of the poem:

> *Rise like Lions after slumber*
> *In unvanquishable number —*
> *Shake your chains to earth like dew*
> *Which in sleep had fallen on you —*
> *Ye are many — they are few.*

Suppressed in England, but he would publish those words and others like them here, in the magazine that he and Hunt and Byron were launching, and his words would get back to the people. Who would one day rise.

Thanks at least in part to his poem, and he'd needed her and maybe Claire, too, and Italy, to find the strength and courage write it. Needed them both to flank him here. And they'd needed him, too—to face the forces they'd unleashed against themselves.

And she knew something else now, too, that if she'd died that day, three weeks ago, if she'd bled to death and Claire had stepped into her place, tried to step into her place, it wouldn't have worked. Because Claire could stand as Shelley's "3," but not his one. She, Mary, was that. She was the one he'd come to Skinner Street for that day, the one who'd captured not just his heart but his imagination. Which with Shelley was absolutely key.

As it had been with her. He, too, had captured her imagination, which is the most solid of all foundations for true love between people like them. It took them both to another plane, where everything else—all their faults, all their failings, as well as the whole world ranged against them—had become very small. Details, that is—even Claire, she saw now, was just a comet in their cosmos. From which height they had been able to defy the world, together.

But without him? If he didn't come back? She didn't know, couldn't see it. Without him, none of it made any sense. Maybe she could have been happy if she'd never met him. In a house in the country, married to someone smart, like Peacock or Hazlitt, living the kind of life Marianne Hunt lived, with friends and children and dogs. She wouldn't have written *Frankenstein*, or *Mathilda*, but maybe she'd have taken up her mother's cause. Social justice. Women's rights.

Without Shelley. A worthy life, interesting even. But outside "the still cave of the witch, Poesy." No one's "Child of light and love."

There was some noise below, some shouts and splashes, that meant the arrival of the boat with the mail. She took hold of the sofa, carefully, carefully. She could hear Jane Williams, already out on the rocks to meet it. Her stomach heaved and her heart seemed to almost stop, but she steadied herself, and went over to the arches and looked out.

# XII.

Jane Williams came running out onto the terrace. "A letter—"
"From him?" she asked her.

Jane Williams was very white. The fever spots were back on her cheeks. "No, for him."

From Hunt, but addressed to Shelley, how could that be? Shelley was there, with him—why would Hunt be writing to Shelley?

Jane handed her the letter and she ripped it open. It was dated Tuesday, the ninth. Today was Friday, the twelfth.

"Pray let us know how you got home the other day with Williams, for I fear you must have been out in the bad weather and we are anxious."

But what could that mean—"how you got home"? The "bad weather"? Then Shelley had left? "The other day"—when? Monday, if the letter was written Tuesday? Then where was he?

She dropped the letter. Jane Williams grabbed it, started sobbing—"Then it's all over!" Claire came running out onto the terrace.

They were talking, crying, but for a moment she didn't hear them. She was remembering a bit of a poem he'd written, not long before:

*Many a green isle needs must be*
*In the deep wide sea of Misery.*

But how did it go from there?

*Ay, many flowering islands lie*
*In the waters of wide Agony.*

Had he found one? He loved this place, it couldn't have betrayed him. He had written, not long ago, on the back of one of her letters to the Gisbornes, "We drive along this delightful bay in the evening wind, under the summer moon, until the earth appears another world . . . and if the past and future could be obliterated the present would content me so well that I could say w Faust to the passing moment, 'Remain, thou, thou art so beautiful.' "

She could see him now, in his striped jacket, his long soft curling hair, sailing off from Livorno, to a fair wind, waving to Hunt. Alive.

"No, it's not all over," she said to Jane Williams. They had to get to Pisa—not to Hunt, a man of bad news, she could see now, but to Byron. Byron was a man of good news, strictly. "Oh, Shelley went—" somewhere, he would tell her. To attend to something. The bank, the magazine.

She walked, carefully, to her room, swept up a few things. Claire would stay with the children, Jane Williams's two and her little Percy. Not poetic like the lost Willmouse, but nearly three and alive that day.

The bay was rough, but someone would row them across. Then a carriage to Pisa. She would be all right, if she concentrated and sat as still as one could over these roads. What mattered was to get to Byron. And even at midnight, he would be awake, drinking, dining, and he would tell her why it was all right. The details.

That's what it had been about with him, all along—for Byron to give her this good news today, she was thinking, as she went carefully down the steps and, clutching at Jane's arm, climbed with her into the unsteady little boat.

# XIII.

It was midnight as they brushed past Byron's servants and climbed his stairs. He rose, staring, from his table, and stood, wordless. Afterward he described her face as "pale as marble, & terror impressed on her brow." It was Teresa who rushed to her side.

"Where's Shelley?" she asked her in Italian, but Teresa didn't know. Byron pulled himself together then, and tried to calm her, tried to get her to lie down, wait for Shelley there, but she refused. Refused, too, to let him wake Hunt—she knew Hunt's news, didn't have to hear it again, nor would she take a bite of food or a sip of wine. Once she realized that even Byron had no good news to give her, she turned and made her way, somehow, with Jane Williams, back down the grand stairs. They didn't speak, just climbed back into the carriage and told the driver to take them to Livorno, where they dozed in their clothes and waited.

When dawn broke, they went out looking for Trelawny. He told them he'd started off in Byron's *Bolivar*, to accompany Shelley back on Monday, but had been stopped by Italian customs agents for lack of papers. Shelley and Williams hadn't wanted to wait and had sailed on without him. Trelawny knew nothing more, except where to find Roberts.

Roberts, the boat builder, told them that he'd been following the boat through his spyglass as it sailed from Livorno. As he was watching, he saw a storm move in with great rapidity and break over the boat, and when it cleared, "There was no boat on the sea."

Jane Williams started sobbing then, but she held Roberts's gaze. "Meaning what?" she asked him point-blank. He was silent. She was coming to distrust him anyway. Wasn't he the one who'd rigged the extra sails? Made the boat "tippy"?

And just because he couldn't see Shelley's boat, that didn't mean it wasn't there, somewhere. Trelawny agreed—he claimed to know of someone whose boat had caught an offshore current near here and been carried to Corsica. Which Roberts quickly agreed might have happened to Shelley.

And this was what got her and Jane Williams back home. Trelawny accompanied them, and stayed on a few days, to help her bat away each bit of bad news, as "the calamity," as she would put it, began to "break over us in pieces." First came word that the boat's dinghy had been found, five miles out to sea.

But, "Jettisoned on the way to Corsica," she could still say, and Trelawny could agree.

Then a water cask was reported to have washed up—did anyone ever throw their water overboard? Maybe, or maybe it had washed over. It was possible, Trelawny agreed, but decided to head back to Livorno then, to see if there was anything more to learn.

A day passed, another—good, she thought, the longer the better. Corsica was far. Jane Williams had taken to her bed, but she stayed up, waiting. As far as she was concerned, no news was good news. As long as they heard nothing, Shelley was still alive.

Trelawny did come back, though, finally. Climbed the stairs in silence, with each footstep tolling like the dead bell. He came out onto the terrace. Jane Williams and Claire were already weeping, but she sat silent and waited. Let him speak. Let him say it.

He didn't for a while, and then said too much. They found Williams first, knew him by his boots.

*His boots? Why his boots? What about Williams's nice face, his mustache?* she only just stopped herself from saying. Because that, too, was breaking over her in pieces, what happens to a body after ten days in the water.

She didn't say, *And Shelley?* Just sat for one last moment with the thought that Williams had washed overboard with the water casks while Shelley was being carried to Corsica, or one of his "green isles." So she didn't ask, just sat and watched Trelawny. She'd found him handsome at first, even waltzed rather madly with him once in Pisa. How could that have been?

"Shelley," he said, and she felt her ears close, though still she heard, from a distance. Something about Viareggio, the beach there, just up the coast. Something about washing up. Something about a striped jacket. She took a breath.

"There must have been other striped jackets out sailing on a summer's day near Viareggio," she said. Other Englishmen.

Afterward Trelawny described the way she'd looked at him, with "her large gray eyes." Funny, some called them gray, some hazel. She herself would never know. You can't know the color of your own eyes, not really.

"Other striped jackets," she repeated.

"Not with Sophocles and Keats in the pocket."

And there it was. Shelley.

She suddenly remembered the wave that had broken over this house in one of Shelley's dreams. The way it had come roaring in, to carry them all away. Towering, unstoppable.

She took a breath. Another. He was right, the wave had come, but she was still breathing, and little Percy was asleep in his cot.

"Which Keats?" she asked. ·

"*Lamia*," said Trelawny. Keats's last book. You couldn't get it yet in Italy. Hunt had promised to bring it from London, and he must have. She'd heard it was about a woman turned into a monster, a snake. Had Shelley read it? Another woman in the shape of a monster—the opposite of Coleridge's Geraldine, a monster in the shape of a woman.

She got to her feet then, and felt the blood, suppressed till now, starting to trickle down her leg. It would be horrifying to Trelawny—a monster in the shape of a woman. The locals had doused Shelley in quicklime where he'd washed up, Trelawny was saying, and buried him in the sand, because of the plague.

But they would dig him up, he and Hunt and Byron, and burn him, and then she could bury his ashes in Rome, beside Willmouse. Which would be good, Trelawny seemed to be saying. Byron had offered to take it in hand.

She nodded, she must have. Didn't say anything, because what was there left to say? Shelley had told her that he'd seen Allegra one night here, soon after she'd died, naked, coming out of the waves.

He had been horrified, but she was prepared. A monster in the shape of a woman, or was she a woman in the shape of a monster? Either way, she was ready to meet him, however he came. The sun was setting, and eventually, she knew, Trelawny would stop talking and go to bed—somewhere. Claire would see to it.

She, however, would stay on the terrace, and keep watch.

# JOAN OF ARC
# IN CHAINS

# I.

The cemetery in Rouen outside the cathedral was crowded, so crowded you could hardly move. It was May 24, 1431. They'd come to burn Joan of Arc.

"Joan, do you submit . . ." a preacher was droning on the platform. She was standing in chains, toward the front, but gazing not at him but at the executioner, nearby with his cart. Now she turned and looked at him for the first time.

"What?" she asked, in a whisper. She had always spoken loud and bold before.

"Do you submit," he repeated. Not bothering to make it a question—she wouldn't submit, everyone knew it. It was simply part of the formula for burning.

But she turned to him. "Can I?" she said.

He looked up—"What?" Heads turned. A silence spread through the crowd.

Jean Massieu, the young priest closest to her, rushed over and grabbed her hand.

"Can I submit?" She searched his eyes. She couldn't burn. She knew it only now. "Can I live?"

She was nineteen. Massieu was almost as young as she was.

"Yes," he said.

. . .

The faces around her were shocked, all of them. It was true that they'd been asking her that same question for months, they'd even asked her yesterday. And yesterday she'd answered, as she always had, "Even if you brought me to the stake and tied me there, and the fire was lit, and I was in the fire, I would never deny my deeds and my saints!"

But that was yesterday, when she'd been safe in her cell, and today she was standing on a platform in a cemetery, with a black-hooded man at her feet. Waiting to put her in his cart and take her to the stake, right then, that morning, and suddenly none of it made sense anymore.

She was surprised herself. She'd thought till now that she loved her saints more than life. But her saints had promised that they would save her. "Saved," they'd said, all through her captivity, never "burned."

She looked up. She hadn't seen the sun in five months. It was May, her favorite month. A beautiful day in May, though if a storm were to come up, suddenly, with thunder and lightning and the kind of rain that would make burning impossible, she could take it as a sign.

As her miracle—Saint Catherine and Saint Margaret had said it might be like that. *Maybe you'll be saved by a miracle*, they'd whispered.

But the sky was clear, it wasn't going to rain. The heavens wouldn't open, and the fire could burn. Burn her feet first, and then her legs, her virgin body, untouched, till now.

*Maybe by a great victory*—they'd said that, too. *Be brave, daughter of God, you'll be saved*. She scanned the crowd. Enough people for a great victory, but the only ones armed were the English soldiers, her enemies.

Still, if the French townspeople picked up their hoes and sticks, and used their dogs—but they wouldn't. They weren't looking at her that way. When men are ready to fight for you, they fasten on your face with open eyes, hungry, excited. No one was looking at her like that today.

Except maybe the henchman, in the blackest hood she'd ever seen. The black of death, and he was already thinking she was his. He'd woken up that morning and put on that hood for her. Brought out his cart, thinking she'd say, "I'll never submit!" and then he'd have her.

They all thought that. She looked across the platform at her judges, the French priests, and English captains, her enemies, sitting there waiting—like cats, she thought, and she was their mouse. She'd never been afraid of them before. "You tell me to beware," she'd taunted them, all through her trial, "beware yourselves! For I shall be saved, and you will all be brought low!"

They'd come to watch her burn alive this morning. The worst of all deaths—had they never believed her, then? All the times she swore to them that Saint Margaret and Saint Catherine would save her? It seemed impossible, it made no sense—nothing did, suddenly.

Where were her saints? *Go, daughter of God, we are with you—* where, Saint Catherine? *Be brave, daughter of God, you will be saved—*when, Saint Margaret?

It had to be right now. She passed her hand over her face. Her face. Her hand. "I shall be saved." They must have believed her, her captors. They'd locked her in their deepest dungeon, surrounded her night and day with their fiercest guards, and still kept her chained hand and foot—which she took as a tribute.

"As you like," she'd told them, "and still I shall be saved!"

. . .

Burning was the worst death. To be put alive into the fire, and wait while it rose, getting hot first, while you try desperately to get away, but you are tied fast, you can't move, only toss your head back and forth, and then your feet burn, but you are still alive, for more burning.

"I can't burn—" She turned to Massieu, the young priest.

"Just submit!" he whispered back.

Submit—that meant standing here today, in front of them all, and admitting that they, her enemies, were right, and she'd been wrong. Agreeing that everything, her life, her deeds, her saints, had come from the devil. Her Saint Catherine and Saint Margaret were, she'd have to say, devils who had led her to the sin of insubordination, and to the stake.

But they had, in a way, led her to the stake, and it was diabolical here.

"Yes, maybe . . ." She looked into Massieu's eyes. They looked kind. Sympathetic. She hadn't noticed it before, but then, she hadn't been looking for sympathy.

"Will they take me out of the dungeon? Will they put me in a Church prison, with a woman guard?" She'd been in a state dungeon till now. The Church's prisons were said to be "gentler."

"Yes, yes, right away, they have to, that's the law!" swore Massieu, who would spend the rest of his life telling the tale, in tears.

"Submit to the Church now, Joan," he urged her, "and you'll be the Church's prisoner."


Bishop Pierre Cauchon, on the opposite platform, was watching this consultation, with an unease that was turning to

fury. It was all he could do to keep from snatching up a dagger
and stabbing them both through the heart. What was wrong
with that idiot Massieu? Advising her like that—didn't he know
that the English would burn Joan of Arc over the dead bodies of
every French priest in Normandy? If not today, then tomorrow
or the next day, and why drag it out?

He glanced sideways at the English cardinal, Henry
Winchester, and the English captain, Richard Warwick. No
longer at ease, no longer chatting. Picking it up that something
was not quite right. Even the English soldiers had started looking from side to side, hands tightening on their pikes. They'd
come out this morning for a celebration, but now the smiles
were passing from their faces to the French crowd. Who had
assembled—dutifully—to see Joan of Arc burn, but were just
as happy, Cauchon knew, to watch her trounce the English one
last time.

S he scanned the sky, and the crowded churchyard. No miracle in sight, no great victory. As opposed to the hooded
man, who was right there before her.

It wasn't supposed to end like this today. She suddenly knew it.

"I submit." She turned back to Massieu. "I submit." It was
simple, once she'd said it. Louder now: "I submit!" She smiled
for the first time in the year since she'd been captured. Suddenly everything fell into place. She wasn't going to burn. "I
submit." No thunder, no earthquake. On the contrary, everything was firm again. She was no longer hanging by a thread
over the fire. A new life was starting. She stood there smiling.
She was alive.

.  .  .

The English soldiers turned to each other. "Look how she mocks us, the witch! She's laughing at us!"

Cauchon turned to Winchester—"What should I do?" Not that he didn't know perfectly well what had to be done. They were burning her on a technicality, not as a witch but as a heretic, and a heretic had, technically, one chance to submit.

Still, there they all were, all the English, in what was left of their power and glory in France, Winchester, and Captain Warwick, even the Duke of Bedford, the regent of the realm. They and all their horses and men had come out this morning to burn this girl who'd not only disgraced them in battle, but had also, for all intents and purposes, put a decisive end to their hundred-year dream of combining the French and English crowns, by beating them to Reims Cathedral and crowning a king of her own, a French king. A hundred years of English victories, and all the careful marriages, all those miserable French princesses dragged to London to produce half-French English heirs—all turned to dust by Joan of Arc. The English had come out this morning in full regalia to return the favor. Cauchon wasn't sure that a legal technicality would stop them.

But it did, it had to, for the English wanted not only to burn her, but to burn her legally, in an attempt to delegitimize the coronation of the king she'd crowned. Negate it, as the work of a heretic, whom the Church had legally burned.

Cauchon turned to Winchester: "What should I do?"

Winchester, cardinal of England, didn't look at him. Just snapped, "Admit her to penance, of course."

He didn't say, *Fool*, though it was implied. His secretary took a scroll from his sleeve, with a standard recantation. Hastily written—lucky he'd brought it. They'd all thought she'd go down like a fanatic. He handed it to Cauchon.

Who took it and started forward toward Joan of Arc. "Perhaps you *favor* her!" one of the English lords called out to him.

Cauchon threw down the scroll. "You lie!" he cried. Favor her? He hated her! Sinned, actually, in hating her so much, for them, his friends the English.

"You insult me!" he shouted.

Richard Beauchamp, Earl of Warwick, stepped in. "Gentlemen." He was captain of the English garrison in Rouen. His soldiers had already started picking up rocks, understanding that something was wrong, and that Joan of Arc might not burn this morning. They'd been waiting for a year.

"Look how she laughs at us, the witch!" one of them had shouted to him.

Warwick turned. She did have an idiotic smile on her face.

"Look how she mocks us!"

It had been hard, almost impossible, to recruit men to fight in France once she'd taken the field. She had terrified the English soldiers, disgraced them in battle. These men had come out this morning to get even.

And now she was escaping them, as their own lives were escaping them, those promises of wealth and glory that had enticed them to France—a few rocks started flying. Warwick wasn't entirely sure that he could stop them. The French crowd was already melting away.

And now this: "He insults me!" Cauchon was crying. "I'm a bishop of the Holy Church! Of course I seek her salvation, and not her death!"

*Ha!* thought Warwick. "Beg forgiveness," he muttered to the English lord. Quickly. He picked up the scroll and handed it to Cauchon. "Proceed," he said, glancing at his soldiers. Quickly.

.  .  .

Cauchon, red in the face now, stepped forward to Joan of
Arc. He didn't even look at her as he rapped out the standard formula for repenting heretics: "The Church unbinds you
from the chains of excommunication. But since you have sinned
rashly against God and the Church, you are finally and defi-
nitely condemned for salutary penance, to a life of perpetual
imprisonment, on the bread of sorrow and the water of affliction, so that you weep for your sins and sin no more."

Joan of Arc nodded. "Bread and water"—better than fire.
"Perpetual prison"—much, much better. Someone handed her
the scroll. She turned to Massieu. "I can't read it."

"It's all right," he whispered. "Just sign and save your life."

He gave her a pen, and she signed, either a cross or a circle,
an X or an O, she couldn't remember afterward. There were six
or seven lines written on the paper. Someone took it from her.

Rocks were flying. One of them grazed her face, but she
wasn't afraid. She'd been so frightened this morning that she
had a whole new standard for fear. She looked around—the
hooded man was gone, without her. She laughed.

Cauchon looked over at her now, standing there, smiling
like a monkey, or like a crazy woman and he was the monkey, he,
the bishop of Beauvais.

The exiled bishop, ever since Joan of Arc had liberated his
town from the English two years ago, and he, a known collabo-
rator, had had to flee, a refugee.

"Now take me to your Church prison," she called out to him,
almost gaily.

Cauchon stared. Invincible ignorance. Impressive, really.
"Church prison"—how should they get there? Fly? Over the

heads of the English soldiers, half savage in the best of times, and now within an inch of falling on them both?

"Take her back where she came from," Cauchon snapped.

"Where she came from"—for a moment she wondered if he could mean Domrémy? Where she'd been just another farm girl, straggling up and down hills after the sheep, not someone anyone would ever burn. Until her saints had come and told her, *You were born to save France.*

Another rock hit her, a solid blow this time. Cauchon was gone. The soldiers were shouting, pushing, but someone led her off the platform and away. She was alive.

# II.

Though she soon realized that they were taking her back to her cell in the dungeon, not the "mild" Church prison with a woman guard to which she was legally entitled, and as she'd been promised. But it could have been worse. They could have been taking her to the stake.

She looked around—birds, trees, sky! She hadn't been outside since they'd brought her here in January, and now it was May.

May! The trees in full leaf, like June, but still the freshest green, like April. She sniffed the air. Where she grew up, they treasured May, day by day—the day of planting, the day of lambing, the day of the fairy tree, and then the Pentecost. Each day better than the last, longer, with midsummer still to come.

"They'll come later, Joan, and take you to the Church prison," said Massieu.

She looked at him with some surprise—he seemed to be speaking almost like a friend. She knew him—that is to say, recognized him, he'd been one of the ushers, all through her trial, escorting her back and forth from the dungeon, but he'd barely spoken to her then. Always looked past her, which had been fine with her.

But now she was grateful to have him by her side, watching her face almost like a partisan, a follower. Like old times. Like Joan of Arc.

She winced. Joan of Arc was over. She realized she didn't even feel like Joan of Arc anymore. Though till now, even in shackles, she'd still been Joan of Arc.

Joan of God, Joan of the saints, savior and lover of France, and nearly burned this morning.

Yes, that was what she had to remember. Joan of Arc would be burning on this May morning, to cinders, her flesh and bones turning black, even now, as she was smelling the May flowers and catching glints of sunlight in the tops of the trees.

Who, though, she wondered, was smelling May flowers, if not Joan of Arc? But who cared? She laughed again. Girl X, or O— how had she signed that paper? It occurred to her that something strange had happened that morning. Joan of Arc had been dragged out of the dungeon, and someone else would be dragged back in.

Where was Joan of Arc, then? Hard to say, though she hadn't burned, couldn't burn, it turned out. There had been the executioner, dressed in black, and then a sudden terror so big it had covered the sky and turned it black, too, and in that darkness, Joan of Arc had disappeared.

Had there been a miracle, then, after all? Her enemies thought they had her, but maybe Joan of Arc had gotten away. What was left might look like Joan of Arc, but it wasn't. It was Girl X, the one who'd submitted that morning. Joan of Arc would never submit.

She laughed. It was true. There had been some kind of miracle—did anyone know but her?

They came to the dungeon, Massieu still by her side. Had he seen? she wondered. Did he know? He'd been right there. She searched his eyes.

"Don't worry, Joan, you'll soon be out of here."

He still called her "Joan." Maybe he meant a different Joan. Joan of the Chains, Joan of the Dungeon, Joan of the Bread and Water.

Clearly he hadn't seen. Though he'd been there, closer than anyone. And still he had no idea that Joan of Arc was gone.

"They'll come later," he said, "and take you."

"Take who?" she asked him, but he didn't seem to hear. It was such an amazing thing, this miracle, so clean, seamless, perfect. She almost told him. He seemed trustworthy, though if her saints had wanted him to know, they'd have shown him.

They went down the seven steps to the dungeon.

"I'll stay with you," Massieu said.

*With who?* she almost said.


Later, amid the church bells, "They should be coming now," said Massieu. He walked over to the door again. One of the guards looked up.

"What are you doing, priest? Think you can slither under?"

"It's all right," she said quickly, to Massieu. The guards were quiet, in their corner now, playing their game, some kind of lots. Let the sleeping dogs lie.

Massieu came back and sat beside her. He was unused to the long rhythms of prison life. "Soon," he said to her, "soon."

She nodded. She had time. She'd learned that over the five months she'd been here.

"It'll be a gentle prison, maybe with a window, you'll be able to see out, it won't be dark like this, or damp"—poor Massieu; he wasn't accustomed—"and they'll bring you a dress."

She turned—"No!" Not this again! All through the trial, they'd been at her relentlessly.

"To show that you're penitent, and you've renounced your former error."

She felt suddenly ill and had to take a quick breath.

"But you won't need men's clothing in the Church prison, you'll be safe there."

Ah! So he understood? Did they all understand, then? Not one of them had acknowledged even once during her trial, as they berated her, endlessly, for the sin of wearing men's pants—"insubordination" and "an abomination," they called it—and none of them admitted once that they understood why she wore them.

Not one of them granted that she was a prisoner, alone in a cell guarded by English soldiers so brutal that the people called them *houspilleurs*, goons, brutes, from the phrase "to abuse, to maul and throw about." Known in Normandy by their signature treatment of girls of the countryside: gang rape, followed by disembowelment.

Horrible, and why? Why did they hate the girls after they'd attacked them that way? She'd seen pictures in the Bible, the tiger beside the snake, hate and lust, and she knew her guards hated her, but they'd kept their hands off, thank God.

But then, she wasn't a woman to them. Women didn't wear pants.

Which was the point, though she hadn't wanted to talk about rape during her trial. In fact, it had sickened her altogether to sit in a room with fifty men sworn never to "know" woman and discuss what covered her nether parts.

She had tried to keep to the high road. "I wear pants," she repeated, in the early days of her trial, "because my saints command me. Saint Margaret and Saint Catherine—"

But the gavel would always crash down when the talk turned to her saints. Though that's where it all started, the pants and the hair—with her saints.

Because the first time she'd set out to save France, she was still wearing the red skirt and long braids of her native Lorraine. When she went to the local captain and told him that she needed a horse to ride to the king, he'd laughed at her and told her to go home.

"And tell your father to spank you, or I'll spank you myself," he'd said.

But then her saints told her to cut off her hair, and change her skirts for men's pants, and when she went back a year later, dressed as a boy, that same captain gave her not just his horse, but his sword as well. Just as her saints said he would.

B ut the priests wouldn't listen. So she tried different tacks. "There are plenty of other women, let them wear skirts!" Or: "Clothes are a little thing! God doesn't care what I wear!"

But, "Your pants are the sign of your sin," they squawked back at her. That, and Deuteronomy: "The woman shall not wear that which pertaineth to the man . . . for all that do so are an abomination unto the Lord. . . ."

"An abomination," they called her, and then threw her back, alone, to the houspilleurs. Who hadn't raped her, though they knocked her into walls, pulled her chains till they cut her, forced her to relieve herself in front of them.

"The skirt," said the priests. A roomful of men with their eyes below her waist.

She got to her feet that day. "I stay in my pants to be ready for my escape! For it may be by a great battle, and my saints have commanded me to be ready to fight against you!"

But, "Take back the skirt," was all they repeated, over their shoulders, as the prison door clanged shut on her.

And the houspilleurs, who occasionally would let her know just how it would be, when they finally did do it. Just what they would do to her body, some dark night, when she was asleep, and too bad if she was a virgin, not that they believed it, they knew she was a whore. But either way, they'd had virgins before, young and old, children, nuns.

And then the priests by day: "Take the skirt."

Once she even tried to tell them. "My pants are my protection! You keep me among men, my enemies, they say terrible things! They threaten me—"

Crash, the gavel. "Take back the skirt."

As if she'd been speaking Greek, or Babel.

So she gave up trying to make them understand, but had they understood all along? Massieu had; he'd said she wouldn't need pants in the Church prison. Admitting that he understood why she needed them here.

What did that mean, his understanding? They'd almost burned her this morning for the heresy of her dressing like a man. Were they so false, then?

And now they were coming with a dress—she couldn't do it, couldn't "take the skirt," as they put it. She wore pants, had to wear pants, just like the English captains, like all soldiers! She couldn't change her fighting pants for the wretched, submissive skirt.

Massieu took her hand. "You did well this morning, Joan, when you submitted and saved your life."

"Not Joan!" she pulled back her hand. Joan of Arc wore pants.

Massieu just looked at her, uncomprehending. "Don't you see?" she wanted to cry to him, but he didn't see, couldn't, but she could. See that Girl X could wear a skirt, a shift, a robe, whatever they brought her. It didn't matter, so long as she was alive.

# III.

Massieu crossed to the door. "They're here!" The guards threw down their lots—"Bloody priests!" "Goddamned French!"—and hauled open the heavy door.

Cauchon came in, robes muddy, hat askew, face as red as it had been that morning, even redder. There'd been a scene just now, outside the castle. He'd been surrounded, he and his party, just as they were entering, by English soldiers with unsheathed swords and pikes.

"Hey you, priests! Our king has wasted his money on you!"

Cauchon hadn't wanted to come, had tried not to come. Tried to send the inquisitor, the scribe, some other high-ranking clerics, but then Winchester had made it clear that only Cauchon, chief judge in this affair, could exact penance correctly, legally, from the prisoner.

Thus Cauchon found himself outside Rouen Castle that afternoon, surrounded by the rabble. He looked around, at first more offended than afraid, for someone to call them off.

"Hey, priests! Anyone who throws you into the river won't be wasting his time!"

Cauchon turned in fury—where was Captain Warwick, to

call off his brutes?—but froze when he saw that Warwick had been there all along. Watching, with a very cold eye.

"The king stands badly in this!" Warwick called loudly.

Cauchon caught his breath. Warwick was his friend. They spoke English together.

"My lord, don't worry!" Cauchon tried to make his voice sound natural, light. As if it were nothing for Warwick to be standing off, looking on as his soldiers threatened the bishop's life.

Cauchon took another breath. This would soon be behind him, and he would be archbishop of Rouen. Winchester had promised it to him, in exchange for burning this girl.

"Don't worry, my lord," he called back to Warwick, "we'll soon have her again!"

Warwick said nothing, but Cauchon was allowed to pass unharmed through the soldiers into the castle, with his men, and down to the dungeon, where he stood outside her cell a moment, still breathless with fear.

Which turned to rage when he walked inside. More English soldiers, worse ones, and Massieu. What was he doing there? All soft around the eyes—the idiot, the biggest fool of all time. It was a wonder he could feed himself.

And her, too, still with that half-crazed smile, but why was he even looking at her? She was already dead.

"The Church unbinds you. . . ." He had to do the whole thing again. Where was the dress? That thing they'd brought. Someone held it out.

"Do you submit, Joan?"

"Don't call me Joan."

He looked at her.

She looked away. "Only let the dress be long."

Long, short—Cauchon passed it to her. The creature put it

on, over her pants, then slipped them off. These were handed back to him. What was he supposed to do with them? He didn't want to touch them.

He motioned to the barber.

"Do you agree, Joan, to the removal of your short haircut, offensive in the sight of God and man?"

Joan never would. But Girl X nodded.

The barber shaved her head. Now Cauchon really couldn't look.

"You are condemned to perpetual imprisonment, on the bread of affliction and the water of sorrow."

She listened abstractedly. "Bread and water"—she had never eaten much more, really, not even at the table of the king of France. When she'd been Joan of Arc.

And "perpetual imprisonment"—well, that's all Girl X had ever known, since her strange incarnation this morning. At least her guard would be a woman now. She would be relieved, at least, of the constant fear. Terror, really.

Cauchon moved to the door.

"The Church prison," she reminded him.

One of her guards grabbed the pants roughly away from Cauchon. He had never been treated this way by the English before. He was frightened again.

"The Church prison!" Joan of Arc cried to him. "A woman guard! Now that I'm in a dress—"

Cauchon turned. Couldn't she *see*?

"She submitted to the Church, she belongs in a Church prison now!" cried the idiot Massieu, deaf and blind, too, both of them. He made no move to leave with them, but the guards pushed him out with the rest of the churchmen.

Then one of the guards walked over and punched her, hard, in the face. Deliberately, before they shut the door, so the

French priests would see. Cauchon gasped, in spite of himself. One of the guards raised a stick at him, as if he were a dog. Still, he stared for a moment, before he turned away.

"If you fall again, you are dead," he called back to Joan of Arc, then fled. The door slammed shut behind him, in the face of Massieu, who stood there, frozen, until one of the priests grabbed his arm and pulled him up the seven steps.

# IV.

She lay on what they called her bed. She wasn't quite sure how long it had been since the priests had left. A day, maybe. Half a day. Maybe two.

Time had changed. She lay on her back and breathed in and breathed out. She was proud of that—she'd gotten that for herself. She had no one else to thank for the fact that she was still breathing.

Not even her saints and angels—well, that was something new. Even here, in this black hole, *quelque chose de nouveau*. One just had to look. She passed her hand over her head—this time, she remembered. Last time, she'd forgotten, and when she felt the stubble, her shaved head, tears had sprung into her eyes, and that had been bad. But this time she was prepared, and it was all right. "My hair is a small thing," she'd said, throughout her trial, when they complained that her short hair, too, "men's hair," was "an abomination." "A small thing," she said then, and it still was, especially when compared to the stake.

She touched her eye, gently. It had swelled shut. The guards had never hit her before. They'd struck her just as the priests were leaving, probably more to scare them. She'd had a glimpse of Massieu and Cauchon, just before the door was slammed, looking back at her, frightened, but nothing frightened her anymore.

Except the stake. Fine. She'd admitted it, publicly. They all knew it, they'd all seen: she couldn't burn. Some people could, Saint Apollonia, and Saint Cyril. But not Joan of Arc.

She'd thought she could. She'd said it all through her trial: "I'd rather burn than deny my saints!"

It had sounded good, and she'd meant it when she'd said it, with all her heart, or so she'd thought. But it turned out to be just words.

Which, she now knew, were easy—words. For five months: "You may burn my body to cinders," or "You may torture me so that you separate my soul from my body," or "Even if the executioner comes to take me and I am in the fire," and so forth, "I shall never deny my saints!"

Fine, bold, shining words, until the first real intimation of what she'd been talking about, the fire. And then those words had given way so fast, to other words, words she didn't even know she knew.

"Your saints led you to the sin of insubordination—"

And she'd said, "Yes," just as fluently as she'd said, "No," before.

"—and heresy."

She, easily: "Yes."

"They caused you to defy the Holy Church—"

She, eloquently: "Yes."

"They are devils."

One hesitation, and then finally, loud and clear, "Yes."


Girl X turned over. But those yeses were just words, too. Maybe Joan of Arc's saints understood that, would have understood, if they'd been there. Understood at least that it was Girl X who was talking by then, and she knew nothing of saints. Her words, too, were just words.

And her legs were cold. Joan of Arc's never were. She wore pants. Always and by first definition: Joan of Arc wore pants. Take away the pants, and you've got—what? Girl X. Anyway, not Joan of Arc.

The priests must have known that during the trial, the way they dwelled on it so. Every day, pants and hair, pants and hair.

"Why do you wear them?"

"Which saint commanded you to wear them?"

"Wouldn't you feel more honest in a dress?"

"Don't you know it's a mortal sin to dress the way you do?"

"Don't you care?"

"Won't you at least take off the sinful pants on Easter?"

"And why, once again, have you abandoned the clothes that are fitting to your sex?"

She had answered them variously, with passion, with common sense, with theology, from the bottom of her heart, and the furthest reaches of her brain. Fool that she'd been. Trying to make them see, when she was the one who wasn't seeing. She finally did see, that morning in the cemetery behind Rouen Cathedral, where they'd stood ranged, ready to kill her. Saw at last that they were out to destroy her. Willing, even, to burn her alive.

What a fool Joan of Arc had been, what a child! She hadn't seen that the priests were her enemies, simply because she saw them first as priests. Holy men, that is, sanctified by the Church. Every one of them—it took her breath away even now— had been consecrated by the Holy Spirit, which, she'd been taught as a girl, changes men forever, like water into which one has dropped even a bit of wine.

"Gentle priests," she had called them. Girl X hit the wall with her fist. Joan of Arc brought tears to her eyes.

"If only you could see my saints!" she'd said to them, her enemies, taking them into her deepest confidence, opening her heart to them, her soul. To the point of wishing that these deadly enemies could be blessed with a sacred vision of her saints.

"For if you could only see them once," Joan of Arc had testified earnestly, "you would know, right away, just as I do, that they are holy."

Girl X cringed. How could she have dragged her beloved saints into that wretched courtroom? Served them up in that unholy place, her "beautiful" Saint Catherine and Saint Margaret, "gold crowns on their heads," smelling "fresh and sweet," speaking in voices "beautiful, worthy, and good."

And to what avail? For then Cauchon would bang down his gavel and repeat, "Your saints are devils. Your pants are the proof that they lead you into sin."

And then, rather than standing up and saying, as Girl X would now, You men are my enemies! This trial is the devil's work! Joan of Arc, poor thing, would try then even harder.

"No, no, if only you could see, even once, gentle priests! My saints aren't devils! They're Saint Catherine and Saint Margaret—"

And so on. She should have seen it, of course. She almost did, that day with Saint Gabriel and Saint Michael.

"You say Saint Michael came to you," the priests began. "How did you know it was a man?"

"Did he come to you naked?"

At least she hit back on that one. "Do you think our Lord has no clothes for him?" But they went on.

"Did you kiss him?"

She: "Yes, of course."

"Where?"

She: "On the knees."

"Did he smell good?"

She: "Of course, he was a saint."

They were interrupting each other: "Did you feel his body?"

"What part of his body?"

"How did you know it was a man?"


Poor Joan of Arc. "Gentle priests!" she'd cried. "Please! I know it was Saint Michael, the very one who suffered passion and death for us! I believe in him, as I believe in Jesus Christ, our Lord—"

The gavel.

She closed her eyes. That was over now. And they hadn't gotten her in the end, even though they'd all gone out there to kill her, to burn her. Well, she didn't burn.

They had all been shocked. That was at least some measure of their respect, she supposed. So brave did they think Joan of Arc, they even thought she would go to the stake.

She'd thought so, too, not that she'd ever expected it to come to that. She hadn't once considered the possibility. She had gone out that morning still believing that a last-minute miracle was more likely than a trip in the cart to the stake.

And even then, when it came to her slowly, gradually, that she was alone, that there were no angels there, no saints, and there weren't going to be any miracles in Rouen that morning, she was still surprised when she sold her saints for her life.


Or rather, Girl X's life. "Perpetual prison." Bread and water. Skirts among rapists who had already started hitting her. No saints or angels now—she hadn't heard a word from them since her recantation, not even a whisper. She missed them badly, missed even the promises of salvation that had turned out to be untrue.

What had been true, however, was that she'd been publicly revealed to be a coward who didn't have the courage to burn.

But she wasn't supposed to burn! She was supposed to be saved.

But now she was thinking like Joan of Arc, and Joan of Arc was gone, as gone as "the snows of yesterday," as she'd once heard a bard sing at the king's court. "*Où sont les neiges d'antan?*" Maybe where Joan of Arc is—fine, let her go. She was brave to a point, though not, it turned out, to the end.

And anyway, she had understood nothing.

# V.

B ut maybe that was the only way it could have been. If Joan of Arc had known anything, she wondered if she'd ever have left her father's house.

Wouldn't she have run from her saints, when she first heard them? Called them witches, or fairies, or the wind? Run down from the hills, inside to her mother? Or turned, at least, to other children, whose voices might have stopped her from hearing, even once, *Daughter of God, you were born to save France.*

For, once she heard it, everything else fell away. Everything she knew, that is, all the cautionary tales, the stories, the sayings. The whole canon of common knowledge that advised "slow and steady," and kept most French peasants from lives of art and danger—"the Grasshopper and the Ant," "the Crow and the Cheese." All this safe-and-sound advice gave way to, *Go, daughter of God, to the king.*

If Joan of Arc had been wiser, Girl X realized, she wouldn't have listened. Wouldn't have even been able to hear her saints in the first place, but she did hear them, from the time she was twelve. The cautious voices of the village wise women were replaced by Saint Catherine and Saint Margaret, the same two who stood carved in stone beside the altar of her church in

Domrémy. At first they spoke to her in general terms of her destiny. *You were born to save France.* Joan of Arc would lean against the trees, standing among the fields, listening, dreaming.

But when she was sixteen, the situation in France worsened. The English laid siege to Orléans. It was the last stronghold of the Dauphin, the uncrowned French heir to the throne; if the English took Orléans, they would have France.

At that point, Saint Catherine and Saint Margaret became specific. *Go to the Dauphin, and tell him to give you an army. You will raise the siege of Orléans, and then crown him king. We are with you.*

S he heard this, and went. How? Girl X marveled. With not the first preparation, not a thought of the near future, or even of where she'd sleep that night, Joan of Arc placed herself in her saints' hands, and set out.

Lightheartedly, you might even say, in the coarse red skirt and long braids of the Lorraine countryside. Thus she slipped away from home, from parents and chores and sheep, with no fare-wells; walked, trekked, scrambled, the ten miles to the French garrison at Vaucouleurs; and presented herself, as she thought her saints had commanded, to the captain there, Robert de Bau-dricourt. Who took one look, and sent her home for a beating.

She was mortified, and, worse, confused. Her saints had said, *Baudricourt will help you.* Were they lying? Was it all a deceit? Was she a fool, or, worse, mad? Overreaching? Some of the stories came back: Was she the girl who comes to a very bad end, out chasing visions while her sheep were left to the wolves?

Her heart was heavy and her mind clouded, and she returned home to worse than a beating. She found herself betrothed.

News had traveled from Vaucouleurs to Domrémy: Jacques d'Arc's daughter had run away to join the French army. A girl, the army—a camp-follower, then? A prostitute? What else could there be? Everyone was shocked. Her father went shouting through the village that he'd "rather see her drowned," he'd drown her himself!

Though by the time she got back, he'd turned from homicide to the standard remedy for wayward young women: he found a young man, and arranged a marriage.

"I'd rather die!" cried Joan of Arc. She refused the marriage in terms that left neither doubt nor hope. But to her dismay, her suitor sued her.

"Breach of promise," he claimed, in the ecclesiastical court at Toul. Not only was she betrothed to him now, he told the court, but she'd sworn to marry him when they were children, under the ancient beech tree where the fairies danced in May.

Even her father testified against her, agreeing that this might have been so.

No one expected her to plead her own defense. Girls in these cases mostly didn't. What they did was cry at their own weddings and then settle down to real life, dreams of the king of France, or convents, or poetry in the streets of Paris giving way to swaddling cloth and mutton stew.

Joan of Arc, however, trudged to Toul, where the records noted only that a local peasant girl, Jeannot, "little Joan," daughter of Jacques of Arc, appeared before the court, defended herself with vigor, and was not, in the end, sentenced to marry.

Thank God!
Or not?

Still, the point was that Joan of Arc didn't hold back after that. It had been too close for comfort, this brush with the fortune of all womankind.

Her saints were in a hurry now, too. *Go before mid-Lent*, they whispered. It was February. She had turned seventeen. It had been hard, saying goodbye to her mother, who must have sensed something. She'd held her close to her breast and wept over her head. She'd had to lie to her, tell her she was going off to assist with the birth of a girl cousin's baby, when in fact she went to a boy cousin in a neighboring village, whom she got to cut off her hair.

Straight around, with a bowl, definitive. No one could look at her now and think marriage. But then it was done. Her hair was off. She'd explained to this boy cousin that he had to give her his pants as well, and when she went to Captain Baudricourt this time, it was in pants and a black cap, hair cut short. No longer an errant shepherdess, but Joan of Arc.

On her way to the Dauphin. Baudricourt didn't laugh at her this time. "When?" he asked her.

"Better today than tomorrow," she told him. "Better tomorrow than the next day."


Mid-Lent, the saints had said. Baudricourt sent a letter to the Dauphin, and refused to let her go until he got word back. She felt the loss of every day. Just the fact that he was willing to send to the court should have cheered her; but she was visualizing big victories, and didn't notice the small ones.

Meanwhile, excitement was rising around her in the town. There was a prophecy going through the countryside then: "France, destroyed by a woman, will be saved by a virgin."

Everyone knew who the woman was—the Dauphin's mother, Queen Isabeau, wife of the late king of France, Charles VI the Mad. She had declared her own son, the French Dauphin, the heir, "illegitimate" in favor of her daughter's English son. This essentially gave the throne of France to England.

But who was the virgin?

"I am," Joan of Arc told the people of Vaucouleurs. They started gathering in the evenings at the wheelwright's, where she was lodged, to listen to her tales of saints and angels. She told them that she would set out any day now, from their town, to save France.

Their town! They wanted to help, but first were obliged to confirm her holiness. They called on the priest, who waved his stole in front of her, and commanded her to fly off if she was from the devil.

But she stood firm, and then the people of Vaucouleurs started raising money to buy her a horse.

The powerful young Duke of Alençon heard the talk and came to meet her one evening. "Well, sweet friend," he said to her, "it looks as if our king will be chased away, and we turned to Englishmen."

"No!" she cried. She would get to the Dauphin before mid-Lent, "even if I have to wear my legs down to the knees! For no one, no king, no duke, no daughter of the king of Scotland can save France. Only me!"

Finally, word came from the court. Let her come, why not? The Dauphin had just lost another skirmish with the English, called the Battle of the Herrings, for the Lenten provisions that had been among the spoils. A bit of a joke, if it hadn't been his last stand. He had no possibility of raising another army. He was so broke that his shoemaker had refused him credit for a pair of stockings.

And then came the news of this girl. A virgin sent by God to save France? Well, why not? Everyone knew that virgins had special powers. Unalloyed. Concentrated. As for heaven's personal concern with the state of the realm, France had always been God's "eldest daughter," so no one was surprised. On top of that, Marie d'Avignon, a celebrated mystic at the Dauphin's court, had recently reported a vision of a virgin and much armor. It was agreed that the Dauphin should send for the girl.

The word came in February, a bad time for traveling, Baudricourt pointed out to Joan of Arc. The roads were in ruins, the bridges all down, the land either "deserted or infested with soldiers."

"Better today than tomorrow," repeated Joan of Arc. The Duke of Alençon, who stood to recover his own lands should she prove successful, decided to seize the adventure and accompany her. He contributed a group of fighting men. The whole town gathered to see them off. The people presented her with the horse, and Baudricourt gave her his sword.

"Go," he said, "go, and come what may."

Actually, she told him exactly what would come. She would cross France safely, despite the civil war and all the raiding parties that made travel so perilous; she would enter the little town of Chinon, where the Dauphin had taken refuge; she would have an immediate and successful audience with him; he would give her his army, with which she would hand the English their first major defeat in France in a hundred years. After which she would march the Dauphin down the Loire Valley, with one town after another throwing open its gates and declaring loyalty, all the way to Reims Cathedral, where she would see him anointed with the sacred oil and crowned Charles VII, king of France.

And it turned out that she was right.

# VI.

The beginning. Girl X opened her eyes, then closed them. She coughed. There was blood in her mouth. One of the guards had pushed her into the door the last time she'd had to get up. She'd fallen then, and hurt her knee as well. But she was alive.

That spring, two springs ago—but it hadn't been spring yet, when she set out for the court in the beginning. She and her small party left Vaucouleurs, traveling at night because the roads were too dangerous during the day, too many soldiers. The men who slept beside her on the trip were inflamed neither by "desire nor carnal motive," they informed her, in wonder.

But that was why she'd cut off her hair and put on pants, she told them.

"Do you know what you'll say when you get there?" they asked.

She didn't, but, "Don't fear, my brothers in paradise will help me," she said. And sure enough, eleven days later, when she arrived in Chinon, that far corner in France where the Dauphin was holed up, they did.

Or so it had seemed to her at the time. She'd felt protected, almost surrounded by help, and when she was ushered into the throne room, she wasn't afraid. She was trembling, true, but with deepest reverence, not with fear.

It was night—the giant hall was lit by fifty torches, the kind of splendor she'd never seen before. In her previous life, one torch was a luxury. There were more than three hundred knights in attendance, to see her. She was led past them, up to the throne, as her saints had said she would be, but just as she was about to throw herself at the feet of the man sitting there, something stopped her.

It must have been her saints, but what she found herself suddenly thinking of, there in the throne room, surrounded by all the knights and ladies of the realm, were not her saints, but her sheep.

And the wolves who crept down from the hills, and the foxes who lurked occasionally in the brush around the barnyard. The sheep and chickens always knew it first, before you could see it. Before anything happened—probably they smelled it. "They dream it," the old tales claimed. Anyway, if you paid attention, you could always catch the signs. The animals couldn't speak a word, but they didn't have to.

Nor did these strange creatures in the throne room that night. Something was wrong. Jeannot, the keeper of sheep, daughter of Jacques d'Arc, knew it.

She turned away from the throne, from the man posed there, and walked slowly around the room until whatever it was, whatever was happening there that night, made her stop. She stood before a man, hardly princely, with a long nose, thin lips, and skinny bowed legs. Wolf or sheep? She could feel both power and fear. But she held the rod and the staff that night.

"God grant you a good life, gentle king," said Joan of Arc.

"I am not the king, he is the king," said he, pointing to one of the knights.

"In the name of God, gentle prince, it is you and no other. You are the king."

Silence. What had started as a little joke was no longer funny.

"How do you know?" he said. Meaning not *How did you guess me out in this little game?* but *By what authority do you call me king, if my own mother calls me illegitimate?*

His father, Charles VI, Charles the Mad, had spent extended periods of his life, weeks, months at a time, lying in darkness, completely comatose, "turned to glass," as he would afterward put it. The king's wife, the Dauphin's mother, Isabeau of Bavaria, barely spoke French. She had few friends among the courtiers, who mocked her sauerkraut compote, to which she was "more faithful," it was said, than to the king of France. When she confessed that her son's father was someone other than her husband, no one had reason to doubt her.

Except for the timing of her statement, made to coincide with the signing the Treaty of Troyes with her friends the English, a treaty that not only declared the French heir to the throne illegitimate, but also married her daughter to Henry V of England and gave him, through her, the French throne.

"France destroyed by a woman"—the thing was knotted, and then tangled, and knotted again. Whether the allegation was true or false or both, for it was also possible that the queen had no certainty as to her son's paternity, it had done its work for the English. It had rendered the French heir to the throne impotent. Under the shadow of illegitimacy, the Dauphin, upon the death of his father, had been unable to muster either the will or the support to push forward to his own coronation.

"Charles the Weak," they called him, "King of Bourges," an

obscure provincial town. His court was impoverished, his king-
dom rent by civil war. His two powerful uncles, the Dukes of
Orléans and Burgundy, had murdered each other. Paris was in
English hands.

But, "You are king," said Joan of Arc that night.

"How do you know?" the Dauphin more begged than asked.
He took her hand. No one spoke.

"Saint Catherine and Saint Margaret have assured me. It is
the will of God that you be crowned king of France."

"Saved by a virgin." Slash, the knots cut. In one fell swoop,
all doubt sundered. Girl X tried to remember if Joan of Arc
had even understood the question, the concept of illegitimacy,
when she refuted it definitively that night.

Anyway, what did that one man's bloodline matter, to her
or to any of the poor people, the common people, across whose
lands these endless wars of succession had raged? The ones
who starved and froze and watched their farms that in the best
of times produced only by a miraculous combination of good
seed and just the right weather, knowing the moon and when to
plant, and then getting the right sun for growing, and enough
rain, at the right time, these people whose crops then, having
survived, having been blessed by all these miracles, were stolen
or burned by every army that came through, "ours" or "theirs,"
both had to eat—these people needed a king more than they
needed a king's legitimate son.

"Saint Catherine and Saint Margaret say you are king," said
their girl, Joan of Arc, to the Dauphin that night. She herself
had had to flee more than once with her family and neighbors, to the castle at Neufchâteau, leaving homes, flocks, crops,

everything they'd worked their red hands to the bone for, there below, to the passing soldiers.

"You are king," said Joan of Arc, who knew nothing, only what everyone knew. "Now give me an army, and send me to Orléans."

Orléans was the first step to Reims, where the Dauphin had to be anointed to become king.

When? he asked her.

"Better today than tomorrow," but there were factions in the court. She hadn't known it then, would learn it only too late, the next year, when they pulled her up short, checked her when she was still moving forward—dear God! Why? Why? Was the devil so strong? She hadn't understood it, until the second spring at court, but that first spring, the beautiful 1429, she still understood nothing.

Lucky her! Joan of Arc, before her—what? Her education? Simple Joan of Arc—how beautiful she was! She welcomed the priests from the University of Poitiers who wanted to examine her "against witchcraft." They waved stoles again, and threw holy water—so far, so good. She neither melted nor flew away.

But the court was too divided for these university men, clerics and dependent, to give themselves over to early enthusiasm.

They tried a twist of logic: "If God wills victory for France," they asked her, "why do you need soldiers?"

"The soldiers will fight in God's name," she answered, "and God will grant them victory."

"Bravo!" shouted her partisans, mostly from Lorraine and Anjou, who would recover their lands should her campaign prove successful.

But, "Give us a sign," demanded others, whose loyalties were more complicated.

202 { VICTORIA SHORR

She stood up. "I didn't come to Poitiers to make signs," she said. "Give me an army, put me in front of Orléans, and I'll show you the sign I was sent to make."

The clerics were impressed, but by good or evil? They couldn't agree, pointed out that goodness did not preclude the devil's having a part in it. Examples were cited. Three weeks passed. Joan of Arc despaired, half mad with impatience. "Better today than tomorrow!" she was crying to the Dauphin.

"Yes, yes," from the Dauphin. Never inclined to exertion, he was starting to wonder aloud if the effort should after all be made.

Queen Yolanda, his mother-in-law and chief advisor, said nothing for the moment. She was waiting for a private exploratory party to get back from Domrémy. When they returned with the word that the girl was just what she claimed to be, a simple peasant of impeccable reputation said to commune with saints and angels, Queen Yolanda made her move.

She convened the priests and reminded them that God was known to work through virgins, though the devil could not. Why not refer the case to the midwives?

Silence from the clerics then, silence from the court. It was a checkmate, they knew, a brilliant move with no possible rebuttal—no surprise, coming from the skilled hand of Yolanda, queen of Sicily, Aragon, Jerusalem, and, more to the point, Anjou, a province wholly and entirely sympathetic to ridding France of the English. "The man of the family," the courtiers called her, behind her back.

But, "Why man?" she said with a smile. She led in her personal midwives to examine "the secret parts" of Joan of Arc's body, and emerged with the confirmation that Joan of Arc was a virgin, "whole and entire." Queen Yolanda then advised her son-in-law to make the girl some armor, put her in front of his army, and send her to Orléans.

# VII.

Orléans—"Or-lé-ans," she whispered. Even the name rang like a bell, calling back her very best days. "Orléans." Inseparable from Joan of Arc. Even from dreams of Joan of Arc, for she'd known, as soon as she knew that she had a fate apart from the other girls of the village, that she would raise the siege of Orléans. That was how Joan of Arc would save France.

She left the court for Orléans in late April 1429. She was seventeen.

The English had been besieging the city for over a year. It was nearly surrounded. The people were half starved—her first victory was simply to send a party of soldiers to skirmish with the English just as night fell, while she slipped into the town with a herd of swine. There was wild rejoicing. Food, and a virgin, both from God! The people of Orléans feasted and crowded around, kissing her feet and even her horse.

"This is the beginning," she told them with tears in her eyes. "We shall be free."

"Saint Catherine and Saint Margaret are with me," she said, and went out on the ramparts to look over the English army she was soon to defeat.

The savage, invincible English army, whom the French

hadn't beaten in a hundred years. She stood there, and was overcome with it all. With the mystery of life, and of her presence in Orléans with an army, just as her saints had said, most improbably, absurdly, really, when she was a shepherd girl, no different from the rest, unlikely to go anywhere, much less to Orléans.

But here she stood, at the head of the king's army, with God's grace upon her. She would win. She looked out at the English soldiers, the doomed.

"You soldiers!" she called to them. "I have great pity for you! Listen to me! You don't have to die in France!"

What?

"Go back to England, soldiers, so we don't have to kill you!"

Orléans was the last significant pocket of resistance in France. The English had only to win here—mop up, really—and then they could put their own king, Henry VI, son of Henry V, on the throne of France.

"Saint Catherine and Saint Margaret send pity! They are crying for you! But you can go back to England, you don't have to die here now!"

Die? The English didn't die in France, they killed in France, even if outnumbered, even when surrounded. Crécy, Poitiers, Agincourt! "Few in number but valiant in war"—these soldiers could even say it in Latin. "Ten Englishmen equal a hundred French"—that was the first mathematics they'd learned. They'd followed their fathers to France to do what the English always did there: lead the French to slaughter, "like a flock of sheep."

And now, this girl? With pity for them? They were dumbstruck at first.

"Go back to England, where God loves you, too! For Saint Margaret and Saint Catherine have promised that we shall win!"

Now the English soldiers found their voice. "Slut!" they shouted at Joan of Arc. "Whore!"

"When we beat you, we'll put you back in skirts and use you like the whore you are!"

She was stunned. She'd come to them in good faith, dressed in pants! And still, they insulted her like—a woman.

"God is with me!" she cried.

"The only ones with you are pimps and infidels!"


She climbed back down from the walls after that in tears, but her words had found their mark. She was a "whore" to the English soldiers that night, but by the next day, when the fighting started, she had become a witch. And then she was invincible.

The battle lasted for three days. The English were scattered in small forts outside the city, which turned out to be impossible to defend against the large French force that Joan of Arc had inspired. The English didn't bother to concentrate their own forces, relying on their usual courage and luck, but their courage was flagging in the face of the witch, and the luck this time was with Joan of Arc.

*Go, daughter of God*, her saints were whispering to her throughout, *we are with you*, and she felt them, always. The English left their outlying forts, one by one, and concentrated their army in the tower, Les Tourelles, on the bridge in front of the city.

It was the eighth of May, 1429. The night before, Joan of Arc had led her whole army to mass, confession, and Communion. The townspeople had come, too, crowding in, overflowing the church, receiving the blessing, being blessed. Beseeching, together with God's virgin, what they felt might truly be granted—deliverance.

Victory. "I could die here among you happily," said Joan of Arc to the people of Orléans that night. It was all she'd hoped, dreamed even, out there alone in the hills of Domrémy. She found that battle agreed with her. She fought hard, feared nothing, sought always to be in the thick of things. She was wounded once, in the soft flesh between her neck and shoulder, but though she bled, she scarcely felt it, and it didn't stop her. She remained in the field.

That day, she refused to stop fighting, even in the evening, when they'd been at it since dawn. The generals assured her they could do no more that day, and when she refused to call a halt, they held a council without her, and sounded a retreat.

She was furious. "You have been with your council," she cried to the generals, "and I have been with mine!"

She turned directly to the soldiers. "My saints have promised us victory tonight!" She rallied them despite the high command, and led them herself on another sally, out of the city. And when the English saw the French, the timid, weak, home-for-dinner French, ready to fight on as though possessed—"The witch!"—they panicked and fled.

Stampeded, terrified, out of Les Tourelles, onto the bridge, in their armor, too many of them, until the bridge collapsed under their weight, and they fell into the Loire and sank like stones.

The Siege of Orléans was lifted. Bells rang, people danced through the streets, laughing, singing, cheering—Joan of Arc! She ate nothing but bread dipped in watered-down wine. She led the townspeople to a mass of thanksgiving, still in her armor.

Her armor, her standard, her sword—they seemed almost

part of her now, like her strong arms and short hair. Much later, when some women were helping her to undress, they were shocked to see her entire body battered black and blue.

"From the armor," she told them. She'd had to sleep in it on the journey from Chinon to Orléans.

No one slept in armor, not the boldest of knights, not the hardest among them, but Joan of Arc always did, she'd told her men on that journey, "to be ready," she'd said. They were impressed.

She told the truth, however, to the women: she'd found herself there among men, her first night on the march, and couldn't figure out how to take off her armor without—undressing. Turning from a soldier into a woman who was taking off her clothes.

The first night had been the worst, she said, and the next morning she'd had to grit her teeth even to stand up, much less get on her horse. But that had proved a small price to pay for what she had gained.

The women of Orléans understood her perfectly. "Men don't feel desire around me," she told them. "I am free."

They nodded, and bathed her limbs tenderly, and laid her in their softest bed.

# VIII.

One of the guards threw her a crust of bread. She couldn't eat right now, couldn't chew. Her jaw.

Does it help to remember? she wondered. "The Pucelle," they'd called her, the Girl, the Maiden, as if there were no other, as if she were the only girl in France.

Everyone knew her, in those days of glory right after Orléans. Everyone followed her, wanted her, but all she wanted was more. More Orléans. More days in battle, more nights deep in prayer. More horses, more soldiers, more comrades by her side.

Like the Duke of Alençon. He'd marched with her from Vaucouleurs, then stuck with her in court, and was always beside her in battle. He knew how to fight, and he was brave in the same way she was.

Did he know, she wondered, about her now? He had gone back to his estates in Normandy when it all broke up. She sat up suddenly—Normandy! Near here? Did he know she was chained in a dungeon in Rouen? She, his ally, the best fighter he knew, he said. If he found out she was here, mightn't he at least try to save her? Even now?

For they had really been friends then. She could still almost see them, Alençon and herself, Joan of Arc, that is, laughing, riding, thundering like war gods, from Orléans straight to Reims.

Though it hadn't been straight. She'd thought it would be. After Orléans, they'd rushed back to court, where she expected to find the Dauphin mounted and ready to ride out with them. He wasn't. That is, he almost was, or claimed he would be soon, and would like to accompany them now, if only the roads were safer. Or the English not likely to be reinforcing, even as they spoke. Or if the towns along the way were his, not theirs.

"But they will be yours!" she cried to him. "All France shall be yours!" She was in a great hurry to get him to Reims Cathedral, where one drop of the holy oil there would turn the Dauphin from questionable pretender to the king of France, the point of her mission. She would ride in front, she assured him, and "win by battle" what didn't come "from love."

"Saint Catherine and Saint Margaret will be with us!" she assured him, swore that she stood ready to leave, morning or evening, it didn't matter, just the sooner the better, that was all.

"Let it be today," she prayed, every day, before breakfast, but the Dauphin was wavering. His chair was soft, his horse was hard, plus there were his councillors, all of them, advocating delay. Some were false, he suspected, some lazy, others afraid, but their consensus—that if he sat still, the crown, Reims Cathedral, would come to him—was not without resonance in his own heart of hearts.

Still, against all this there was one clear voice, positing saints and angels, and a holy coronation, and towns where people were waiting to throw open their gates to him. All of France would receive him as the duly crowned king, that voice repeated, for a month, longer, until finally, one night, just after midsummer with Scorpio rising, the Dauphin crossed to a window and looked out.

He stood there for a while, sniffed the air, and must have sensed something. Change, for though he'd never been moved before, and hardly would be again, that night as he retired, he announced to the court that he would set out to Reims with Joan of Arc in the morning.

They went first to Jargeau, which Suffolk was holding for the English. She and Alençon charged, and Suffolk surrendered. On to Meung, which they took easily, and then to Beaugency, which surrendered without a fight. They arrived next at Patay, where Lord Talbot himself, who had fled from Orléans, was captured, after his reinforcements retreated to Paris, terrified of the witch.

"You didn't expect this to happen this morning, did you?" Alençon asked Talbot.

Talbot shrugged. "The fortunes of war."

No, no, not fortune, said Joan of Arc, the way it would always be! That summer of dreams, dreams more than realized but surpassed. That march through France, with her army swelling daily, not just with knights and regular soldiers, but also with civilians, her people, more of them every day. Peasants, "jacques," with their sticks and stones, and women and children. For them, the campaign was a pilgrimage to Reims Cathedral, where they would finally get their king.

They were stopped before Troyes, though, the biggest city on their way. The English were there in force, but Joan of Arc wasn't daunted, and the feeling was that "nothing could resist her anymore."

But after two days of inconclusive fighting, the Dauphin's military advisors wanted to withdraw. This time, though, she was prepared. She refused them further audience, and went around them, right to the soldiers.

"Fill the moat with brush," she commanded. "Saint Catherine and Saint Margaret say the city will be ours!"

The people of Troyes watched nervously through the night as their moat disappeared under brush and wood, and with the first light of morning they surrendered directly to "the Pucelle," notwithstanding their strong English garrison.

"All through fear of her"—the English garrison was granted permission to withdraw with their "possessions," but when Joan of Arc saw them leading away the manacled French prisoners which this included, she revolted. She was taxed with this during her trial; the prisoners, soldiers taken in battle, properly made part of the English possessions, argued the priests.

"But the hair on the back of my neck stood on end when I saw them," she explained.

"They are French!" she cried, there at Troyes, and her cheering army set them free. The common soldiers had never been cared for by a commander before. Nor had they ever cared for one as they cared for her.

Loved her, even—every true French heart loved her that summer. The next few cities sent her their keys without further fighting. Her march now became a procession, a triumph. The army hadn't been paid, but no one wanted to leave her. They entered the town of Reims to the ringing of bells and cries of, "Noel!" Praise and joy, as she'd foretold.

Foretold, too, dreamlike, the way it swirled all around her. Only the coronation itself stood out clearly in her memory from those days. It was July 17, 1429, high summer by then. The cathedral was thronged with the people, as well as the priests, bishops, abbots, canons, white and purple and gold. The archbishop of Reims stood at the front, flanked by two knights of St. Remy who held the ampoule of holy oil, given by God directly into the hands of Saint Louis specifically for anointing the kings of France. Joan of Arc, in new white armor, knelt right behind the Dauphin, and she wept, and he wept, and he was crowned king of France, Charles VII.

And it was over.

S he could see that now. It was too bad she hadn't seen it then, in Reims Cathedral. Her mission had been specific, "Orléans and Reims," and she'd fulfilled it. She should have gone home.

But she was seventeen. People were calling her their "Hector," their "Alexander," their "Caesar!" "O France," bards were singing, "though you've had many heroes, you may stop now with this Pucelle!"

"Singular virgin! Marvelous, brave, the glory of France, of all Christendom!" Looking back, she should have thanked them all kindly and said adieu, but what she said was, "Let's take Paris!" to Alençon.

But her saints hadn't said "Paris," and she didn't take it. Could have, said the generals, if she'd listened to them and marched straight from Orléans, instead of to Reims.

Might have, she felt, when she finally did get there, if they hadn't carried her from the battlefield when she was wounded, just slightly, in the thigh. She could have fought on, she felt sure—how many hundreds of times had she seen it in her mind? Her rising to rally her holy army, and Paris wanting her suddenly, as Troyes had wanted her, and throwing open its gates. Welcoming her, and her king, who would have marched beside her into his capital to greater rejoicing than either of them had known till then. And then, surely, she would have gone home.

But the generals ordered her carried from the field, and then it was shouted through Paris that "the witch" had "bled red blood!" The defenders took heart from that, and her own soldiers lost their way without her. They remembered, suddenly, that they hadn't been paid.

And her army broke up after that. It was September. Summer was over. Even Alençon went home, and though they had great plans to rejoin in the spring to launch a new campaign for Paris, she never saw him again.

# IX.

Her winter at the French court was a nightmare—the
beginning of the nightmare. The factions of conserva-
tism regrouped against her. The archbishop of Reims had
started speaking down to her at council meetings. Worse,
the king was no longer meeting her eye. Nor did he show
the slightest interest when she spoke of her projected
spring campaign.

"Saint Catherine and Saint Margaret say we shall take
Paris!" she urged him—not knowing that he even then had a
secret envoy in Paris, treating with the enemy, and no one cared
about Saint Catherine and Saint Margaret anymore.

She tried believing in small favors—an exemption from
the poll tax for her native village; a position for her brother
in nearby Vaucouleurs. She tried to keep her head. She was
asked to raise a dead child, decide between the two Popes,
touch crosses and rosaries—"Touch them yourselves," she
said with a laugh to the village women. "Your touch is as
good as mine."

Her family was ennobled, she was granted the fleur-de-lis.
The king presented her with richly embroidered men's clothes,
woven in gold—meaningless to her.

. . .

Joan of Arc. The truth was she didn't really want to go home anymore. She had acquired a taste for the action. She was, Girl X realized, a very different girl from the one who'd hoped to take Orléans without killing any English soldiers. Even her sword had changed. It had been "holy" when she first went into battle. Now it was "excellent," both "for thrusts and cuts."

She longed to be fighting again. Her only consolation at court was her plan for her spring campaign. She and Alençon would meet again—they could start in Normandy. She was just waiting for the rains to finally stop. Once they did, she felt sure the king would grant her an army.

But then he didn't. Wouldn't? Couldn't? She couldn't comprehend it. His ministers were against her, were always against her—why?

True, she had been having trouble hearing her voices in the din of the court, but even without her saints she thought her case for another campaign was a sound one. The English were still afraid of her, Alençon had confirmed it, now was the time to take the rest of France back for her king! For their king, too, she cried to the ministers—why not?

Why not? Well, for one thing there was the secret deal that Georges de La Trémoille, the king's chief minister, his trusted favorite, had made with the English just that spring. They would refrain from laying siege to any town that belonged to him, or interfering in any way with his personal income, in return for him keeping Joan of Arc in check while their men were still terrified of her.

. . .

Treachery and perversity—she had been in over her head there. Neither her practical country upbringing nor her saints had prepared her to fathom those depths. She pressed on, begging to be allowed to continue a victorious campaign. The English were in disarray, Paris was waiting, the Duke of Alençon and all the rest of them were standing by to march, to fight, to fly with her again. The spring had come, the time was right. And still—and still—her king refused to move.

"Perhaps I will go home," she murmured, for the hundredth time, to her page.

But it is only the oldest and the wisest, she knew now, who go home. And she was the youngest and the simplest, and she was floundering there at court, and when she heard that the town of Compiègne was besieged, she grasped at it, though it proved a straw.

A small town to the east, of no importance, really. Still, she remembered how the good people there had thrown open their gates to her last summer, when she was the Pucelle of Orléans, on a victory crusade through France. She had been in her glory then, and they had responded, they had been part of that time, and now they were besieged, and she resolved to go to their rescue.

Compiègne—it would go to her rescue, too. She would be on her horse again, at the head of a group of fighting men, doing what she did best, what nobody did better. Once they started fighting, God would be with her again, her voices would come back, and none of this would matter. This court scene where she couldn't find her footing would fade back into nothingness, and she would hold her famous banner high again and know why she'd been born.

What she was living for—as at Orléans, when she rode a white horse through the streets, bells ringing, "Te Deum," people thronging to kiss her hands, her feet. As on the way to Reims, when her voices were still saying, *Go, go, daughter of God.*

She gathered with her the few she could inspire—her brother, some other loyalists from home—joined up with a small army at Lagny-sur-Marne, and arrived at Compiègne in such a state of excitement that she rode into battle that very first day.

Before she'd looked around properly—before she'd done even rudimentary reconnaissance. So desperate was she to prove that nothing had changed, that she changed everything. Joan of Arc had always paid close attention. She had always looked carefully around.

But at Compiègne—maybe it was that year at court, the ease, the flattery. Or maybe she'd heard too many versions of her own myth. Joan of God, Joan of the Saints—at Compiègne she didn't ask even the first questions, which would have informed her that the Burgundians outside the town had been reinforced the night before by some allied forces who were passing through.

Not the best time for an action; and one might sit in one's chains and wish, till one nearly went mad, that Joan of Arc had stopped and asked a few questions. Or that Saint Catherine and Saint Margaret had been there with her.

But they weren't, and all the wishes, all the regrets to the dregs, change nothing. Joan of Arc still rides out that bad day in Compiègne. She holds her banner high, crying, "Forward! They're ours!" as before—but instead of the brilliant clarity that had always preceded her, there was a sort of fog, smoke, dense confusion. She never could quite get a sense of the battle in its entirety that day.

Though she knew fairly soon that something was wrong, but by the time she figured out what it was, she was trapped. The enemy had gotten between her men and the town. All her experience till then had been with forward movements, offense, and when she finally realized that a retreat was in order, it was too late. The captain of Compiègne had already been compelled to draw up the bridge to save the town.

She rode off wildly then, helter-skelter, into some fields, but she found herself surrounded, increasingly closely. "Saint Margaret! Saint Catherine!" She spurred her horse, tried to break through, called desperately on her saints, her colleagues, her brother, but they were held off at a distance, horrified, unable to help. A party of Picards, who were closest to her, chopped madly at anyone near her, even killing soldiers who would have made valuable prisoners, in their frenzy to be the man to take the maid.

"*Rendez-vous!*" "*Rendez-vous!*" "Surrender!"—and then an archer, "permitted by Fortune to end her glory," got close enough to grab the side of her golden tunic. He pulled her from her horse, "flat onto the ground."

He led her off, "happier than if he had a King in his hands." It was the twenty-third of May, 1430—little more than a year since she'd ridden in full glory into Orléans. She was eighteen.

# X.

Girl X looked up. There was someone coming. No one had been there since—whenever it was.

Footsteps, voices. Massieu, maybe? She moved in her chains a bit, and tried to sit up. She wouldn't mind talking, even hearing her own voice, though her lips were parched. There had been no water for some time. She'd even dreamed that she'd been at the well at home, and she was hauling up water, it was splashing, there was so much, and she was just about to drink it.

She heard the lock turn outside, then laughter. English, not French. She lay back. English. It wouldn't be anything good.

An English lord came in with some men. Laughing. "*Kah, kah, kah, kah.*" Like crows. A bad language. Rough and cruel.

One of the guards yanked her up. Her chains caught, she half fell. More laughter.

*Funny to you, yes, you people of the law. Of the book, because you need a book to tell you right from wrong, so empty, so dry, is the desert that makes your hearts.*

"So you've got a dress on, harlot," said the lord to her in French. "Are you any prettier now?"

What was he saying?

He walked closer. "Let me see you."

Her stomach clenched. No man had ever looked at her this way. What was he planning? "Holy God, help me!"

He came closer. She could smell the beer on his breath. She started to cry. He touched her neck.

"Preserve me, Mother of God!" She fell to her knees.

The guards pulled her up. "What did you say, little whore?" The lord put his hand on her breast.

"Saint Catherine! Saint Margaret!" She swung her manacled hands, and caught him—on the arm, on the chest. He staggered back.

"Slut! Whore!"

One of the guards hit her, hard, on the side of the head. She fell.

"The filthy slut"—the lord was on her, they were grabbing her legs, pulling them, but she was chained.

"Holy Mother of God! Hear me now!" Someone hit her again.

She closed her eyes. Just as she fell, though, she saw it—the ray of light that came in, through the tiny little slit of window, once a day now. Now that the days were getting longer. Just one ray, but it came every day, and she could ride it out of there, as far away as it went.

Back to her mother's house, her mother who had held her close and cried in her hair when she left. And to the woods, with her friend, the sweet Mengette. It was May, they could gather flowers for "the ladies." The fairies who danced around the beech tree, in spite of the priests' holy water.

Speaking of miracles! Walking free, unchained, through the woods in May! Birds and beech trees, and flowers! Sun and rain, and sky. Friends and mothers, and no English. No one shouting in English, anywhere.

Was it possible—such grace? So much happiness? Could it

still be there, that miraculous place? Maybe that was where Joan of Arc was now.

At home, with her mother, and her friends, and her sheep. She opened one eye. The light was gone. It came and it went, and no one saw it but her. The guards didn't notice—or if they did they couldn't keep it out, though they'd covered most of the window. But still, that ray of light came every day now, as it pleased, and they couldn't stop it. Couldn't chain it, or hit it, or throw it on the ground and grab its legs. It was free, and, since she was still alive, it would shine tomorrow for her.

# XI.

Night, though it had just been day. It was funny, how things happen so quickly. Absolute change, in the blink of an eye, no time at all, the flash between past and future. A man is alive, a good fellow, full of blood and muscle, with a name, a family, maybe a horse, and plans to be a miller as soon as he gets home—and then, one arrow, one spear, one thrust from an ill-fated sword, and that good fellow, who knew the words to all the songs and could dance like an elf king, is a pile of dirt, soon to start smelling.

Joan of Arc hadn't been happy that afternoon when she'd charged out from Compiègne. Her life had gotten complicated, and she forgot first principles in favor of second ones. She rode out that afternoon seeking her own happiness—fighting, shouting, banner high. At the head of a group of soldiers again, the greatest pleasure, she thought, in life. Having forgotten how infinitely pleasurable it was to sit simply in one's house, to walk by the way, to lie down in one's bed, and then to rise up in the morning.

Until all that was taken from her, and she could take its measure, but by then she was on her back, on the ground, with an enemy archer standing over her. *"Rendez-vous!"*

She almost said to him, No, no, this is all wrong! Just a mistake, I see it now!—and she still thought it would come out all right in the end, when she made her official surrender to Jean de Luxembourg, the Count of Ligny and Saint-Pol, the highest-ranking knight there that day.

S he hoped at first he would extend her his protection, at least from the English. He was, after all, French, though allied to her king's enemies. She wasn't unduly alarmed when she heard that the English had sent him a message, by swiftest runner, offering him a "whole King's ransom, to be paid at once" for her. Or that, even before he could reply, they'd sent another runner, offering another king's ransom. Joan of Arc was worth two kings to them.

She was more flattered than uneasy at first. Luxembourg moved her from one of his towers to another, farther from the English. She took this as a good sign.

She didn't know, of course, that he was simply removing her from danger while he negotiated the details of the fortune that had fallen into his hands. He had only to preserve his prisoner alive until all was settled. He had a wife, an aunt, a daughter, all named Joan. To them he entrusted the care of his great prize.

They went together to visit her, the three Joans, and then separately, and then together, for they were always there, up the long winding stairway to her cell in the tower. They would arrive wordless, breathless—with food, sponges and water, to care for their namesake prisoner, whom they were coming to regard as holy. They began to love her. They begged her, for mercy's sake, for holy charity, to change her offending pants for a skirt.

She started telling them of her saints and angels. They

listened to the descriptions of Saint Catherine's dress, Saint Margaret's hair, the sweetness of their saintly breath, which she had smelled—"as sweet as, no, sweeter than the flowers in the woods in May."

"If ever I took the skirt again," she told the three Joans of Luxembourg, "it would be for you." They would come in the morning and bring their needlework, and at the end of every afternoon they would kneel together, all of them, her, too, in prayer. And she began to feel safe.

"Yes, of course! Fear nothing at our hands," the Luxembourg ladies assured her. "Our family would never sell you for gold!" She believed them.

She shouldn't have. The wonder, Girl X understood now, wasn't that Luxembourg gave her up, but that he managed to keep her as long as he did. She had been captured in late May. He still had her in his tower in November, when Richard Warwick, commander of all the English forces in France, paid him a call.

He brought with him a fortune—ten thousand gold francs, gathered mostly from the captive estates in Normandy—and a large armed escort.

"We'll refuse the gold!" the three Joans swore to their prisoner. They went to Luxembourg, citing the cardinal laws of chivalry, their family's ancient honor, and his own oath as a knight, sworn on his aunt's jewel-encrusted Bible, to protect prisoners of war and damsels. Joan of Arc was both.

They trusted in that, and so did she, and together, she could see now, they were the biggest fools in all of Gaul. Chivalry was dying. Hadn't she heard its musical horns giving way to the mechanical beat of drums on the battlefield? As well as the hateful new proverbs making the rounds in the court of her king: "Big fish eat the little ones." "In time of need, one takes help from the devil." "Who serves the common weal is paid by none." "If your coat is thin, turn your back to the wind."

Still, she believed she was safe. Luxembourg's women, maiden, mother, crone, threw themselves at his feet. They were great ladies all, in their own right. He himself was just the younger son of a younger son—his whole inheritance came from his aunt. His wife had brought her own wealth and title. These ladies knelt before him and took the hem of his garment. "Release her!" they pleaded. "Don't take gold for her—it will be cursed!"

Jean de Luxembourg was really just a man of his times, it occurred to Girl X. A man for changing times, he tried to explain to his ladies. Tried, too, to explain that it wasn't as if he had any choice. He pointed out the strength of Warwick's army. Warwick would have Joan of Arc whether Luxembourg took his money or not

The Luxembourg ladies were horrified. They vowed never to speak to him again. Never to extend to him the hands that had bathed and fed his prisoner. Nevermore to let him hear the soft voices that were forced to break to her the worst of all news— that their family had sold her to the English.

The three Joans left the tower that evening weeping, and she was left to pace desperately, back and forth, trying to make sense of what they'd told her. "Sold to the English, sold to the English"—what now, what now? She wasn't hearing her saints, clearly—had they abandoned her here in this predicament? Or was it more that she couldn't quite hear them? Maybe she needed the wind in the trees, and the church bells, needed to be inside a church again, and then they would come back to her clearly.

"Sold to the English"—was this possibly to be part of her mission? "Maybe Saint Catherine and Saint Margaret are saying that I won't be freed until the English take me to London to meet their King Henry. . . ."

Joan of Arc actually said that. Girl X almost laughed. Almost funny, that—her initial conception of what her English captivity would entail.

That hadn't lasted long. Her forebodings increased, though not enough, she knew now, for her to have any real sense of what was in store for her, how bad it would be.

Still, she had been sufficiently appalled to climb out onto the parapet that evening. The tower was high, sixty feet or so, but not impossible. Maybe she hadn't been hearing her saints because she wasn't meant to be a prisoner. Maybe they would help her again if she helped herself.

She looked down. A long way, but if her saints came to her, she could do it. She took heart and decided to try. She climbed up on the ledge, called on Saint Catherine and Saint Margaret, commended herself to God, and, looking up, not down, leapt.


When she finally opened her eyes, it was into the kind eyes of the three Joans, full of tears. She had been found lying unconscious on the ground, and they had been terrified that she would die in mortal sin, a suicide.

No, no, she whispered to them. She hadn't been trying to kill herself, she had been trying to escape. She'd thought that maybe her saints would catch her. Then she closed her eyes again and nearly did die.

The English were outraged. "The king," fumed Warwick to Luxembourg, "has paid dearly for her. The king"—six-year-old Henry VI—"doesn't want her to die, except by his justice."

She didn't die then, thanks to the loving care of the three Joans. Still, she wouldn't eat or drink for three days. That had been only last November. What would they say now? she wondered.

"You must eat, dear girl," they'd said then, "drink this water, this tea, otherwise we fear greatly that you will burn in hell."

And she'd done it, for them, but hadn't she been in hell since then anyway? Locked in a dungeon, chained. No light, no air.

Though no fire, put in Girl X. Yes, there was that.


The three Joans were there, when Luxembourg finally turned her over to the English. The old one tried to speak, but couldn't. "She has sickened, she will die soon," the young one whispered. She herself vowed never to forget, ever. She was in black—she would never wear colored clothes again, she told Joan of Arc, tears running down her pale cheeks.

The middle one's eyes were dry. She didn't answer when her husband addressed her. She turned away when he moved to take her hand.


As for Jean de Luxembourg, he had his gold—and a new coat of arms. A camel, staggering under its load. His new motto: "*Nul n'est tenu à l'impossible.*" No one is held to the impossible.

"Goodbye," sobbed his daughter to Joan of Arc. "Take our love."

And she would, thought Girl X. She'd take it tonight. Wrap it around her, though it was rightfully Joan of Arc's, not hers, and cover her legs with it, sleep with it tonight. It would be her pants, and her evening prayer, mass even, and Holy Communion. It would protect her and defend her, from all the English—they could do it, her three Joans. She would wrap their love around her, and sleep that night and maybe dream.

# XII.

She awoke the next morning. Still alive. Arms and legs, hands and face. Everything hurt—it had been bad yesterday. But her perspective was a long one now.

"Unchain me," she called to the guards. It was routine, every morning. They let her up to use the latrine.

"Unchain me, let me get up."

Whispering, mumbling. Finally, one of them came and unlocked her chains. The best part of the day. She rubbed her wrists and ankles.

"Give me the dress first," he said, "before you go."

"I can't go without it—" It was all she had on, besides a short shirt. She would have to walk half naked, in front of them.

But he started pulling it off, over her head. The other one grabbed the dress, then pulled her old pants out of a sack, and threw them to her. "Now get dressed."

She covered herself, as best she could, then sat there, shaking. If they got her to put on the pants, they could report that she'd broken her promise to wear the skirt. And then she'd be a relapsed heretic, and she would burn.

She wondered who'd thought of this scheme. She looked at their dull faces—it occurred to her that they must have names.

They'd been together, truly intimate one might say, for months. Long, bad months, bad for them as well. The dungeon was cold, and damp, and dark.

"You know I can't put these on! They'll burn me!"

"Get up and get dressed!" One of them stuffed the dress into the sack, and tossed it into the corner.

"No, no, you don't understand!" But she could see they understood perfectly.

"Was it your idea?" she asked in fast French, which they didn't catch. She knew, anyway, that it wasn't. It was sophisticated and clever, this ploy, worthy of Warwick, or perhaps the lord who'd been here yesterday. Murder with no trace.

"These pants are my death," she said, more slowly. They nodded. They knew.

S he didn't put them on at first, just sat there till noon, trying not to think, just to sit, calm, quiet, made of stone, until the exigencies of nature insisted that she was not stone, but alive. She finally put on the pants, and went out to relieve herself. When she came back, she turned to one of the guards.

"What's your name?"

The other, cutting in: "Shut up, whore!"

To him, then: "I beg you, in the name of God, give me back my dress!"

He, the smarter one: "What dress?"

The dumber: "The dress is gone." He pointed to the corner. It was true. The dress was gone.

T hey forgot to chain her—or anyway didn't. They weren't playing their lots, or laughing, or drinking their beer. No one was looking at her. They wouldn't hit her anymore now, she felt. And then it came to her that Joan of Arc was back.

In her pants. At least that. Dear God, it was good to have them on again. She would die now.

We all die, said Joan of Arc.

You didn't, said Girl X, you couldn't.

Then, said Joan of Arc.

But to burn?

But to rot here? Chained like a dog?

Better than to burn!

I burn once. I'm chained here forever! And what choice is there anyway? said Joan of Arc. Where's the dress?

Someone had put the guards up to it. Cauchon, or probably Warwick, it was more English than French, this murder of prisoners. Hadn't these kings of theirs come to power through the murder of allies, even archbishops? Her eyes filled with tears.

They were tricking her, murdering her! She would at least accuse them!

So—die kicking and screaming? said Joan of Arc.

Better than as a lamb to slaughter! You know nothing! cried Girl X.

No, no, I knew nothing before the stake.


All the things that happen to a person in life. Born naked, and die naked, too. Even in pants. Church bells were ringing. It was Sunday.

*Be brave, daughter of God. . . .*

She leapt up—they were back! Saint Catherine and Saint Margaret! She fell to her knees. Tears streamed down her cheeks.

They're murdering me!

*Just be brave, daughter of God. . . .*

I have been forsaken!

*No, no, daughter of God, be brave. . . .*

Don't leave me again!

*Never, daughter of God. . . .*

The ray of light came in. It hit the same spot every day, just a little bit later. She got up tentatively—they still hadn't chained her. The guards didn't look up as she walked across the cell to the place where the light hit the wall. She crouched down. She could frame the place where the light came in, where just by luck, or the grace of God, or both, the sun passed just once a day at just such a height as to hit that tiny slit of a window, and bring her—everything.

To be murdered by them—Girl X motioned at the guards. Cruel, stupid faces, though somehow assuaged now. As if it were over.

Well, it mostly was.

The door had been opening and closing all day. Faces looking in at her, confirming. She was in pants. She had fallen.

No, no, it won't be like that, said Joan of Arc.

Don't tell me you're still expecting your miracle? said Girl X cruelly.

Joan of Arc half smiled. Who knows?

# XIII.

Eight priests came in with Cauchon the next day. None of them had been there since last Thursday, and they all stopped short, even Cauchon, when they saw her. The Dominican friar Isambart de la Pierre turned away in tears.

She put her hand to her face gingerly. She knew it was bad.

Cauchon cleared his throat. "You are in men's clothing."

She: "Yes, I took them recently."

Cauchon: "Who made you do it?"

She: "No one. I took them willingly, without any constraint."

Cauchon: "Why?"

She: "I like them better."

Cauchon: "You swore not to take them."

She: "You swore to put me in a Church prison. But it is more licit that I wear men's clothes here, among men."

Cauchon: "Have you heard your so-called voices since Thursday, when you abjured them?"

A question both leading and fatal, and they all knew it. There was a pause, and then she said, "Yes."

Cauchon breathed. "What did they say?"

She: "They brought me God's pity for the treason I committed to save my life. But Saint Catherine and Saint Margaret have told me that I damn my soul this way."

The priests looked up. It was done now. The scribe wrote "RESPONSIO MORTIFERA"—fatal response—in big letters in the margin. She watched the quill: *Yes, write. I don't read, but I don't have to.*

She: "They told me to be brave, and answer boldly, for the preacher that day was a false one, and when he said that I hadn't been sent by God, that was a lie, for God sent me. I was damning my soul, and my saints came, and told me to confess my sin, for they understood that I did it all from fear of the fire."

Cauchon: "Yet you denied your saints on the scaffold."

She: "It was because I saw the executioner there, with his cart. I didn't know, after that, what I was doing, but now I know I'd rather die once than suffer any more in here. And I'll never deny God or my saints again."


Joan of Arc stood before them, radiant again.

Liar, said Girl X to her silently.

Maybe, said Joan of Arc, maybe at first.


The priests stood, silent. No one moved, or even seemed to breathe.

"Well?" Cauchon said finally to them. "Anything to say?"

But there was nothing. "Then let us go."

Still, they didn't move. They stood there, like choirboys, like newborn babes. Isambart looked like he was going to be sick.

Cauchon wanted to kick him, all of them. "We have our work." Idiots! He nodded to one of the guards, and the brute let them out at once, with no unpleasantness. Good. These days, one no longer knew.



Cauchon didn't look back at Joan of Arc as he left. Why look back, when he was looking forward? Soon he would be archbishop of Rouen, with all this behind him. Winchester had promised.

He walked out of the castle and spied Warwick there, waiting.

"Be of good cheer!" called Cauchon, loud enough for everyone to hear, as he crossed the few steps to his English colleague. "We've got her!"

Warwick gave the barest nod. Everyone knew that the girl was back in pants. The question now was how much longer these Frenchmen could dither. "When?" asked Warwick.

Right away, said Cauchon. There was one small formality that they'd take care of tomorrow, Tuesday, and they could burn her the next day. Wednesday. First thing.

Warwick didn't smile at his former friend, but he dispatched a military escort to see him home. Cauchon was relieved. They all knew the streets wouldn't be safe until after the burning. A group of his priests had been chased to the Seine and nearly drowned by English soldiers. Several had already fled Rouen.

"*Farowelle!*" Cauchon called gaily now, in English to Warwick. Bad English—Massieu, who was lingering there outside the castle, looked up.

"*Farowelle*, my lord!" Yes, Cauchon's lord, thought Massieu.

"It's done now! Be happy!" called Cauchon.

*Is there a God?* Massieu wondered, as Cauchon hurried off with his military escort.

# XIV.

Massieu managed to stay close, just outside the castle. The other French priests, Isambart, Martin Ladvenu, others, had been chased off by the English soldiers—"Traitors!" "French dogs!"—but the English didn't seem to mind Massieu. It occurred to him that he'd become invisible against the castle walls, the way beggars do. He'd been keeping watch since Thursday, waiting, hoping, praying—anything to see her again.

"Let's go in," he heard Warwick say to the French priest Jean d'Estivet, who was, as usual, trotting at his side. Warwick and d'Estivet—the worst of both lots. What would she think if he, Massieu, slipped in with them? That he was one of them?

Still, it was his chance, and he took it, followed them in, Warwick marching erect in his power, d'Estivet submissive, curved toward him, the two of them a perfect portrait of England and France that day. Warwick had, in this sordid affair, at least the excuse of being English. Doing his duty, burning her for "his king," as he was wont to put it.

In a way, perhaps, he was right. He had been given charge of the boy-king's education, when his father, Henry V, had died, and Massieu had heard that he'd beaten the child so badly that he stopped speaking. Warwick's king.

The great knight Richard Warwick—he'd hosted one of chivalry's most famous tournaments not long ago, in Calais. Ridden around bedecked in pearls and ostrich feathers, bested all the other knights at the jousting, and feasted all the people afterward. A day already renowned for its pomp and chivalry, but what was Warwick here but a glorified guard?

Top brute, like the ones he'd selected to guard her, and it was Warwick, after all, who had ordered the chains.

But why, since he knew she couldn't escape? No one had ever escaped from that dungeon, it was impossible—unless, of course, Saint Catherine and Saint Margaret decided to take a hand in it, and then chains and brutal guards would be as nothing.

But Warwick didn't fear Saint Catherine and Saint Margaret. He was English—and Massieu had come to see that what the English feared was disgrace. Hence, Joan of Arc. Did she know, Massieu wondered, that she'd given Warwick the fright of his life? Disgraced this flower of English chivalry, sent him and his men fleeing in terror from what turned out to be a seventeen-year-old girl?

Massieu wished he'd been there when Warwick first laid eyes upon her. Once he'd spent more English gold for her than had ever been spent on any prisoner, once he got hold of her and she was his, and he saw—a French country girl. Nothing more. The typical stocky build, the dark hair—Warwick must have been expecting a witch with a broomstick, showering sparks.

And here instead was this plain girl, simple, solid, already brought down, and hardly dangerous—and Warwick had her clamped in irons anyway. Hand and foot, all the tighter, once he saw that his disgrace had come at such unpracticed hands. The cruelty with which he imprisoned her tempered only by his ultimate goal—keeping her alive long enough to burn her.

Warwick and d'Estivet stopped at the dungeon door, d'Estivet giving way, elaborately, to Warwick. Warwick, who took this submission as natural, as his due, barely acknowledged it—did he know, Massieu suddenly wondered, that the last laugh between them had nearly been d'Estivet's? Was the great and all-powerful Lord Warwick aware that this minion bowing and scraping by his side had very nearly murdered Joan of Arc, just last month, during Lent?

Warwick knew that she'd gotten very sick and almost died. He'd even sent his own doctors, the best doctors, and then every doctor in Rouen, to her bedside. "The king has paid high for her," he warned them, "the king does not want her to die but by his justice."

The doctors suggested that the prisoner's chains be removed. Warwick hesitated—"Make her swear not to escape first," he said.

She refused. Anyway, she murmured, it wasn't the chains that had made her sick, it was a poisoned carp that d'Estivet had brought her, from Cauchon.

D'Estivet was there, at her bedside. "Slut! Whore!" he shouted. "You lie! You made yourself sick, stuffing yourself with herrings, you trollop!"

She tried to rise then, tried to speak, but she began vomiting so violently that the doctors, panicking, took off her chains even without permission, and bled her, bathed her, their whole repertoire, but she fell into a higher fever still.

She begged feebly for last rites. D'Estivet, as resident priest, refused them. "Die like a Saracen!" he spat.

"I was baptized a Christian, and I shall die one," she murmured. And then she commended her spirit to God, and turned her face to the wall.

And didn't die. Alas, thought Massieu. She told him that

her saints had come back to her then, renewing their promises of salvation. So she found the strength, somehow, to get better.

*Why did you do it?* Massieu asked d'Estivet silently now, as they descended the seven steps to her cell. *Pity? Mercy?* No chance of that. D'Estivet had addressed her regularly as "filth" throughout the trial. When he got wind that Massieu was letting her pause in the doorway of a little chapel they passed on their way to and from the trial, he waited one day, hidden, until she had fallen to her knees and started praying tearfully, even joyfully, to her saints and angels—then jumped out and blocked the door from the "ex-communicant whore!"

They'd both lost their breath then, Massieu and Joan of Arc. D'Estivet was Massieu's superior, Cauchon's "Promoter General." He warned the usher that if he ever "let this whore" stop to pray again, he'd put him in "such a tower" that he "wouldn't see the sun or the moon for a month." And then d'Estivet took the trouble of having the chapel closed up, lest she be gleaning some modicum of comfort from simply looking in as she passed by.

So why had d'Estivet done it—the poisoned carp? For it surely would have been a mercy, for her to die in her bed. And there was always the chance, too, that Warwick would discover what he would consider highest treason—why did he risk it? Or rather "they," d'Estivet, and Cauchon, too, for d'Estivet had come from Beauvais with Cauchon, and scarcely scratched his own ear without the bishop's consent.

Was the idea to get Cauchon off the hook? Make a swift and relatively easy end to what was moving each day further from the bishop's finest hour? For Cauchon, unlike Warwick, could understand every word of colloquial French Joan of Arc said during her trial, all the nuances, and he had to know, as did every French priest there who could understand her words in a way their English lords and masters could not, that she was holy, and it was not only a crime but a sin to burn her.

"Say nothing to her," Warwick warned d'Estivet now, as they entered her dungeon. Fearing what? wondered Massieu. That she could still die of rage, insult? Warwick motioned the guards to one side, away from her.

She was in her pants. They could see it. She favored her visitors with only the briefest of glances, but it was enough for them to take in her blackened eyes, her cut and swollen lips. Her bruised and tear-streaked face. Warwick opened his mouth to speak, and closed it.

*Now leave*, said Massieu silently. *You got what you came for, you can see it plainly. The combined might and power of the English army and the established Church of France have brought down this formidable enemy. This girl.*

And how many men had it taken? Massieu had counted over a hundred and fifty churchmen during the various sessions of the trial, working very hard, all of them, since January, to burn her. To say nothing of the secular force of the English, and now they'd just about done it. *One girl*, he said silently to Warwick.

But rather than making "good cheer," as Cauchon had advised, even Warwick stood silenced. She didn't dignify him with another glance, but he had seen her face.

*Well done, Captain Warwick, flower of English chivalry*, thought Massieu. *Your big guards beat a girl in chains, and now you'll burn her. Have you nothing to say to her now?*

But the silence was unbroken. Massieu looked from one to

the other. *D'Estivet, Warwick—nothing? No crowing?* They looked like ravens, or more, cormorants. Envoys from hell.

Finally, Richard Warwick turned on his heel and walked out. D'Estivet followed so closely he bumped into him when Warwick paused to bark something at a guard. They forgot Massieu—or maybe he really had become invisible. Whichever it was, he uttered a prayer of thanks.

He crossed to her then. No one else was there but the guards. He knelt and took her hand. "Tell me," he whispered.

"You didn't come."

"They wouldn't let me in. I've been here, day and night, outside—"

She looked at him. "Yes, I can see."

"You took back the pants! They're going to kill you now!"

"They always were."

"You promised to wear the dress!"

"It's better this way."

"Where's the dress?"

A long pause. He looked into her eyes. She had been his enemy, it was true. He was a Norman, from Rouen, under English rule his whole life. He'd grown up hating the king she'd crowned. But as he looked at her now, he felt he'd give his right arm to have ridden out from Orléans beside her.

Behind her, near her, following her that glorious summer up the Loire to Reims. There must have been all the magic, all the light in France around her then. And as he looked at her now, bruised and beaten, he saw that, somehow, she seemed to be in the light again.

She told him the truth about the pants.

# XV.

He was still there that night, when they brought her bread and water. They had been praying together, and she'd shown him the little ray of light—she'd even startled him, the way she jumped up when it came in through the crack in the window. He, too, took it as a gift from a God who hadn't entirely forsaken her, and they'd given thanks for it together, but mostly they'd sat in silence.

"You didn't tell Cauchon—or anyone? About the dress?" he asked her, for the tenth time, when the guards finally came over to chain her.

"Would it help?" Girl X had asked him earlier that afternoon, but now Joan of Arc said, "It's better this way."

Massieu just shook his head. He, too, had been simple, the same way she had. They'd grown up together in the last few days. His world, too, had turned from white to black, black to white. He was considering leaving the monastery. He would not, at any rate, stay in Rouen with Cauchon as archbishop.

"Still here, priest? Get out!"

The guards were still houspilleurs, though less avid now. Done with their job, less watchful. What if he traded clothes with her? Gave her his cassock and hood, and she could simply walk out? The main obstacles were the chains. But if he brought some tools from the blacksmith tomorrow, and then figured out a way to distract the guards, and then put on her clothes, himself, and something over his head—

"When will it be, do you think?" she called after him.

"I—don't know. There's still some procedure—"

"Will you come tomorrow?"

"I won't have to come!" He crossed back, grabbed her hand. "I'll still be here—just outside, all the time! Even now. I won't leave! I'll be there, just outside the castle. I'm like a beggar, the English don't even see me anymore—"

She half smiled. He touched her swollen cheek. "I'll get in tomorrow somehow. Be brave, and try to sleep." The guards pushed him out, slammed the door.


She was brave then, but she didn't try to sleep. It came on her sometimes, now and then, but she no longer sought it. Heading as she was for so much sleep.

Massieu seemed more frightened than she was. Maybe because she was still in this dungeon, where change was very slow in coming. Change, she had learned, was a stranger here. Here, there was long, slow time, redefining itself constantly, as each hour was a day, each day a year.

So maybe she was old, then. Old and gray—or would be, when her hair grew in. What if time really had changed—not just for her, but for everyone? What if not just one year, but long years had passed? What if they opened the door tomorrow, and let her out, no longer Joan of Arc but an unkempt hag with long gray hair over her shoulders, blinking in the sun and babbling of great victories and a girl in pants whom no one remembered?

She took a deep breath. It was done now, she knew it. Still, she didn't want to die. More tears, she couldn't stop them. What is life—what is it? Why had she ever been born?

*To save France*, whispered Saint Margaret and Saint Catherine.

# XVI.

May 29, 1431. A Tuesday, full of grace. Not a burning day. Cauchon decided to hold the last session in the archbishop's palace, since it was as good as his, he figured. He was already permitting his underlings to address him as "my lord the archbishop."

A priest from Rouen, a preaching friar with nothing to lose, had asked him if he wasn't perhaps presuming. "Tempting fate?"

But Cauchon no longer believed in fate. "Make sure you get enough judges there tomorrow for one last session," he'd instructed d'Estivet.

"Any particular ones, Your Grace?"

"No, any of them will do." Just as long as there were enough bodies present to condemn her again. It was a mere formality. They weren't even going to trot her out.

D'Estivet drummed up forty—fine. Cauchon recognized most of them, though some he hadn't seen for months. Some he'd never seen—maybe they hadn't even been to the trial. There were even a few medical doctors in the mix—that was all right, too. You didn't need a Parisian legist to know which way this wind blew.

Cauchon saw no need for preamble. He simply repeated the facts. He had heard that Joan of Arc was back in pants, he had seen that she was back in pants, and she had admitted to him that her voices were back. It was sad but true, as well as indisputable and undebatable: she had fallen. There was nothing for the judges to do now but pronounce her a relapsed heretic.

"Should we perhaps read to her her abjuration again?" suggested Gilles, the abbot of Fécamp, the inquisitor, so to speak. "Remind her of her promise not to wear pants? Try, perhaps, to preach to her?"

Yes, yes, that would be nice, said Cauchon, we can even do it later. But now, right now, shall we simply declare her relapsed? Unanimously?

They would—they did. Cauchon looked beyond the men, his minions, to the beautifully furnished room, the tapestried walls, the thick carpets, gilded chairs, silver candelabras, gold chalices, everywhere his eye might flit. All this was his now, or would be, once Winchester gathered the Rouen chapter to confirm him as their archbishop.

"Shall we go prepare her?" d'Estivet asked him.

Cauchon looked at d'Estivet and remembered that day in the torture room. They'd felt obliged to have her dragged down there to illustrate the lengths to which the merciful Church would go to redeem her soul. The session would be, Cauchon had trusted, strictly formal. A station on the way to the stake.

In fact, Cauchon's fear hadn't been that Joan of Arc would stand firm under threat of torture, but that she wouldn't. He didn't want to have her tortured, much less watch it—not to mention the fact that any wavering in the face of the rack, pincers, the whips and chains and flayers, any sign that she might, under torture, be brought to see the error of her ways, would have to be pursued, with all the messiness and delay that this would entail. Cauchon had neither the time nor the stomach for that.

But she'd spared him—she'd been splendid in there, completely undaunted. Stood there and declared, "You may tear my flesh from my bones, you may even separate my soul from my body. I will never deny my saints!" And then, examining the "instruments of torment" again, one by one, with her practiced country eye, she'd precluded any doubt with, "And even if I do say something under torture, I shall deny it afterwards, as having been forced from me."

*Bravo!* Cauchon had nearly shouted. He could now have inscribed, in the official record, that "the Church has decided that even the torments of torture would not serve to bring this errant lamb back to the fold." Thank God. Since they were going to burn her anyway.

But d'Estivet had been disappointed. Cauchon had seen it in his eyes. A yellow gleam.

"My lord the archbishop?" D'Estivet now waited. "Shall I go and tell her?"

Cauchon looked at him. You'd like that, wouldn't you?

Tomorrow morning, Cauchon told him, would be soon enough. They would reassemble early at the Old Market Square, where she would be brought before them at eight o'clock and burned.

# XVII.

Joan of Arc waited all that Tuesday. No one came. She thought of Massieu, outside, or had he gone home? Did priests have homes? She did—but she wasn't going to think of that anymore. She'd thought it up and down, into every last corner, under every bed and cupboard already, and there was nothing left there to think.

About anything, really. She'd thought it all. Thought childhood, thought the king, thought Orléans, thought Reims. Thought her saints—hadn't figured it out, but was done thinking about it.

Anyway, it was all very far away now, all of it, even her captivity, even her trial. All part of her life on the other side of the river. She saw it now in a sort of golden light, the light of late sunsets on the hills in high summer. Beautiful, but she wasn't there anymore.

She'd crossed that river, away from her whole life—not, as she'd thought at first, when she stood there at the stake on Thursday and denied her past, for she'd still believed then. Believed just as she had before, though the details were different. She'd gone to the stake believing in saints and angels, and come back believing in priests and Church prisons. But when she stood here and lied to Cauchon about the pants, that's when everything changed.

And though it had been better there, much better, in that golden place where she'd been young and innocent enough to do all that she'd somehow managed to do, what was interesting to her was where she was now. Strange, too—she was glad Massieu hadn't gotten in. It was good to be alone for a bit.

Though she wasn't entirely alone—that was the puzzling part. Her saints had come back. She was trying to sort out exactly when, and even why. She'd told Cauchon that they'd come before she took the pants, that that was why she took them, but that wasn't true. Or was it that it wasn't quite true?

She wouldn't have taken them, granted, herself. She wanted to live, of course, but once she'd been forced to do it by the guards—surely the angels had never used less likely agents— then, gradually, by steps, her saints were there again, saying exactly what she'd told Cauchon they'd said.

*God sends you forgiveness, through us, daughter of God. But you damn your soul if you deny your holy mission. . . .*

Girl X wanted her to ask them what happened to the escape they'd promised.

But that, too, was back there, behind her. History. She was studying something else right now. The meaning of life.

Since we all die, she reminded Girl X.

Girl X: But to die like this? To burn? Why not to have died, then, in battle, or at the tower, or even here, in bed, from the poison? It would have been better! Much better!

I'm not sure. This week has been enlightening—

Girl X: For what? The beatings? The attacks?

—and, I think, important.

Girl X: You should have stood there and taken it the first time, then! It would have been simpler, and over by now!

Yes, there's that, but I would have died on that side of life. Not knowing what I know now.

Because she was glad for this chance to see beyond. It was different here, on the other side now, and quiet, and a strange thing had happened with time. There had, this week, been time for everything, time to grow old, and wise. A thousand days in May, she'd had this week—two thousand. Her whole "three-score and ten's" worth of Mays.

You mean this whole endless nightmare! said Girl X. You're just saying it seems like a lifetime and you've grown old in one week—like the man in Domrémy whose hair turned white over-night when his wife ran off with the fiddler. Do you remember?

No—that is, yes, she remembered him. He wore a blue cap then, and tried to dye his hair afterward with some red mud.

But no, she didn't mean time seeming endless, days drag-ging out. Just the opposite, really. When she was sleeping, half sleeping, she saw them all—what might be called all her natural Mays. First the flowery Mays, then the fighting Mays, and the court Mays, the captive Mays—

Girl X: But that's just memory! You just lay there and reminisced!

—and then the Mays, all the ones that would have come after, as if they were granted.

Girl X: When?

Last night, this morning. . . .

Girl X: Where? Here? A thousand Mays in the dungeon? Not here.

Girl X: Where, then? If you're so free, what are you doing here?

I am so free—and I'm here.

Girl X: You say that here, now. Alone, chained to the bed— but you'd run so fast if you could, from the stake!

Yes, who wouldn't, though where? she'd been thinking. Domrémy? The court? The red skirt or the armor? She couldn't see how either of them would fit her now, though she'd give much for one more night in her mother's house. Or a talk with the king, for that matter, if it could be honest, and face-to-face.

But both were over for her now. Life had carried her along.

And life had been good, her own life extraordinary.

Beg them to save you still! Call on Saint Catherine and Saint Margaret! Tell them to take you away, or send the army as they promised! a voice, Girl X, was still pleading.

Joan of Arc sat up in her chains, shook her head. She no longer thought that was how it happened.

You did!

Yes, but I'm thinking now that that was childish, to think that escape meant leaving this place, or that victory meant a real battle, with men at arms, like something from a child's tale. Since now she had grown up and put away childish things.

But the glass is still dark!

Unless maybe the saints were granting her both, escape and great victory. Do you see? she asked Girl X.

Who was silent for a while. Then, finally, There are better ways to die than burning.

My saints didn't choose that for me, any more than God chose the cross for his son. It's just the way it is, and it won't last forever. It will start, and it will happen, and it will end. And then, if I'm right, if I'm hearing my saints correctly now, I'll be free and victorious.

What if you're not?

Then it will be something else. Something I don't know now, but will know then.

What if you're wrong?

I can't be.

. . .

Joan of Arc was calm that night, on her knees, eyes closed, when the compline rang, the last bells of the evening. That's when she always heard her saints best. The guards came in to chain her to her bed, and then paused.

They knew it was her last night. Funny, they seemed almost regretful now, around her. Like they'd lost the will, or maybe they no longer believed the same way, either. They'd done what they'd been called to do—treated her with all the cruelty and hatred they could muster, for king and country. They'd hit her, called her names, subjected her to whatever degradation was at hand—watched her piss, helped that drunken lord attack her, and for what, in the end? Their king was a stuttering boy who'd never notch an Agincourt, and they were still them, guards in a dungeon. Poor forever. Stuck in France.

And she was going to die in the morning, and they knew now, after all this time of wanting it badly, that that wouldn't help any of it, either. And now they were supposed to chain her to the bed.

"Let it be," one of them muttered to the other. For once. They turned and walked out.

# XVIII.

Wednesday dawned, full of woe. May 30, 1431. Martin Ladvenu arrived at the castle at first light. Massieu was still there. "They sent me to tell her," Ladvenu said.

They stared at each other. Ladvenu was a Dominican monk. "I'll go in with you," Massieu said.

Although, he thought, as they descended to the dungeon, *Instead of telling her, we could run, the two of us, right now, away from Rouen, and not have to witness the end.* Hear about it, maybe, but that was different from truly seeing the face of the Gorgon, which strikes men dumb, he'd heard. Old tales.

He would tell her king, confront him. He should leave now, today. Not wait, but head out of Rouen before the sun was properly up, and follow the Seine to Paris, and then past, to—where was he, her Charles VII? Somewhere on the Loire, and Massieu would find him and lay her death at his feet. The horrible death of the girl to whom he owed everything. For whom he'd done nothing.

Ladvenu was shaking like a leaf. Muttering something, some prayers, a plea for strength. They arrived. Massieu took his arm, and they went in.

She jumped up when she saw them. "Today?"

She started to cry at once. "How?"

Didn't she know? Of course she knew! What could she be hoping for? A reprieve? A change of heart among her enemies? Mercy?

"How?" she asked again.

Why make them say it? Tears started down Massieu's face. Ladvenu took several breaths, then stammered out, "The fire."

She fell to the floor. Massieu noticed she wasn't chained. At least that. He knelt down, took her hand.

"No, no, please no!" she cried to him—she hadn't thought she'd panic like this, had thought she would be all right. But now she couldn't stop herself. "Anything else, anything but that! Let them behead me seven times!"

"I know," he whispered.

"My body," she wailed, "burned to ashes—"

Massieu suddenly found himself thinking about his mother, whom he very rarely saw. If she were here, maybe she would know what to say. Something calming.

"To be ashes! Cinders! Dear God, please no!"

Massieu was frightened. He didn't want her to die like this. Kicking and screaming. It would make it easier for Cauchon, the English.

"Let me confess you," broke in Ladvenu gently.

"Yes, yes!" She grabbed at his sleeve. "And let me receive my savior! Let me eat and drink of the Lord—"

Yes, thought Massieu, that might help. "I'll go," he said to Ladvenu.

"To Cauchon," Ladvenu said, low. "Beg him! Be quick."

They were supposed to have her at the stake by eight.

Massieu ran out, he would run through the whole town

to find Cauchon if he had to, and then run back again—but Cauchon was already there, outside the castle, escorted by Warwick's armed guards. The soldiers were already gathering, milling around, though no one was smiling. It wasn't a picnic this time.

Massieu stopped and swallowed hard. He took Cauchon's hand. Kissed his ring. "My lord."

He begged his favor: Communion for the condemned? "If it please Your Grace, Your Royal Highness . . ."

"Yes, why not?" said Cauchon.

"But she is a relapsed heretic, Your Grace!" called d'Estivet, elbowing in. Massieu wheeled on him. Burn in hell!

"No, but Your Grace—" Massieu began.

Cauchon silenced them both. "Consider, gentlemen. The law on heretics clearly states that they may receive one last Communion if they ask for it 'with all humility.'" To Massieu, "Did she ask thus?"

"With all humility," said Massieu, "the greatest humility—"

"Then," Cauchon to his clerk, "go and fetch what they need."

The clerk went off to the church.


*Thank you, Jesus*, whispered Massieu silently. It occurred to him that this was a day for Jesus, not God. Jesus, who'd cried out himself, "My God, my God, why hast thou forsaken me?" Did she know that psalm? "I am a worm"—that was the psalm that Jesus was quoting. That could be a great comfort to her now. Maybe if he recited it for her, it would calm her a bit.

Bishop Cauchon and the rest of them proceeded in, to the dungeon. The bishop looked considerably more relaxed. He had his armed guard back. He was dining once again with Warwick.

Massieu wondered why he was going to see her now. Was he obliged by law? But wasn't it enough that he see her at the stake, when he sentenced her? Why now? Curiosity? Perversion?

They walked in.

"Bishop, I die through you!" she cried to Cauchon.

*Finally!* cried Massieu in his heart. Let him hear it!

"No, Joan, you die through your own wickedness," returned Cauchon. Milder than usual, his mildness more terrible than his passion. Signifying, as it did, no further concern that Joan of Arc wouldn't burn today.

Of course she would. Massieu knew it. Unless—Saint Catherine! Saint Margaret!—there was a miracle.

"I call you before God as your judge!" Joan of Arc was crying to Cauchon. "I call God to judge how horribly you've treated me!"

Massieu wondered again if Cauchon even believed in God. If he did, Massieu though wildly, maybe he would still stop this, even now.

"Bear it bravely," Cauchon snapped to Joan of Arc, "with forbearance," and walked out.

*Good*, thought Massieu. Let them all leave. He wanted to get close to her, wanted to tell her about Jesus.

"Where will I be this evening, Master Pierre?" she cried to a priest lingering there. She was sobbing again. Massieu had never seen her like this. Be here now, Jesus!

"Don't you have good faith in our Lord, daughter?" asked the priest.

"I do! I do!" Nervously. Talking very fast. "God willing, I'll be in paradise this night."

Massieu pushed his way through. "Joan!"

She was still crying to the priest, "God willing, Master Pierre, please God! Please, God—"

"Joan!" She still didn't look at him. "I have to tell you—" He touched her hand. Ice-cold. He knew the condition, "scared out of one's wits."

*Don't let her die this way*, he prayed. *Jesus.*

"Joan," he said aloud, "I was thinking that Jesus will be here today, with you. It's not unlike what happened to him, that day. 'My God, why hast thou forsaken me?'"

She seemed to hear him then. To stop a bit—did she? The clerk arrived with some of the accoutrements for Communion, but he hadn't bothered to bring candles, or a stole for Ladvenu. Without them, the Communion would be questionable. Incomplete.

"Just do it," said the clerk. Time was short, and the streets weren't safe for him, he said.

But Ladvenu was a stalwart that morning. "Do you mean for me to give her Communion lightly? Are you insulting her, or me, or God?"

The clerk hesitated, looked from face to face, and then went back for what he'd neglected, the candles, the stole. Good, thought Massieu.

"Joan," he said, "I'm not thinking of God. I'm thinking of Jesus the man, alone and forsaken. He never thought it would be that bad—"

She still hadn't looked at him. Would it end this way? Wouldn't he get just one more look?

"If he came here right now, in the flesh, I mean, you could talk to him, I think. You're the only one who might know what to say. To make it better, for him—"

Massieu no longer knew what he was saying. But he saw her take a breath.

"You could walk with him, up the hill, the two of you, alone and forsaken. . . ."

"No!" sobbed Girl X. "Anything but burning! Anything but burning—"

Massieu took her hand.

# XIX.

The clerk came back, breathless, with the candles and the sacred stole. "The streets are filled with people," he said, "all praying for her soul! The priests from the cathedral followed me in procession, calling, 'Pray for her, pray for her!' And people have lit candles everywhere!"

Joan of Arc looked up.

"Truly?" she asked the clerk.

"Everyone in Rouen is praying—"

She turned to Massieu—looked, at last, into his eyes. *Thank you*, he whispered.

"They're praying for me," she said slowly. "The people of Rouen—"

"Yes," he said.

"My enemies—"

"No, not the people. Never the people. They love you. They will never forget you!"

"It could be that way—"

"It is!" said Massieu. What else was there? Since there was nothing else. And, "He felt forsaken, too."

*Yes*, thought Joan of Arc, *that's true. He felt forsaken, but they're out there, singing for me. The people of Rouen, not even my people. People who had been my enemies.*

She remembered her first dream at Orléans, that the English soldiers would heed her warning. Come over to her, and she would bring them all together, in peace and prayer, for God and for France, and England, too. Was that dream being realized here, now? Could it be?

Funny, that, amazing, maybe even a gift. Joan of Arc resolved then to think no more about the details of her death. She would be the "daughter of God" again. She would come out again, from a castle, with the townspeople praying for her soul once more.

She was holy again, though in a different way. Almost sanctified. Few people knew the hour of their own death, though everyone would die. She would try to be brave.

But you can't be brave! They're going to burn you at the stake! cried Girl X. Don't you remember your horror? The executioner? The cart? The bundles of wood!

I said I wasn't going to dwell on the details!

That's because you've forgotten! It's the worst death—you couldn't do it! Remember?

But I've had time now, this week, this lifetime, to become brave.

You were brave before! Joan of Arc was always brave!

I'm braver now.

No! cried Girl X.

Yes, said Joan of Arc firmly.

Massieu was looking at her. "We all die," she said to him softly. He looked terrible. "Don't worry," she said. "They'll kill me today, or I'll die some other way tomorrow, or the next day, next year. It's our fate."

. . .

Ladvenu was ready now with the Communion. Some English soldiers were outside, banging on the door. The priests knew they were late.

Joan of Arc knelt down to receive her last Communion. Ladvenu suddenly turned to Massieu. "Her pants?" That had been the pretext upon which Cauchon and d'Estivet and their men had refused her Communion throughout her imprisonment. Even though they knew she loved the sacrament, took true comfort—probably because they knew she would take comfort. "God doesn't care what I wear," she had pleaded with them all through her trial, to no avail.

"God doesn't care what she wears," Massieu repeated now to Ladvenu, who nodded, and they began.

She was crying again, but it was different now. There was no trace of the terror. She prayed and wept softly, and they all wept with her, and it seemed to Massieu that time had stopped, and by secret miracle, this moment would never end. This would be his life, and her life, praying here, together, in tears of awe forever, and the candles would never burn down.

But then, the executioner, hooded, all in black, came into the dungeon.

She jumped. Massieu turned—Holy God!

*Just a man*, Joan of Arc took a breath and told herself. It was all right. She knew him now. He was just a man, under a very black hood. A man with a name, and a birth, and a death, too, like the rest.

He had brought a sort of shift for her to wear—a shroud, Massieu realized, his tears falling faster than hers now. He helped her put it over her head.

Massieu wished he'd followed his earlier instinct to flee.

This was worse than he'd feared. They took her out from her cell. He looked back as she was leaving. The chains were there, lying on the floor, open now. They looked almost beautiful like that. As if she'd flown away.

She followed his gaze, and asked, half joking, if he thought her chains would notice that she had gone. Did things? Things that had figured large in one's life?

She suddenly remembered a caged bird in Domrémy, a little songbird, a lark, if she remembered correctly. Just a bird in a cage—what did it care for anyone? But when the old man who'd cared for it had died, the little lark stopped singing. "Saddened," her father had told her. Even though people still fed it just the same.

What is life? There was the street, and the cart. She would go in it now—which was at least action. Better than imagining it, terrified.

Massieu got in with her—she didn't expect that, but was greatly relieved, not to be alone. It was another gift, and maybe even a sign. Maybe it wouldn't be so bad.

Ladvenu climbed in as well—good, too. He'd heard her last confession. She was glad to stay close to that, especially now, with all these English soldiers surrounding them. Lots of them, shouting—just men, after all, who should do what she'd told them at Orléans. Go back to England, while they still could.

For there was no chance now that they'd ever win in France, and she knew it this morning, and they must have known it, too. In their hearts, known that every Englishman who died in France after Joan of Arc died in vain.

There was the river, the Seine, its blue waters coming from Paris. Paris had almost been hers, but she'd lost control by then. Her own generals had carried her off against her will when she was only slightly wounded, and then it had been over.

She had been at her most desperate after that. In that confusion, at the court that winter. It had seemed so big to her then, high treason, that her king's men wouldn't move, wouldn't fight with her or let her fight, but now it seemed a small thing, almost personal. It wasn't granted her to march into Paris, true, but as she looked at the Seine now, here in Rouen, on her way to the stake, she saw clearly that Paris would be hers anyway. Sooner or later—the English could burn her a thousand times, and Paris, she knew now, would be hers in the end.

# XX.

They arrived at the Old Market Square, and there was the stake, high on a platform—why so high? It was so big, and there was so much wood, and something smelled bad. Sulfur? Pitch? Boiling?

Please God, no! Girl X started to whimper.

Don't look, whispered Joan of Arc, turning away. Just take each moment, each moment. No good looking ahead. Like the cart. It had been terrifying at first, and now she'd done it, gone in the cart.

It wasn't the cart that terrified you, it was the stake, said Girl X.

Yes, maybe, but what of it now? She looked across at them, the men of the church, the usual ones. All those priests and bishops and captains, on another platform. They were all in black, but looked small, suddenly.

Like rats, said Girl X.

Small, said Joan of Arc.

But a rat's bite can kill you.

But they're still just rats.

.  .  .

One of them got up and started to preach. From the Bible, Corinthians. The one right before her favorite one.

God's word.

In the mouth of a rat, said Girl X.

Still God's word.

"'For as the body is one and hath many members . . . God hath tempered the body together . . . that there be no schism in the body; but that the members should have the same care, one for another.'"

Yes, that's true, thought Joan of Arc, remembering Orléans, and Troyes, and Reims, when all of France seemed to be one body, caring for one another, tempered together, moving as one to put a crown on its head, the head of France. She had been close to the head then—it came to her that she'd been the heart. The heart of France! She could live long, she thought, and never do better.

"And when one member suffer, all the members suffer . . . or one member be honored, all the members rejoice with it." They had rejoiced that summer, all of France, it seemed to her. She remembered looking out at her army one day, after Troyes, on the way to Reims Cathedral, and seeing women and children trotting along with them, and thinking, Yes, this is fitting. No longer a military campaign, but a pilgrimage, for the love of God, full of people.

Now Cauchon began: "Joan, we declare you a relapsed heretic today . . ."

For she had truly done it for them. She had put their needs first. That's why she marched first to Reims, when she could have taken Paris. The generals said she'd made a mistake, but the truth was that the people needed a king more than they needed Paris.

" . . . we cast you off . . ."

Like a boat down the river. Like the deep blue sky. She'd been nearly overwhelmed with joy then, that summer, she was nearly overwhelmed with sorrow now, and what was either, to the immensity of the deep blue sky? She'd been born nineteen years ago in Domrémy, and could have been kicked by a cow or fallen into a well and died right then. Instead, she'd lived to die here today. And yet another throw of the dice, and she might have lived too long, in some obscure village. Lived to be lonely and forgotten.

"*Johanne, vade in pace*," went the formula Cauchon was reading. Go thou in peace.

Massieu turned to him, her words—"Bishop, I die through you!"—still ringing in his ears. Had Cauchon even heard her? She'd said it to him, straight out, this morning.

"I die through you"—did Cauchon know the truth about the dress? That the guards had taken it, and forced her back into the fatal pants? He must have known, someone must have put them up to it. It was a clever ruse, and the guards weren't clever—or freethinking, or independent. If they had been, they wouldn't have been in there all those months, the lowest of the low, wouldn't have been given the job of kicking around a girl in chains.

No, it was someone clever, someone higher up who'd lost patience, Warwick, or maybe Winchester, and Cauchon would have been told. So he'd known as well that when she stood there in front of his tribunal and declared that she'd taken the pants "freely," she was lying.

So, was he impressed? Massieu wondered. Did he appreciate her progress? She'd come to him a simple country girl, but she'd gotten an education at his hands. And was still heroic.

More heroic—it was a choice now. Her eyes were open.

"Bishop, I die through you!" Cauchon had to know, too, that she had taken measure of the extent of his corruption. How could he live?

Unless, thought Massieu, looking quickly around, he does something now. It wasn't too late—she was still among them, standing there breathing, alive. Surrounded by English soldiers, true, with their lances and swords—*But look at the people, Cauchon! Look at the French here, many more than the English, thousands more.*

*If you say, No! now, Cauchon, if you shout out, No!, scream it, they will rise. All of them.* Massieu could feel it. They were disposed.

But they needed a leader. Someone they recognized—Cauchon could do it, if he did it right now. He could set her free, and turn himself, with just one word—No!—from a wretch to a hero. And he might die here this morning, but he would die holy, redeemed, and people would remember him forever, his name would live. "Saint Pierre," they might call him.

But Cauchon merely cleared his throat. "The Church can no longer protect you," he intoned. He looked up into her eyes then, and quickly away. Massieu knew that Cauchon's life hadn't been without merit. He had been young once, was known to love art, and had even spent one summer among some mystics in Paris, a few decades back. Since then, though, he'd clearly made his way, with much success.

And within the overall narrative of that success, he must have understood this affair as a footnote. Politics, a detail, the price of the archbishop's palace in Rouen. When Winchester had asked him to oversee the trial, which was to say, the burning, of Joan of Arc, Cauchon could have slipped out of it. Pled illness, clerical business, a sore foot—but he must have thought it would be a small thing. Quickly done and soon behind him.

But would it ever be behind him? "Bishop, I die through you." How easily could even a rising prince of the church walk away from that?

And there was the rest of it, every word she'd said to him during the trial. The other day, Massieu had seen the bishop looking over his shoulder, twice, three times, and hitting his ear, as if he were hearing something. "You tell me to beware— beware yourself!" And now, worse, "Bishop, I die through you."

And then there'd been the trick question, the trap Cauchon had laid for her. When he'd gotten one of his men to ask her, cruelly, almost sinfully, "Joan, are you in a state of grace?" There was, of course, no safe answer to that question. If she'd said yes, she would have been guilty of the sin of presumption; if she'd said no, then she was, by her own admission, outside of grace and certainly not, as she claimed, sent by God.

But almost miraculously—yes, miraculously, Massieu would say now—she'd found the answer. "If I am in grace," she'd replied, "I pray that God keep me there. If I'm not, I pray that God lead me to it."

The men in the room had gone speechless at that, and Cauchon had quickly adjourned the trial. And another time, worse, actually, when they'd asked her if she knew the Lord's Prayer and the Ave Maria, and she'd turned to Cauchon and said, "Let my lord the bishop hear me in confession, and I'll gladly say them to him. . . ."

"Gentle bishop," she'd called him then, before she knew, when she still took him for an honest man of God.

Cauchon looked up then, right at Massieu. With a look in his eyes that Massieu had never seen, pleading almost. *What do you want from me?*

*Just one no!* Massieu shot back at him, silently pleading himself now. And Cauchon could have, right then. Shouted, "No!" and lived as a hero, or maybe died there, but heroically. Having thrown it all off, all the hypocrisy, the double-dealing, just come clean and gone down fighting beside Joan of Arc.

*Say no*, Massieu was still praying, *and we'll follow you, and you will live forever and the little children will revere your name—* when Cauchon intoned, "We turn you over to secular justice, and hope it will be gentle," and took his seat.

# XXI.

That was the signal for the executioner to pull up his hood.
Joan of Arc fell to her knees. She was surprised to hear
herself calling out, "Forgive me," to Cauchon, "as I forgive you."

No! cried Girl X.

He's just a rat, Joan of Arc told her. She cast her eye over the
rest of the judges. All rats.

"Forgive any wrong that I did. I meant no harm. And I forgive you all. And you, Rouen"—the people. There were hundreds of them, thousands. At her feet. She looked around.

And saw the stake, higher than she'd remembered.

"Ah, Rouen, Rouen!" broke out Girl X. "I fear you will suffer
for my death!"

Silence! Joan of Arc commanded her. To the townspeople,
she called, "I forgive you all! Pray for me!"

"We will!" they shouted. Tears began to roll down French
faces, sobs to break from French breasts.

"Dear God, and dear Saint Catherine, Saint Margaret,
Saint Michael, help me today! Be here with me now! Don't
forsake me!"

She turned to Massieu. "Is there a cross?" she asked him. "A
big one, that I can see till the end?"

Isambart came up. "I'll see if they'll give me one, from the cathedral."

"Beg them!" Massieu said. "Take it by force if you have to!"

Massieu was worried that the executioner would take her before Isambart came back with the cross, but the man seemed to be waiting for something, too. Joan of Arc was kneeling, praying, forgiving.

"Holy Jesus, who died on the cross! And Holy Mother—"

The English soldiers were muttering, stamping. They'd been told eight o'clock this morning: "Without delay."

"Hey, you priests!" one of them shouted. "Do you want us to have dinner here today?"

They tightened their hold on their pikes and their swords. They were greatly outnumbered by the weeping French crowd.

Isambart came back with a cross six feet high—perfect, big enough for her to see across the heads, should the priests be pushed back. Massieu took it up to her—she threw her arms around it, hugged it, kissed it. Wouldn't let go.

"Come on, priests!" the English soldiers were shouting. "Get on with it!" they cried to the executioner.

But he was waiting for the bailiff to pronounce the secular sentence to burn her. The Church had formally cast her off; now the state, to which it fell to burn the Church's prisoners, had to formally sentence her. Only then could he burn her legally.

The executioner was a formalist. It was how he justified his work. He relied on procedure to turn what he did from torture and murder to law. He had taken this profession, following his father, who hadn't much liked it, either. His father used to cry out in the night. He'd died young, from drink.

This executioner didn't drink, and he understood, better

than his father, that the law was complicated. There was a need for his work. Someone had to do it. He accepted his role, that it had fallen to him to flay his fellows, break their backs, even burn them, for the law.

But since he enjoyed none of these activities, he relied on certain consolations. The legal formulas, for example, soothed his soul and quieted his heart, always pounding right before, always beating to him, *Run! Don't do it!* But the ancient words of condemnation, sounding biblical, and intoned always so solemnly, so dispassionately before what were surely the least dispassionate of events, gave him a profound reassurance, every time, that what he was about to commit was necessary, and even for the good.

For the law, which he revered and served. Just like Joan of Arc, it occurred to him. With her march to Reims to have her king crowned legally. Turned from man to king.

Now he, the executioner, was waiting.
"Hey, priests!" The soldiers were shouting louder now.
The executioner turned back to the bailiff. He didn't like any of it today. First of all, the stake was too high. How was he supposed to reach her, to smother her, put her out of her misery before the flames reached her, as was customary? The way he always did it, always—didn't the English know this?

Or worse, did they actually want the girl to burn alive? Why else would they have built it like this? It wasn't right. He'd never had to burn anyone alive before.

And then there was the strange order he'd received in writing from the English—to pull the clothes off her body as she burned, so that everyone could see her naked. One of the priests had read it to him: "Her woman's body, and all the secrets it contains," it said.

He didn't like it. Everyone knew she was a virgin—it was unseemly. And what did they think they'd see? He'd nearly cheered the other day, when she recanted. And in the torture room, too, he'd gone to church afterward and thanked God that he hadn't had to torture her, though he would have. It was his job.

She'd smiled at him then, that day. Said her saints were going to save her. Well, he wished they would. Right now. He truly wished it, more than anyone here, probably, except maybe her.

"Hey, you priests!" Two English soldiers mounted the scaffold and pulled her to her feet. That was clearly out of order.

She was praying, clinging to the cross. The executioner turned back to the bailiff. What about the sentence? The words that would turn her from a flesh-and-blood girl to the condemned? As good as dead?

One of the English lords said something, and the bailiff then shrugged and muttered to the executioner, "Just do your job."

The English soldiers pulled her off the scaffold, pushed her toward him. He turned, shocked, to Cauchon. "There was no sentence!"

But Cauchon just waved his hand. "Take her away, take her away!"


The executioner went, unconsoled, up to Joan of Arc. Good that he'd poured so much pitch on the wood. It had been hard work, but it would make it go faster.

He took her hand. "Forgive me," he said. He always asked forgiveness, and they always gave it, no one ever blamed him. Well, sometimes in the torture chamber, where there was still passion, but there was never passion here. "Forgive me."

Yes, of course, she forgave him, she forgave them all. He led her to the stake. Girl X started crying again. Sobbing aloud— well, let her, decided Joan of Arc. They were all crying now. She looked back—even Winchester. Even Cauchon.

Holy God, it was high! He led her up to it. No! No! No! No! Girl X was going to start screaming.

But Joan of Arc didn't want to die screaming.

"The cross!" She turned to Massieu, who was right there, weeping as well. "Keep it where I can see it!"

"Yes," whispered Massieu.

"Don't leave me!"

"Never!" he cried.

# XXII.

Joan of Arc stood, looking up at the stake. Don't start screaming, she begged Girl X, please don't scream. I want to do it
without screaming.

The executioner stood her up against it. It was hard, rough.
Hurt her back—that didn't matter anymore, she realized, even
if it cut her.

He put a fool's cap on her head, with writing on it. Bad
words, she knew—"Heretic, schismatic, apostate," something
like that. That was all right. She couldn't read it. Hardly anyone
there could. Anyway, it was meaningless now, just more lies.
Someone touched her arm. She turned—an English soldier.

He held out a small cross, two pieces of wood that he'd tied
together. She hesitated—was it a joke? Some last insult?

But his blue eyes were filled with tears. He wasn't much
more than a boy. The battle was over between them. Around
the stake, there seemed to be a lake of peace.

She took the cross, kissed it with passion, and put it under
her clothes, right next to her skin.

"Jesus," she whispered. Jesus alone, in the wilderness. A
wandering monk had told them about it, back in Domrémy—
how Jesus had faced down three dreadful monsters, the lion

of anger, the goat of lust, and the seraph of fear, but had been defeated by the fourth, the white bull of haste.

She, too, it came to her now. She had been hasty, that day at Compiègne, when she was captured. If she had been patient—but Joan of Arc wasn't patient. She was brave and strong and bold, and she acted. Others would be patient. Their lives would be long. Hers would be short.

A short life, but not a bad one, all told. She had been born an obscure shepherd girl. She was dying with a thousand people at her feet. In between, she had commanded kings and dukes. Maybe it always ended this way—for her, for Jesus, for Saint Catherine, Saint Margaret. The executioner started tying her to the stake. More tightly than usual, he knew. For this one would be worse.

Why? he wondered. There were all the priests who'd wanted her burned, crying, and slipping away, one by one, leaving, they couldn't watch—why do it, then?

He took her hands now. "Please." She was just a girl. "Show all her secrets," the English had commanded him. What did they expect to see? Her courage? What they'd run from in battle?

At least she wouldn't know. "Please." He had to climb over the wood to tie her hands. She wasn't screaming yet. Most of them scream. Well, he'd get it over with as soon as he could for her, throw on the extra pitch he'd brought. He glanced around, almost prayerfully, for some sign of saints or angels—nothing. "Forgive me," he whispered, as he climbed back down and picked up his torch.

Isambart climbed up on top of the wood next to her, with the big cross. "Make sure I can see it till the end!" she begged him. The wood was high around her legs, scratching her feet, cutting them. The executioner must have lit the fire. She knew it, she could hear it.

And now feel it—it was bad, worse than she'd thought. Much worse, much, much worse—Massieu was still here, and Isambart, with the cross. "Get down!" she cried to them. "Don't get burned!"

For it was rising faster than she'd expected. All that pitch— "Water!" suddenly screamed Girl X.

"Holy water!" cried Joan of Arc. The fire was burning her feet. The smell came through the crowd.

"Jesus!" cried Joan of Arc loudly. That's how she'd do it— she saw it now. It would be all right. Every time Girl X was going to scream, No! or Help me! or I was betrayed! She would cry, "Jesus!"

She could burn, she saw. She could do it. "Jesus!" Suddenly she wasn't afraid any longer—of anything, she realized. She could burn, like they could, the great saints—was she one of them? When her saints had said they'd save her, did they mean for this?

She coughed. "Holy water!" The smoke was rising. A soldier came running toward her—my God, the fire! He was shouting, angry—didn't he know that it was over?

What harm did he think he could do her now? He had a pile of sticks—he shouted that he was going to throw them on the fire, make it worse.

But it wouldn't be worse. It would be better, faster. He spat at her as he threw his sticks on the fire. She smiled at him.

He froze. What was the matter? He stood, staring at her. "A dove!" he cried. "A dove flew out of her mouth! It's flying toward Paris—" He fainted.

A dove? That was nice. "Help him," she murmured, though whether anyone could hear her any longer, she didn't know.

Someone carried the soldier off. She looked up at the cross that Massieu and Isambart kept in front of her. "Thank you," she whispered to them. "Saint Margaret! Saint Catherine!"

Her head felt light now. There was beautiful light all around her. "Water! Holy water!" The sky was as blue as water, as the sea, which she'd never seen. She imagined it blue, like the sky, though someone had told her it was gray.

Rouen was close enough—a giant wave could come up, right now, a holy wave. Cool, cold. Wet. "Jesus!" She looked at the people, all standing silently, weeping. So they did love her! And so much—she loved them, too. She looked over to Cauchon, but he was fleeing, his head down, weeping, from the platform. Winchester, Bedford, and Warwick, too—all running.

From her. "The English run from Joan of Arc," she murmured, smiling now. In the light. Funny, how long they'd worked to burn her, Cauchon, Winchester, Warwick, and now they ran from her.

Winchester's secretary came up to the base of the stake, staring strangely. "Go on, throw more wood if you'd like," she tried to say, but he stood, transfixed.

"We are lost!" he cried. "We have burned a saint!" He, too, turned and ran.


"We have burned a saint—"

*Is that how they see me?* she wondered. She looked for Massieu—too much smoke now, to see anyone. But there was the sky.

Deep blue. She remembered once as a child, when she, and all of them, had had to flee from marauding soldiers to the castle at Neufchâteau, and there'd been a storyteller there.

Who'd told them of a princess, in a castle, who was allowed anything her heart desired, except to look into one room, which became the only thing her heart desired. She looked, and came to a very bad end.

"Life's like that," her mother had said. "She shouldn't have looked"—but Joan of Arc had looked. She'd looked into all the rooms. The king's rooms, the priests' rooms—and yes, look what had happened to her. She was burning.

But no! she wanted to say. That is, yes, she was burning, but we all die. And Joan of Arc had worn pants and looked men straight in the eye. She hadn't cast down her eye to anyone, and had looked in all the rooms.

And she'd come to a very bad end, they might say. But only because they didn't know. She could still see the sky. The perfect sky!

They didn't know that she had been granted transformation, one last time. She looked out at the English—she could hardly see them. Her life as Joan of Arc was over. It shouldn't have been. Her king should have fought on with her, but he didn't, he was finished fighting, and her mission there was finished— though not for the English. The English had actually believed in her longer than the French.

That was funny, too. She wanted to shout to everyone, to the girls, Don't be afraid! You can cast down your eyes for seventy years, keep out of all forbidden rooms, wear the skirt, and you'll still die in the end.


We're born to die. But she had the people at her feet, calling her name, praying for her. All the kings and queens, good or bad, true or false, all the French, all the English. The horse that carried her to Orléans, Cauchon, Warwick, d'Estivet who'd tormented her. He would die badly. She could see that, drawn in the flames, just as he'd lived. A cruel death.

But hers? Glorious! she tried to say. There was no more air, but her death was glorious. She could climb it like a ladder straight up to the deep blue sky, climb it like a stairway. She would go straight where they went, those who died gloriously.

And she'd be where she wanted to be, then—among the bold ones. The fact that she'd been so scared last week just made it better now.

There couldn't be more than another breath or two. It had to be nearly over, this death she'd been so dreading. Nearly over.

So you see? she whispered to Girl X. I could burn.

"Jesus!" cried Joan of Arc, for the seventh time, and then her head fell forward. She was dead.


The people of Rouen rioted that afternoon. The English soldiers stayed inside Rouen Castle, knowing to a man that it was over. No one went out, except the executioner. He had to find a priest. He was in mortal fear for his soul. He had burned Joan of Arc's body, as commanded, and her bones, but he hadn't been able to burn her heart. No matter how much pitch and sulfur he had poured on it—her heart wouldn't burn.

He had panicked, and thrown it into the Seine. Now he feared eternal damnation. He, too, was quite sure that he had burned a saint.

# AFTERWORD

It is said that the men who burned Joan of Arc died very bad deaths. Several got leprosy, a few the plague. D'Estivet was found in a sewer outside Rouen, his head bashed in. Cauchon died of apoplexy, in his barber's chair. He never did become archbishop of Rouen. The local churchmen wouldn't have him.

But her king, Charles VII, lived long—long enough to still be on the throne, in Paris, twenty years later, when an old woman was escorted down the aisle to him, in tears.

"I am Joan of Arc's mother," she said, kneeling before him. "I come for justice."

And justice was granted her. Hearings were held, from 1450 to 1456, in Domrémy, Orléans, and Rouen. Everyone who'd ever known Joan of Arc got a chance to come forward and testify. This testimony was recorded, and Joan of Arc's name was officially cleared.

It was mostly here, in the so-called *Process of Rehabilitation*, that I found this story. It comes like the light through the slit in Joan of Arc's window—not much, but if it's what you have, enough.

# ACKNOWLEDGMENTS

First infinite thanks to Starling Lawrence, who gave me a "yes" after my own "long bad season." Then to Joan and Louise, who kept me going, and finally and always, to J.P.

# NOTES

### Midnight and Jane Austen

3 **at least £200 per year:** Equivalent to $13,000 today.

11 **"3 or 4 Families":** Letter to Anna Austen Lefroy, September 9, 1814.

13 **"& my Mother has shewn":** Letter to Cassandra Austen, January 8, 1801.

13 **"I do not think I was v. much":** Honan, *Jane Austen*, 95.

15 **"The sun was got behind":** Letter to Cassandra Austen, May 5, 1801.

16 **deadly in its social fragmentation:** Honan, *Jane Austen*, 171.

17 **"There was one gentleman":** Letter to Cassandra Austen, January 8, 1799.

19 **"I cannot anyhow continue":** Letter to Cassandra Austen, May 12, 1801.

26 **Harris Bigg-Wither's unmarried sisters:** Wither was added to Harris's name as terms for an additional inheritance from Wither relatives.

32 **about £460 a year:** Equivalent to $30,000 today.

35 **then called *Susan*, for £10:** Equivalent to $650 today.

39 **to her sister a few years before:** Sunday evening, April 21, 1805.

42 **received for the four books . . . £684:** Equivalent to $45,000 today.

43 **"very like in disposition":** Letter to Cassandra Austen, January 21, 1812.

43 **"praised [Sir Walter Scott's best-seller]":** Letter from Charles Austen from Palermo, May 6, 1815.

44 **"the pleasures of vanity":** Letter to Fanny Knight, November 1814.

### Mary Shelley on the Beach
Abbreviations: MWS: Mary Shelley;
PBS: Percy Bysshe Shelley; CC: Claire Clairmont

54 **"singing or rather howling":** Hoobler and Hoobler, *The Monsters*, 263.

55 **but she wasn't *unwilling*:** MWS journal, "I had no fear—rather though I had no active wish—I had a passive satisfaction in death"; Hoobler and Hoobler, *The Monsters*, 265.

56 **"but applaud me":** PBS Letter to John Gisborne, June 18, 1822.

57 **"How long do you mean"**: Seymour, *Mary Shelley*, 300.

58 **"I wish I cd break my chains"**: Seymour, *Mary Shelley*, 301.

59 **"lived too long near LB"**: PBS Letter to MWS; Hoobler and Hoobler, *The Monsters*, 264.

60 **"I awoke one morning"**: Quoted in Thomas Moore, *Letters and Journals of Lord Byron*, 1830.

66 **"Mary wrote it"**: Seymour, *Mary Shelley*, 59.

66 **"Yes, and to Fanny"**: Seymour, *Mary Shelley*, 40; May 21, 1800.

70 **"unfolded to the delight"**: William Godwin letter to PBS, March 3, 1812.

74 **"an arrow from the bow"**: Thomas Jefferson Hogg, *The Life of Percy Bysshe Shelley*, unfinished manuscript, quoted in Sunstein, *Mary Shelley*, 72.

76 **"wrapt in excitement"**: William Godwin Jr., *Transfusion*, quoted in Sunstein, *Mary Shelley*, 73.

77 **"very early in life"**: *Maria*, quoted in Seymour, *Mary Shelley*, 85.

78 **auspicious after all**: Seymour, *Mary Shelley*, 83.

78 **"How beautiful and calm"**: PBS, "Revolt of Islam."

78 **"We will have rites"**: PBS, "Laon & Cythna."

79 **offered him £1,000**: Equivalent to $75,000 today.

83 **"very soft society"**: PBS to CC, June 9, 1821.

92 **"so beautiful"**: Holmes, *Shelley*, 281.

93 **"Pray, is Clary with you?"**: Holmes, *Shelley*, 287.

98 **give birth to a baby**: When he visited the child, he was reported to have written to Lady Melbourne that she "is not an *Ape*."

98 **"I place my happiness"**: Hoobler and Hoobler, *The Monsters*, 124.

101 **"I have called twice on you"**: CC letter to Byron, 27, 43, 44.

102 **"A man is a man"**: Hoobler and Hoobler, *The Monsters*, 136.

102 **"On Saturday"**: Sunstein, footnote, *Mary Shelley*, 428, Murray MS.

103 **"Ten minutes"**: CC Letter to Jane Williams, 1827.

104 **allowance of £1,000**: Equivalent to $17,000 today.

107 **"I am sorry"**: Hoobler and Hoobler, *The Monsters*, 135.

110 **"Now—don't scold"**: Hoobler and Hoobler, *The Monsters*, 136.

110 **his school friend Diodati**: Hoobler and Hoobler, *The Monsters*, 138.

110 **"a beam, now black"**: Hoobler and Hoobler, *The Monsters*, 154.

112 **"No person of respectability"**: Hoobler and Hoobler, *The Monsters*, 139.

112 **A volcanic eruption**: Mount Tambora, on the Indonesian island of Sumbawa. It was the largest volcanic eruption in recorded history.

112 **"approach from the opposite"**: Hoobler and Hoobler, *The Monsters*, 137.

114 **"Mary and I will publish"**: Hoobler and Hoobler, *The Monsters*, 144.

115 **"I will die unavenged"**: Translation by David Ferry.

117 **dalliance with Claire**: "The next question is the brat mine" he wrote to his lawyer. "I have reason to think so. She had not lived with Shel-

ley during the time of our acquaintance and she had a good deal of that same with me."

120 **"My dreadful fear":** CC letter to Byron, August 28, 1816.

122 **her mother had once written:** in her novel *Maria*.

122 **"I know not whether":** Seymour, *Mary Shelley*, 114.

124 **"I understand from Mamma":** Letter from Fanny Imlay, May 29, 1816.

125 **"where she was found":** *The Cambrian*, October 11, 1816.

126 **five shillings and a sixpenny piece:** Equivalent to $50 today.

128 **"fully overbalances the plainness":** Seymour, *Mary Shelley*, 79.

130 **"according to the vulgar":** Hoobler and Hoobler, *The Monsters*, 180.

130 **"another incident allows me":** MWS letter, January 13, 1817.

131 **"Three young writers":** December 1, 1816.

131 **"a scholar, a gentleman":** *Blackwood's*, No. 26.

135 **"a thin, patrician-looking":** Hoobler and Hoobler, *The Monsters*, 196.

137 **"Poor little angel":** Hoobler and Hoobler, *The Monsters*, 192.

138 **officially published:** As opposed to its initial, unheralded publication on January 1, 2018.

138 **"The sun shines bright":** MWS, letter to Marianne and Leigh Hunt, from Lyon, March 22, 1818.

138 **"most beautiful oxen":** Seymour, *Mary Shelley*, 204.

139 **"dressed her in trousers":** Hoobler and Hoobler, *The Monsters*, 200.

140 **"undress and sit on the rocks":** PBS letter to Thomas Love Peacock, quoted in Holmes, *Shelley*, 427.

141 **"It is true that . . . it shocks":** Holmes, *Shelley*, 431.

141 **"We rode among chestnut woods":** Holmes, *Shelley*, 427.

142 **"oppressed with wretchedness":** MWS letter, August 22, 1822.

144 **"Get up at four o'clock":** Holmes, *Shelley*, 443.

145 **"persons of a very ordinary sort":** Seymour, *Mary Shelley*, 215.

146 **"Everything on earth has lost":** Seymour, *Mary Shelley*, 232, 235.

146 **"We have now lived 5 years":** Hoobler and Hoobler, *The Monsters*, 213.

146 **earnings so far was £29:** about $2,850.

147 **"but his appearance was youthful":** Hoobler and Hoobler, *The Monsters*, 257.

148 **"3 still/Clare":** Sunstein, *Mary Shelley*, 426, footnote 13.

150 **"a natural child":** Bieri, *Percy Bysshe Shelley*, 230.

151 **"to a life of ignorance":** CC letter to Byron, March 24, 1821.

151 **"Paradise and the *Bambino*":** Bieri, *Percy Bysshe Shelley*, 253.

153 **"hopelessly lingering":** Holmes, *Shelley*, 649.

157 **"We drive along this delightful bay":** Bieri, *Percy Bysshe Shelley*, 310.

160 **"There was no boat":** MWS Letter to Maria Gisborne, August 22, 1822.

160 **"the calamity" . . . "over us":** MWS Letter to Maria Gisborne, August 22, 1822.

161 **"her large gray eyes":** Bieri, *Percy Bysshe Shelley*, 270.

162 **Another woman in the shape:** Adrienne Rich, "Planetarium."


### JOAN OF ARC IN CHAINS

166 **"Even if you brought me":** From Joan of Arc's Trial, May 23, 1431, in Jules Quicherat, *Procès de Condemnation, et de Réhabilitation de Jeanne d'Arc* (Paris: Renouard, 1847) [hereafter, Trial].

166 **"Be brave, daughter of God":** Trial, March 13 and 17.

167 **"You tell me":** Trial, March 13 and 17.

168 **"Will they take me out":** Testimony of Massieu in Jules Quicherat, *Procès de Condemnation et de Réhabilitation de Jeanne d'Arc*, vol. 2 (Paris: Renouard, 1847) [hereafter "Quicherat"], pp. 17–18.

169 **"I submit":** Testimony of Jean de Mailly, in Quicherat, 3:54–5; Jean Beaupère, in Quicherat, 2:21.

170 **"Look how she mocks us":** Testimony of Manchon in Quicherat, 3:146.

171 **"You insult me!":** Testimony of Jean de Mailly in Quicherat, 3:55; Andre Marguerie, Quicherat, 3:184; Jean Morel, Quicherat, 3:90.

171 **"Look how she laughs at us":** Testimony of du Desert in Quicherat, 2:338.

172 **"It's all right":** Testimony of Massieu, in Quicherat, 3:157.

172 **an X or an O:** Testimony of de Macy, in Quicherat, 3:123; Boisguillaume, in Quicherat, 3, p. 164.

173 **"Take her back":** Testimony of Manchon, in Quicherat, 2, p. 14.

178 **"And tell your father":** Testimony of Durand Laxalt, Joan's uncle, in Quicherat, 1:444.

178 **"There are plenty":** Trial, article 16; February 27.

178 **"I stay in my pants":** Trial, 3/17.

179 **"My pants are my protection!":** Testimony of Massieu, in Quicherat, 3:154.

181 **"Hey you, priests!":** Testimony of Jean Favé, in Quicherat, 2:376.

182 **"The king stands badly":** Testimony of Jean Favé, in Quicherat, 2:376.

183 **The barber shaved her head:** Trial, May 24, 1431.

188 **"gold crowns on their heads":** Trial, February 24 and March 1, 1431.

188 **"You say Saint Michael":** Trial, March 1, 1431.

188 **"Did he come to you naked?":** Trial, May 2, 1431.

192 **sent her home for a beating:** Testimony of Durand Laxalt, in Quicherat, 1:444.

193 **"rather see her drowned":** Trial, March 12, 1431.

193 **sentenced to marry:** Trial, March 12, 1431. Also, Jules Michelet, *Joan of Arc* (University of Michigan, 1974), 14.

194 **with a bowl, definitive:** Le greffier de l'hotel de ville de la Rochelle. Simeon Luce, *Jeanne d'Arc à Domrémy*, 312.

194 **"Better today than tomorrow":** Testimony of Jean de Metz, Joan's earliest follower, in Quicherat, 2:436. *"Citius nunc quam cras, et cras quam post."*

195 **"even if I have to wear":** Testimony of Jean de Metz, in Quicherat, 2:436.

195 **shoemaker had refused him credit:** Joseph Fabre, *Procès de Réhabilitation de Jeanne d'Arc* (Paris: Chez P. Jannet, 1858), 52.

196 **a virgin and much armor:** Quicherat, 3:82; also 2:447.

196 **"deserted or infested with soldiers":** Michelet, *Histoire de France*, 17.

196 **"go, and come what may":** "Va, va, et advienne que pourra . . ." in Pierre Tisset, *Procès de Condamnation de Jeanne d'Arc* (Paris: Société de Histoire de France, 1970), 52

197 **"desire nor carnal motive":** Testimony of Jean de Metz, in Quicherat, 436–7.

199 **"In the name of God":** Jean Chartier, *Chroniques de Charles VII, Roi de France* (Paris: Chez P, Jannet, 1858), 52.

199 **"to which she was more faithful":** Luce, *La France pendant la guerre de cent ans*, p. 50.

200 **had to flee more than once:** Testimony of Isabellette, a friend from Domrémy. Quicherat, 2:431. In his *Chroniques*, Juvenal des Ursins tells of soldiers "pillaging, tearing down, setting fire, as they were accustomed to do in Lorraine."

202 **"I didn't come":** Quicherat, 3:204; *Chronique de la Pucelle*, in Quicherat, 4:205, 210.

202 **virgin, "whole and entire":** Testimony of D'Aulon, in Quicherat, 3:209; testimony of Pasquerel, in Quicherat, 3:102.

203 **kissing her feet and even her horse:** Testimony of Tupinier, in Quicherat, 3:227.

204 **"Few in number but valiant in war":** "Exigui numero, sed bello vivida virtus." Virgil, *Aeneid*, quoted in Thomas Basin, *Histoire de Charles VII* (Paris: Société d'édition "Les Belles Lettres," 1939), 39.

204 **"like a flock of sheep":** "Un tropeau de moutons." Thomas Basin, *Histoire de Charles VII* (Paris: Société d'édition "Les Belles Lettres," 1939), 39

205 **"The only ones with you":** *Journal du Siège d'Orléans* in Quicherat, 4:141; testimony of Louis le Conte, Joan's page, in Quicherat, 3:68.

206 **"You have been":** Testimony of Pasquerel, in Quicherat, 3:109.

206 **sank like stones:** Testimony of Dunois, in Quicherat, 3:8–9.

206 **dipped in watered-down wine:** *Chroniques d'Antonio Morosini* (Paris: Renouard, 1902), 101. "Only two ounces of bread each day, and if she

drank wine at all, she put in it three-quarters water." Letter, Pancrazio Giustiniani.

207 **without—undressing**: Testimony of Louis le Conte, Joan of Arc's page, in Quicherat, 3:67.

210 **"The fortunes of war"**: Testimony of D'Alençon, Quicherat, 3:99.

210 **"nothing could resist her"**: *Chroniques de Perceval de Cagny*, 153.

211 **"All through fear of her"**: *Chronicles of Enguerrand de Monstrelet*, translated by Peter Thompson, p. 307.

212 **"though you've had many heroes"**: Testimony Alain Chartier, Fabre, *Procès de Réhabilitation de Jeanne d'Arc*, 2:279–282.

227 ***"Nul n'est tenu à l'impossible"***: Michelet, *Joan of Arc*, p. 68. "Nul n'est tenu à l'impossible."

230 **"You know I can't put these on!"**: Testimony of Massieu, Quicherat, 2:18.

234 **"They told me to be brave"**: Trial, May 28, 1431.

235 **"We've got her!"**: Testimony of Isambart, in Quicherat, 2:5; Ladvenu, in Quicherat, 2:8.

235 **Several had already fled Rouen**: Testimony of Isambart, in Fabre, *Procès de Réhabilitation de Jeanne d'Arc*, 2:98.

235 ***"Farowelle*, my lord!"**: Testimony of Ladvenu, Quicherat, 2:8.

236 **"Traitors! French dogs!"**: Testimony of Jean Favé, Quicherat, 2:376.

236 **beaten the child so badly**: Turner, History of England, 3:27–8.

238 **"Slut! Whore! You lie!"**: Testimony of M. D. Tiphaine, Quicherat, 3:48–9; Delachambre, Quicherat, 3: 51–2.

238 **"I was baptized a Christian"**: Trial, April 18, 1431.

239 **"ex-communicant whore!"**: Testimony of Boisguillaume, Quicherat, 3:162.

239 **"wouldn't see the sun or the moon"**: Testimony of Massieu, Quicherat, 2:16.

246 **"Remind her of her promise"**: Trial, May 29, 1431.

247 **"You may tear my flesh"**: Trial, May 9, 1431.

249 **"God sends you forgiveness"**: Trial, May 28, 1431.

254 **"Anything else, anything but that!"**: Testimony of Toutmouillé, Quicherat, 2:3.

255 **"Consider, gentlemen"**: Testimony of Massieu, Quicherat, 3:158.

256 **"Bishop, I die through you!"**: Testimony of Toutmouillé, Quicherat, 2:4; Ladvenu, Quicherat, 3:168.

256 **"Bear it bravely"**: Testimony of Toutmouillé, Quicherat, 2:4.

256 **"God willing, I'll be in paradise"**: Testimony of Riquier, Quicherat, 3:191.

259 **"The streets are filled"**: Testimony of de Lenozoles, Quicherat, 3:114.

266 *"Johanne, vade in pace"*: J. Fabre, *Procès de Réhabilitation de Jeanne d'Arc*, 2:81.
270 **"Forgive me"**: Testimony of Massieu, in Quicherat, 2:19.
270 **"Ah, Rouen, Rouen!"**: Testimony of Delachambre, in Quicherat, 3:58.
270 **"I forgive you all!"**: Testimony of Massieu, in Quicherat, 2:19.
271 **"Hey, you priests!"**: Testimony of Massieu, in Quicherat, 2:20.
272 **burn anyone alive before**: Testimony of Ladvenu, in Quicherat, 2:9.
272 **"Her woman's body"**: Le Prétendu, in Quicherat, 4:471.
273 **"Just do your job"**: Testimony of Isambart, 1450, in Quicherat, 2:6; testimony of Massieu, 1450, in Quicherat, 2:20.
273 **"Take her away"**: Testimony of Manchon, in Quicherat, 3:202.
275 **right next to her skin**: Testimony of Massieu, in Quicherat, 2:20.
277 **"Don't get burned!"**: Testimony of Isambart, in Quicherat, 2:303; also p. 6.
277 **"Holy water!"**: Testimony of Jean Moreau, bourgeois of Rouen, in Quicherat, 3:194.
277 **"A dove!"**: Testimony of Isambart, in Quicherat, 2:352.
278 **"We have burned a saint!"**: Testimony of Cusquel, bourgeois of Rouen, in Quicherat, 3:182.
280 **that he had burned a saint**: Testimony of Massieu, in Quicherat, 3:160; testimony of Ladvenu in Quicherat, 2:9; testimony of Isambart, in Quicherat, 2:7, 352.

# BIBLIOGRAPHY

*MIDNIGHT AND JANE AUSTEN* SELECTED BIBLIOGRAPHY
The best account of Jane Austen's life is to be found in her own letters—what we have of them. Lamentably, her sister Cassandra burned what we can only surmise would have been the ones we'd most like to read. One might wish to go back, to stand in that doorway—was it dawn when she did it? midnight?—and bring her the news of her sister's much-beloved afterlife, beg her to stop. But she doesn't stop. The letters remain burned.

But no one burned Jane Austen's books. They live on and on, we read and reread, our favorites changing places as we grow older. *Pride and Prejudice* giving way to *Persuasion.* Emma coming into her own as feminist hero rather than the dense, annoying egotist we found her at seventeen. Marianne's marriage to Brandon breaking our hearts now, rather than bringing relief. As we come to our own understanding of life, as did Jane Austen.

There are countless good books about Jane Austen. I read the ones in the Santa Monica Public Library, some of which are listed below. As for the story written in this book, it started when I was lucky enough to sit in on Anne Mellor's brilliant Jane Austen class at UCLA.

Austen, Jane. *Jane Austen's Letters*, 4th ed. Edited by Deirdre Le Faye. Oxford: Oxford University Press, 2011.
Austen, Jane. *Selected Letters, 1796–1817.* Edited by R. W. Chapman. Oxford: Oxford University Press, 1985.
Honan, Park. *Jane Austen: Her Life.* New York: St. Martin's Press, 1987.
Mellor, Anne K. "Jane Austen and her Peers." Lecture series, UCLA.
Tomalin, Claire. *Jane Austen: A Life.* New York: Alfred A. Knopf, 1997.

Woolf, Virginia. "Jane Austen at Sixty." *Nation*, December 15, 1923 (vol. 34), p. 433.

### MARY SHELLEY ON THE BEACH SELECTED BIBLIOGRAPHY

One can always start with Mary Shelley's *Frankenstein* and Percy Bysshe Shelley's poetry, which is why we care about them in the first place. Then there is Mary Wollstonecraft's *Vindication of the Rights of Woman* and William Godwin's book about Mary Wollstonecraft, *Memoirs of the Author of* A Vindication of the Rights of Woman.

I, however, started with Coleridge. First Alathea Hayter's *Voyage in Vain*, which led me to Richard Holmes's two-volume life of Coleridge, which I hoped would never end. There is much intersection here: Mary Shelley knew Coleridge as a young girl. Shelley and Byron could both recite his unfinished *Christabel* by heart.

It was after one such recitation—*A sight to dream of, not to tell!*—that Shelley had a vision, eyes on a monstrous woman's breasts, that sent him screaming from Byron's sitting room. Those words were in the air when Mary Shelley dreamed her own story.

Bennett, Betty T., ed. *Selected Letters of Mary Wollstonecraft Shelley*. Baltimore: Johns Hopkins University Press, 1995.

Bieri, James. *Percy Bysshe Shelley, A Biography: Exile of Unfulfilled Reknown, 1816–1822*. Newark: University of Delaware Press, 2005.

Gilbert, Sandra, and Susan Gubar. *The Madwoman in the Attic*. New Haven: Yale University Press, 1979.

Hay, Daisy. *Young Romantics: The Tangled Lives of English Poetry's Greatest Generation*. New York: Farrar, Straus, and Giroux, 2010.

Holmes, Richard. *Shelley: The Pursuit*. London: Weidenfeld and Nicolson, 1974.

Hoobler, Dorothy, and Thomas Hoobler. *The Monsters: Mary Shelley and the Curse of Frankenstein*. Boston: Little, Brown, 2006.

Johnson, Barbara. *A Life with Mary Shelley*. Redwood City, CA: Stanford University Press, 2014.

Mellor, Anne K. *Mary Shelley: Her Life, Her Fiction, Her Monsters*. New York: Routledge, 1988.

Mulhallen, Jacqueline. *Revolutionary Lives: Percy Bysshe Shelley*. London: Pluto Press, 2015

Seymour, Miranda. *Mary Shelley*. New York: Grove Press, 2000.

Shelley, Mary. *Mathilda and Other Stories*. London: Wordsworth Editions, 2013.

Stocking, Marion Kingston, ed. *The Journals of Claire Clairmont, 1814–1827*. Cambridge, MA: Harvard University Press, 1968.

——— . *The Clairmont Correspondence: Letters of Claire Clairmont, Charles Clairmont, and Fanny Imlay Godwin.* Baltimore: Johns Hopkins University Press, 1995.

Sunstein, Emily. *Mary Shelley: Romance and Reality.* Boston: Little, Brown, 1989.

## JOAN OF ARC IN CHAINS SELECTED BIBLIOGRAPHY
### Primary Sources
#### The Trial and Rehabilitation of Joan of Arc

This constitutes the recorded minutes from the trial of Joan of Arc, in 1431, and then the recorded testimony from her rehabilitation, hearings for which were conducted in and around Orléans, Rouen, and Paris in 1450, 1452, and 1456.

Of the minutes for the trial, there were five official copies made at the time—four of them translations from the spoken French into Latin. Guillaume Manchon, a priest notary, made three copies in Latin, as well as leaving us the *Minuta in gallico*, the French version, from which we get the clearest and most direct picture of Joan of Arc and her prosecutors.

One of his copies was for the inquisitor, one for the king of England, and one for Pierre Cauchon. Guillaume Boisguillaume and Nicholas Taquel, also priests, made and notarized copies as well, Boisguillaume's on vellum. Three copies remained in Paris, one was dramatically torn up by the rehabilitation judges on December 15, 1455, and one was found in Orléans in 1475.

Modern compilations:

Champion, Pierre. *The Trial of Jeanne d'Arc.* Translated by W. P. Barrett. New York: Gotham House, 1932.

——— . "Dramatis Personae." Translated by Coley Taylor and Ruth Kerr. In *The Trial of Jeanne d'Arc.* New York: Gotham House, 1932.

Fabre, Joseph. *Procès de Réhabilitation de Jeanne d'Arc: Raconté et Traduit d'après les textes Latins Officiel.* Paris: Librairie Ch. Delagrave, 1881.

Quicherat, Jules. *Procès de Condemnation et de Réhabilitation de Jeanne d'Arc, dites La Pucelle.* Paris: Renouard, 1847. Quicherat compiled and reprinted, in Latin and the original old French, the entire trial, rehabilitation, and all relevant chronicles of the time. He is Joan of Arc's most devoted scholar.

Tisset, Pierre. "Traduction." In *Procès de Condemnation de Jeanne d'Arc.* Paris: Société de Histoire de France, 1970.

Chronicles:

Basin, Thomas. *Histoire de Charles VII*, vol. 1, 1407–1444. Edited and translated by Charles Samaran. Paris: Société d'Edition "Les Belles Lettres," 1933. Written between 1470 and 1472 by a Norman bishop who, in 1449, enthusiastically embraced the cause of Charles VII.

Chartier, Jean. *Chroniques de Charles VII, Roi de France*. Edited by Vallet de Viriville. Paris: Chez P. Jannet, 1858. Chartier is a Norman chronicler who wrote this history in 1449, after being fired by Louis XI. Quicherat calls him "a bad writer, a poor judge of events, and an inept and incomplete analyst." Chartier often mentions Joan of Arc incidentally among the various captains, when recounting battles in which she took part.

Chastellain, George, *Chroniques*, vol. 2, 1430–31, 1452–53. Bruxelles: F. Heussner, 1863. A Burgundian chronicler.

*Chronique de Jean le Bel*. Translated by Peter Thompson. In *Contemporary Chronicles of the Hundred Years' War*. London: Folio Society, 1966.

*Chronique de la Pucelle*. In Jules Quicherat, *Procès de Condemnation et de Réhabilitation de Jeanne d'Arc, dites La Pucelle*. Vol. 4. Paris: Renouard, 1847. No one knows who wrote this chronicle or where it was found. The author, relating depositions from Dunois, the Duke of Alençon, and Frère Seguin, must have known at least some of the captains who fought with Joan of Arc.

*Chronique Normande*. In vol. 3 of Chartier, Jean. *Chroniques de Charles VII, Roi de France*. Covers the years 1428–1431.

*Chroniques de Jean de Wavrin du Forestel*. In Jules Quicherat, *Procès de Condemnation et de Réhabilitation de Jeanne d'Arc, dites La Pucelle*. Vol. 4. Paris: Renouard, 1847. Jean de Wavrin was a soldier who fought with the English against Joan of Arc. He was the first one to represent her as an instrument of a political maneuvers. He calls her followers "mad," and her a "monstrous woman."

*Chroniques de Perceval de Cagny*. Edited by H. Moranvillé. Paris: La Société de l'Histoire de France, 1902. Perceval de Cagny was attached to the Duke of Alençon, one of Joan of Arc's closest colleagues. Quicherat calls his account the "head of the chroniclers of the Maid," and notes that though he was "poorly educated," his chronicle is the most complete and the most "sincere."

Froissart, Jean, *Chroniques*. Publiées Pour La Société de l'Histoire de France par Siméon Luce. Paris: Librairie de la Société de l'Histoire de France, 1870.

Hall, Edward. *Chronicle: Containing the History of England*. London: Johnson, Rivington, Payne, Wilkie, and Robinson, 1809.

*Journal d'un Bourgeois de Paris sous Charles VI et Charles VII*. Preface and notes by d'Andre Mary. Paris: Henri Jonquières, 1929.

*Journal du Siège d'Orléans et du Voyage de Reims*. In Jules Quicherat, *Procès de Condemnation et de Réhabilitation de Jeanne d'Arc, dites La Pucelle.* Vol. 4. Paris: Renouard, 1847. Though this work touts itself as written "word for word" at the time of Joan of Arc's lifting of the siege (1429), Quicherat points out various anachronisms as well as plagiarisms that date it to about 1467.

*L'Abréviateur du Procès.* In Jules Quicherat, *Procès de Condemnation et de Réhabilitation de Jeanne d'Arc, dites La Pucelle.* Vol. 4. Paris: Renouard, 1847, 254–276. Written around 1500, by order of Louis XII, by an anonymous author, most likely an ecclesiatic.

*Le Hérault Berri.* In Jules Quicherat, *Procès de Condemnation et de Réhabilitation de Jeanne d'Arc, dites La Pucelle.* Vol. 4. Paris: Renouard, 1847. Jacques le Bouvier, herald of the king of France and of "the country of Berri." As Quicherat says, his errors "are those of a man who has seen."

*Le Miroir des Femmes Verteuses.* In Jules Quicherat, *Procès de Condemnation et de Réhabilitation de Jeanne d'Arc, dites La Pucelle.* Vol. 4. Paris: Renouard, 1847. Written about 1498, full of errors, but evidence of the growing legend of Joan of Arc.

*Le Prétendu Bourgeois de Paris.* In Jules Quicherat, *Procès de Condemnation et de Réhabilitation de Jeanne d'Arc, dites La Pucelle.* Vol. 4. Paris: Renouard, 1847. The most hostile chronicler of Joan of Arc in the fifteenth century.

*Les Chroniques de Enguerran de Monstrelet.* In Jules Quicherat, *Procès de Condemnation et de Réhabilitation de Jeanne d'Arc, dites La Pucelle.* Vol. 4. Paris: Renouard, 1847.

Monstrelet, Enguerrand de. *The Chronicles.* Translated and edited by Peter Thompson. In *Contemporary Chronicles of the Hundred Years' War.* London: Folio Society, 1966.

*Chronique d'Antonio Morosini.* Translation by Léon Dorez. In *Extraits Relatifs à l'histoire de France.* Introduction and commentary by Germain Lefêvre-Pontalis. Paris: Renouard, 1902. Morosini's journals took the "day-to-day" to the "universal," touching all he wrote with his knowledge of "all points of the civilized world, even to the city of the Doges."

Sala, Pierre. *Hardiesses des Grands Rois et Empereurs.* In Jules Quicherat, *Procès de Condemnation et de Réhabilitation de Jeanne d'Arc, dites La Pucelle.* Vol. 4. Paris: Renouard, 1847. Written during the reign of François I. Tells of the "secret" between the king and Joan of Arc.

Thomassin, Matthieu. *Registre delphinal.* In Jules Quicherat, *Procès de Condemnation et de Réhabilitation de Jeanne d'Arc, dites La Pucelle.* Vol. 4. Paris: Renouard, 1847. Written for the Dauphin Louis in 1456. Recounts the English threats to Joan of Arc before Orléans, and her brave answers.

Other sources:

Boissounouse, Janine. *Jeanne et ses Juges*. Paris: Les Editeurs Français Réunis, 1955.

Calmette, Joseph. *Les Grands Ducs de Bourgogne*. Paris: Editions Albin Michel, 1949.

Catta, Tony. "Charles VII et Jeanne d'Arc." *Revue des Questions Historiques*, October 1, 1929: 257–330.

Guérard, Albert. *France: A Modern History*. Ann Arbor: University of Michigan Press, 1959.

Huizinga, Jean. "La Physionomie Morale de Philippe le Bon." *Annales de Bourgogne*, vol. 4 (1932): 101–124.

——— . *The Waning of the Middle Ages: A Study of the Forms of Life, Thought, and Art in France and the Netherlands in the XIVth and XVth Centuries*. London: Edward Arnold, 1937.

Jacob, E. F. *The Fifteenth Century, 1399–1485*. Oxford: Clarendon Press, 1961.

Luce, Siméon. *Jeanne d'Arc à Domrémy. Récherches Critiques sur les origines de la mission dela Pucelle*. Paris: Librairie Hachette et Cie., 1887. "Vive labeur!," its inscription.

——— . *La France pendant la guerre de cent ans*. Paris: Hachette, 1890.

McFarlane, Kenneth Bruce. "At the Death-bed of Cardinal Beaufort." *Studies in Medieval History Presented to Frederick Maurice Powicke*, edited by R. W. Hunt, W. A. Pantin, and R. W. Southern, Oxford, 1948.

——— . "England: The Lancastrian Kings, 1399–1461." In *The Cambridge Medieval History*, vol. 8, *The Close of the Middle Ages*. Cambridge: Cambridge University Press, 1959.

——— . "Henry V, Bishop Beaufort, and the Red Hat, 1417–1421." *English Historical Review*, vol. 60, No. 238 (September 1945): 316–348.

Michelet, Jules. *Histoire de France*. 4 vols. Edited by Paul Vaillaneix. Paris: Flammarion,1898.

——— . *Joan of Arc*. Translated by Albert Guérard. Ann Arbor: University of Michigan Press, 1974.

Oman, C. *The History of England from the Accession of Richard II to the Death of Richard III (1377–1485)*. New York: Greenwood Press, 1969.

Pisan, Christine de. *Ballads, Rondeaux, and Virelais: An Anthology*. Edited by Kenneth Varty. Leicester: Leicester University Press, 1965.

Quenedey, R. "La Prison de Jeanne d'Arc à Rouen." In *Etude historique et Archéologique*. Paris: Champion, 1923.

Quicherat, Jules. *Aperçus nouveaux sur l'histoire de Jeanne d'Arc*. Paris: Jules Renouard et Cie., 1850.

Quicherat, Jules. *Historie du Costume en France*. Paris: Chevignard, Pauquet, & P. Sellier, 1877.

Sackville-West, Vita. *Saint Joan of Arc*. New York: Doubleday, Doran, 1936.

Sutherland, Ronald. *The Romaunt of the Rose & le Roman de la Rose*. Berkeley and Los Angeles: University of California Press, 1968.

Tisset, Pierre. "Quelques remarques à propos de Pierre Cauchon, Juge de Jeanne d'Arc." In *Etudes Médiévales offertes à M. le doyen Augustin Fliche de l'Institut*. Montpelier: Ch. Déhan, 1952.

Tupinier, Joseph. *Orléans et Jeanne d'Arc*. Paris: Bureaux de la Revue, 1906.

Turner, Sharon, F.S.A. *The History of England during the Middle Ages*, vol. 2. London: Longman, Hurst, Rees, Orme, and Brown, 1815.

———. *The History of England During the Middle Ages*, vol. 3. London: Longman, Hurst, Rees, Orme, and Brown, 1823.

Vander Linden, Herman. *Itinéraires de Philippe le Bon, duc de Bourgogne (1419–1467) et de Charles, Comte de Charolais (1433–1467)*. Bruxelles: Palais des Académies, 1940.

Waugh, W. T. "The Councils of Constance and Basle." In *The Cambridge Medieval History*, vol. 8, *The Close of the Middle Ages*. Cambridge: Cambridge University Press, 1959.

Williams, E. Carleton. *My Lord of Bedford, 1389–1435*. London: Longmans, Green, 1963.

Wyndham Lewis, D. B. *François Villon*. Garden City: Doubleday Anchor Books, 1958.